Study Guide

to accompany

INTRODUCTION TO

ECONOMICS

AND

INTRODUCTION TO

MICROECONOMICS

Dorothy Siden
Salem State College

D1508162

The Dryden Press
Harcourt Brace College Publishers

Fort Worth   Philadelphia   San Diego   New York   Orlando   Austin   San Antonio
Toronto   Montreal   London   Sydney   Tokyo

Address for Orders
The Dryden Press
6277 Sea Harbor Drive
Orlando, FL 32887-6777
1-800-782-4479 or 1-800-433-0001 (in Florida)

Address for Editorial Correspondence
The Dryden Press
301 Commerce Street, Suite 3700
Fort Worth, TX 76102

ISBN: 0-03-031219-1

Printed in the United States of America

5 6 7 8 9 0 1 2 3 4   095   9 8 7 6 5 4 3 2 1

The Dryden Press
Harcourt Brace College Publishers

Table of Contents

PART I

Issues and Methods

Chapter 1

What Economics is About

Learning Goals

1. Acquaint yourself with some of the numerical facts on the economy.

2. Understand the definition of economics.

3. View a simple example of decision making in the face of scarcity from the perspective of the economic theory of opportunity costs and incentives.

4. Be able to describe the market process, its necessary components (private property and competition) and via the "invisible hand" its expected benevolent outcome.

Key Term Matching Quiz

Terms

_____ 1.   Economics

_____ 2.   Goods

_____ 3.   Free Good

_____ 4.   Scarce good

_____ 5.   Opportunity Cost

_____ 6.   Incentive

_____ 7.   Competition

_____ 8.   Market

_____ 9.   Trading

_____ 10.   Market Process

_____ 11.   Ownership

_____ 12.   Private property

_____ 13.   Property Rights

_____ 14.   "Invisible Hand"

Definitions

a.   Process by which people attempt to acquire goods

b.   Peoples right to decide whether and how to use scarce resources or sell them to others

c.   Study of how society uses its limited resources to produce, trade and consume goods

d.   Coordination of peoples economic activities through voluntary trades

e.   A good is limited when people want more than the total amount available

f.   Through voluntary trades, each person helps others when they attempt to help themselves

g.   Something people want

h.   Things that are not scarce

i.   Value of something you must sacrifice to get a scarce good

j.   Expected benefit of a decision minus its opportunity cost

k.   Activity of people buying and selling goods

l.   Buying and selling

m.   Right to make decisions about a good

n.   Something that a person owns

True/False Questions

_____ 1. The average person in the world is twice as rich as the average person was in 1900.

_____ 2. The average American is 1-1/2 times richer than twenty five years ago.

_____ 3. Government buys five percent of the U.S. economy's output.

_____ 4. Most major political issues involve the economy.

_____ 5. There is no such thing as a free good.

_____ 6. A market is a specific place or store.

_____ 7. Through the market process and its action of coordinating the activities of people pursuing their own self interest, the interests of society as a whole are often promoted simultaneously.

_____ 8. Limiting property rights does not interfere with the results of the market process.

_____ 9. Free goods have no opportunity cost.

_____ 10. The cost of a scarce good is measured by its opportunity cost.

Multiple Choice Questions

1. Investment is
   a. the production of equipment and machinery for production.
   b. buying an old cottage by a lake.
   c. buying a share of IBM stock.
   d. All of the above.

2. When you spend $1 in a specialty store:
   a. 90 cents of your $1 goes to the store owner's profit.
   b. the owner usually makes a profit of 50 cents.
   c. your $1 covers the direct cost of the product.
   d. the markup of 40.5 cents covers net operating expenses and profit.

3. The direct cost of what you buy in a store refers to
   a. its opportunity cost.
   b. the actual cost of materials in the product.
   c. profit.
   d. advertising costs.

4. A free good
   a. is something people want in a greater amount than is available.
   b. requires people to sacrifice something to attain it.
   c. is available in a greater amount than people want, is abundant.
   d. is anything produced in the free world.

5. Economic decisions are influenced by incentives which are:
   a. the value of what someone must give up.
   b. the expected benefits of each possible decision minus its opportunity cost.
   c. attempts to acquire scarce goods.
   d. the activity of buying and selling goods.

6. Property rights are:
   a. essential for the market process to work well.
   b. allow people to decide how to use a scarce resource.
   c. permit people to sell a scarce resource to someone else.
   d. are described by all of the above.

7. Opportunity costs are:
   a. the sum of direct and markup costs plus profits.
   b. the value of what someone must sacrifice to buy a product.
   c. the profits from the sale of a good.
   d. All of the above.

8. The market process involves :
   a. the buying and selling of goods.
   b. competition for scarce resources.
   c. coordination of people's economic activities through voluntary trades.
   d. All of the above.

Chapter Review   (Fill in the Blanks)

Poverty, Wealth & Growth

1. Each year, the world's _____ billion people produce $_____ trillion worth of goods or $_____ per person.

2. How many zeros are in 1 trillion ?_____

3. The average person on earth is: _____ (how many) times richer than the average person was in 1900 and is _____ (how many) times richer than the average person was in 1800.

4. In the U.S., the population of 270 million produces _____(how much) trillion per year or _____(how much) per person.

5. The average person in the U.S. today is: _____ (how many) times richer than the average person 25 years ago and _____ (how many) times richer than a person 40 years ago. If the U.S. continues to grow as it has in the past at _____ % a year, then in 40 years output will _____ (double, triple, quadruple?) again.

6. US income is distributed so that: the 20% richest households earn _____% of the income and the 20% poorest households earn only _____% of the income.

7. _____ (What fraction) of all US children under six live with incomes below the poverty line. A family of four is termed below poverty line if they earn less than $_____ (how much) income.

Where the Money Goes

8. The U.S. economy produces $_____ (how much) per person per year. The government buys $_____ (how much) of that output. Investment buying (machinery, tools) is $_____ (how much). Each person buys $_____ (how much) per year.

9. (What fraction?) _____ of personal spending is on food, housing and medical care.

10. At a specialty store, for each dollar spent: (how much) _____ cents represents the cost of the good (how much) _____ cents represents the mark up (net operating expenses) on the good and (how much) _____ cents represents profit.

Possible Answers (Some are used more than once)

28,000	59.5	13	2.3
19,000	50	12	2
15,000	40	7.5	1.8
7,000	38.5	5.7	1-1/2
5,000		5	1/2
4,000		double	1/4

Priority List of Concepts

Economics: the study of how a society uses its limited resources to produce, trade, and consume goods and services.

the study of people's incentives and choices and what happens to coordinate their decisions and activities.

Opportunity Cost: the value of what someone must sacrifice or give up to get something.

Incentive: the expected benefit of a decision minus its opportunity cost.

Market: the activity of people buying and selling goods.

Market Process: the coordination of people's economic activities through voluntary trades. (buying and selling)

Property Rights: a person's legal rights to decide whether and how to use scarce resources or to sell them to others.

Competition: the process by which people attempt to acquire scarce goods for themselves.

Invisible Hand: through voluntary trades, each person helps others when he attempts to help himself. Even a person who acts in his own self interest is often " led by an invisible hand to promote an end which was no part of his intention. By pursuing his own interest he frequently promotes that of society." Adam Smith, *Wealth of Nations*

Short Answer Questions

MUST GOODS BE SOLD ONLY AT YOUR LOCAL STORE OR MARKET?

1. Given the definition of a market as the activity of people buying and selling goods, list at least five ways people can buy and sell goods today.

THE MARKET SYSTEM WORKS BEST IN SITUATIONS WHERE THERE ARE WELL- DEFINED PROPERTY RIGHTS.

2. What do you see as the major environmental problem of the day. Are there definite, well defined property rights to the item being damaged?

Basic Problems

THEORY

CHOICE AMONG SCARCE GOODS INVOLVES ECONOMIC ANALYSIS OF OPPORTUNITY COSTS AND INCENTIVES.

Whenever you make a choice among alternative activities, you have engaged in economic analysis of the incentives underlying the choice involved.

> Incentive = (Expected Benefit from the choice)
> minus
> (Opportunity Cost of that choice)

APPLICATION OF THEORY

In the following problems, you are to analyze the incentives that directed the choices.

1. What is the opportunity cost of going to summer school each summer while you are in college rather than taking five years to graduate?

(In formulating your answer to this question, itemize the value to you of all the benefits (PSYCHIC, REAL, IMAGINED) of completing college in four years, such as:

BENEFITS $ Value

      one year tuition and board   +

      earning a salary one year earlier   +

      _____   +

      _____   +

OPPORTUNITY COSTS

      Loss of summer job earnings   -

      Tuition for summer school   -

      _____   -

      _____   -

                     _____

TOTAL INCENTIVE

                     _____

2. What is the incentive for a college junior deciding whether to finish his senior year in college or accept a draft by a Pro Team:

BENEFITS $ Value

_____   +

_____   +

_____   +

_____   +

OPPORTUNITY COSTS

_____   -

_____   -

_____   -

_____   -

                                    _____

TOTAL INCENTIVE   _____

Advanced Problems

1. You are marooned on an island with many resources and only ten people. How would you set up the economy? Would you allow as much freedom in decision making as a market economy? Would you trust that the invisible hand would guide the economy to a benevolent (good) result?

Chapter 2

Solving Puzzles: The Methods of Economics

Learning Goals

1. Distinguish the difference between positive and normative statements in economics.

2. Use logical thinking about economic events to formulate an economic model.

3. Appreciate the value of an economic model in providing understanding, interpretation, and prediction of economic events.

4. Become aware of common fallacies that can hinder logical thinking.

5. Understand the statistical concept of correlation and the presentation and interpretation of it via graphs and economic data.

Key Term Matching Quiz

Terms

_____   1.   Evidence

_____   2.   Positive Statement

_____   3.   Normative Statement

_____   4.   Economic Model

_____   5.   Rational Behavior

_____   6.   Fallacy of Composition

_____   7.   Post Hoc Fallacy

_____   8.   Other Conditions Fallacy

_____   9.   Selection Bias

_____   10.   Positive Correlation

_____   11.   Negative Correlation

_____   12.   Correlation

_____   13.   Statistical Analysis

Definitions

a.   If two events always occurred together in the past, they will always occur together in the future.

b.   A measure of how closely two variables are related.

c.   A verbal, graphical or mathematical description of logical thinking about an economic issue.

d.   "What is true for one person must be true for the whole."

e.   A set of facts that helps convince economists that some positive statement is true or false.

f.   Use of math probability theory to draw inferences in situations of uncertainty.

g.   People use data that are not typical but are selected in a way that biases their results.

h.   People do the best they can based on their own values and information under the circumstances they face.

i.   Statements of fact.

j.   Two variables tend to move in opposite directions

k.   Two variables tend to increase and decrease together.

l.   "An event happened before another so the first event must have caused the second.

m.   Value judgment, they state what should be.

True/False Questions

_____   1. A positive statement is a value judgment about what should be.

_____   2. A positive statement is a statement of fact about what would be.

_____   3. A normative statement is either true or false.

_____   4. Logical thinking by itself is sufficient to reach reliable conclusions about economics.

_____   5. Evidence can prove an economic model.

_____   6. Statistical Analysis studies the merits (good or bad) of a model.

_____   7. For a model to simplify an issue, it makes assumptions that some features of an issue are important while other features can be ignored.

_____   8. Unconditional predictions answer the question, "What will happen if?"

_____   9. Economists do not always agree with each other about economic issues.

_____   10. A positive slope refers to a line or curve on a graph that runs downward and to the right.

_____   11. Every economic model requires assumptions about how people behave.

_____   12. "If...then..." statements, that say what will happen if someone does something, are the assumptions of the model.

_____   13. Models help economists to predict economic events.

_____   14. Unconditional predictions answer questions of the form, "What will happen if?"

_____   15. Rational behavior means that people do the best they can, based on their own values and information under the circumstances they face.

_____   16. Rational behavior implies that a person makes the same mistakes repeatedly.

Multiple Choice Questions

1.   Which of the following statements are positive statements:
    I.   Because of the flooding in California, the price of vegetables will rise.
    II. The government ought to place a ceiling on the price of vegetables, otherwise the price will rise too high.
    III. If the price of California vegetables rises, the demand for foreign vegetables, which are substitutes, will rise.
    IV. It is immoral for Americans to import foreign vegetables rather than buy vegetables from flood ravaged California.
        a.   I & II
        b.   II & IV
        c.   I & III
        d.   All the above.

2. If you do what seems best to you at the time, based on your limited information (according to this author), you are acting:
    a.   logically.
    b.   rationally.
    c.   incoherently.
    d.   scientifically.

3. The moon was full the night before the plane crash so the full moon caused the plane crash. This conclusion is invalid due to the:
    a.   Post Hoc Fallacy.
    b.   Other Conditions Fallacy.
    c.   Fallacy of Composition.
    d.   Selection Bias.

4. "What is true for one person may not be true for the economy as a whole." This statement refers to the:
    a.   Post Hoc Fallacy.
    b.   Other Conditions Fallacy.
    c.   Fallacy of Composition.
    d.   Selection Bias.

5. This fallacy occurs when "one event happened before another so the researcher believes that the first event must have caused the second.
    a.   Post Hoc Fallacy
    b.   Other Conditions Fallacy
    c.   Fallacy of Composition
    d.   Selection Bias

6. Selection Bias is a statistical fallacy that:
    a.   compares two or more things in a way that does not reflect their true differences.
    b.   occurs when people use data that are not typical but selected in a way that biases the results.
    c.   claims that if one event happens prior to another, the first event must have caused the second.
    d.   says what is true for one person may not be true for the economy as a whole.

7. Cross sectional data are:
   a. data collected on a single variable over a period of time.
   b. experimental data.
   c. data collected on many people at one period of time.
   d. All of the above.

8. The purpose of a model is to provide:
   a. understanding.
   b. prediction.
   c. interpretation.
   d. All of the above.

9. A model is "good" if it:
   a. makes assumptions.
   b. assumes that people behave rationally.
   c. uses data as evidence.
   d. makes accurate predictions.

10. Disagreements among economists:
    a. usually occur over value judgments.
    b. usually occur over factual statements.
    c. never occur about value judgments.
    d. All of the above.

Chapter Review (Fill in the Blanks)

1. _____ _____ is the use of mathematical probability theory to draw inferences in cases of _____.

2. Every economic model requires _____ about how people behave. The model often uses these _____ to draw logical _____. The _____ are the predictions of the model.

3. Economic models have three purposes: first, to _____, second to _____ and third, to _____.

4. Rational behavior means that people _____ _____ - _____ _____ _____ based on their own welfare as they conceive it.

5. The _____ _____ fallacy occurs when someone says that if two events always occurred together in the past, they will always occur together in the future.

6. Two variables are correlated when they _____ together.

7. Two variables are positively correlated when they move in the _____ direction.

8. Two variables are negatively correlated when they move in _____ directions.

9. _____ _____ are data on a single variable over _____ _____ _____ _____.

10. _____ predictions answer questions of the form, "What will happen if?"

Priority List of Concepts

Positive Statement: statement of **fact**, can be either true or false.

Normative Statement: expresses value judgments, states what **should or ought** to be.

Economic Model: a verbal, graphical or mathematical description of logical thinking about an economic issue.

Evidence: (facts) can disprove or add support to a model, but evidence can **never prove a model**.

Assumptions: general observations about how people behave so that logical (if...then) conclusions can be drawn about what will happen if someone does something.

Conclusions: predictions of the economic model.

Slope: measures the steepness of a line and represents the distance by which the graph goes up or down as you move one unit to the right.

    Negaive Slope: the shape (line or curve) runs downward and the right.

    Positive Slope: the shape (line or curve) runs upward and to the right.

Computing the Slope of a Line: Pick a point on a graph as a starting point (i.e., point A on the following graph). From point A move one unit to the right and then calculate how many units you must move vertically to get back to the graphed line.

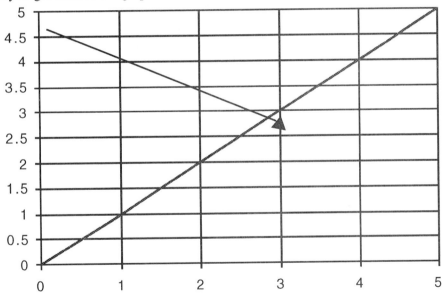

In this graph above, if you move right by 1 unit from 3 to 4, you must move up by one unit from 3 to 4 to get back to the graphed line. Thus this line has a positive slope because you had to move up by 1 to get back to the line.

Slope Formulas: the vertical change divided by the horizontal change
    the rise divided by the run
    $= (+1/+1) = +1$

Reading Points on a Graph: Each point on a graph represents two numbers (variables). One variable is measured on the horizontal axis (quantity) and one variable is measured on the vertical axis (price).

Price	5	4	3	2	1	0
Quantity	0	1	2	3	4	5

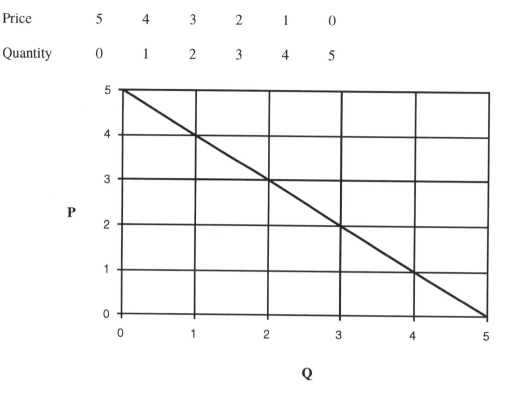

More Than One Curve on a Graph: each curve answers a different question.

A Curve Shifting Position: indicates a change in conditions.

Area Under a Curve: To compute the area under the curve in the graph above, make the triangle into a rectangle, compute the area of a rectangle, (base * height) or (5*5) and then divide the result by 2, equals 12.5 in this example.

Basic Problems (Using Graphs)

For questions 1-6 refer to the graphs below.

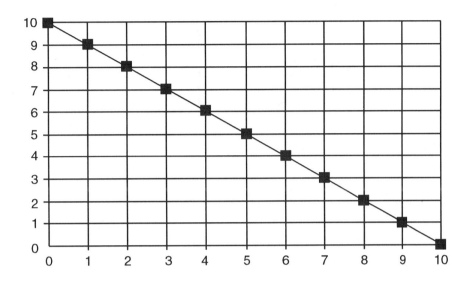

Graph (A)

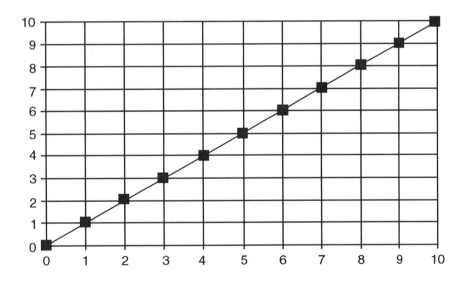

Graph (B)

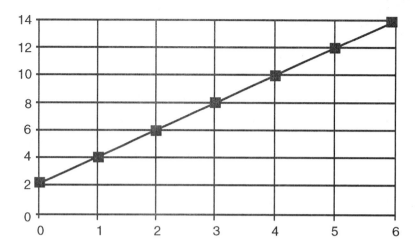

Graph (C)

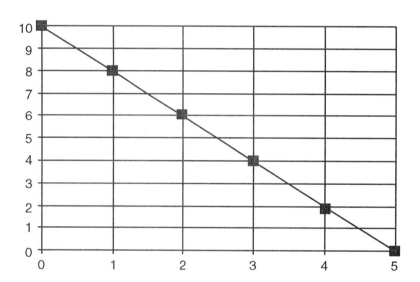

Graph (D)

1. Which graph or graphs exhibit a positive slope?   (A) (B) (C) (D)

2. Which graph or graphs exhibit a negative slope?   (A) (B) (C) (D)

3. Which graph has a slope of -1?   (A) (B) (C) (D)

4. Which graph has a slope of +2?   (A) (B) (C) (D)

5. Refer to graph (C), what is the quantity at a price of 4? _____

6. Refer to graph (D), at a price of 2, what is the quantity? _____

7. Refer to graph (E) below, what is the area of the triangle outlined in bold? _____

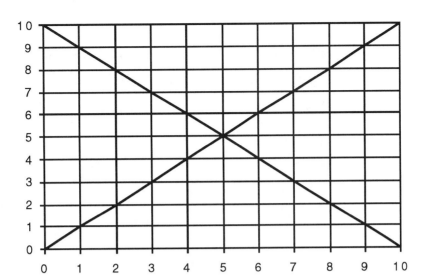

Graph (E)

Advanced Problems

1. Graph the following data. Put price on the vertical axis and quantity on the horizontal axis. Compute the slope of the line. _____

Price	Quantity
10	0
9	5
8	10
7	15
6	20
5	25
4	30
3	35
2	40
1	45
0	50

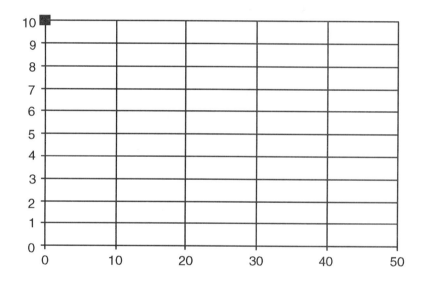

PART II

Fundamental Tools

Chapter 3

Let's Make a Deal: The Gains From Trade

Learning Goals

1. Compute opportunity cost of a trading decision.

2. Evaluate the comparative advantage of producing and trading one product vs. another.

3. Analyze the economic benefits of a trade and the distribution of those benefits, how they are shared.

4. Evaluate the economic efficiency of points on the production possibilities frontier.

5. Explain and illustrate economic growth by changing the assumptions underlying the production possibilities curve.

6. Understand the effect of taxes on efficiency.

Key Term Matching Quiz

Terms

_____   1. Trade

_____   2. Comparative Advantage

_____   3. Opportunity Cost

_____   4. Productivity

_____   5. Zero Sum Game

_____   6. Positive Sum Game

_____   7. Economically Efficient

_____   8. Economically Inefficient

_____   9. Barter

_____   10. Distribution of Income

_____   11. Equity

_____   12. Price

_____   13. Production Possibilities Frontier

_____   14. Economic Growth

Definitions

a. Who gets how much of the goods available in the economy.

b. The process of two people exchanging goods or services in the expectation of gain.

c. One person's gain is another person's loss.

d. Amount of a good that a buyer trades away per unit of the good he receives.

e. A situation which can't be changed so that someone or both gain without anyone losing.

f. What someone sacrifices to do one thing rather than another.

g. Production Possibilities Frontier expands outward faster than population growth.

h. Trading one good for another without exchanging money.

i. Exists when a person can produce a good with a lower opportunity cost than another.

j. Everyone can gain.

k. Equal distribution of goods or income.

l. A situation which can be changed so that all or at least some people gain while no one loses.

m. The amount a person produces per time period.

n. Graph which shows the amount of goods the economy can produce with available inputs and technology.

True/False Questions

____   1.   Whenever two people trade voluntarily, one or both of them expect to gain.

____   2.   Everyone has a comparative advantage at something, even when one person has greater productivity at every task.

____   3.   In a zero sum game, everyone can gain from a trade.

____   4.   An economy is able to produce at any point which lies inside or along the production possibilities frontier.

____   5.   When an economy is producing efficiently, it is producing at some point inside the production possibilities frontier.

____   6.   An inward shift of the production possibilities frontier means that the economy has experienced economic growth.

____   7.   The production possibilities frontier will shift outward if either new technology has been invented or there has been a discovery of new economic resources available for production.

____   8.   A trade is efficient if one or both parties gain and neither party loses.

____   9.   An efficient trade can change the distribution of income.

____   10.   Economic analysis deals with fairness and lets us know whether outcomes are fair or unfair.

Multiple Choice Questions

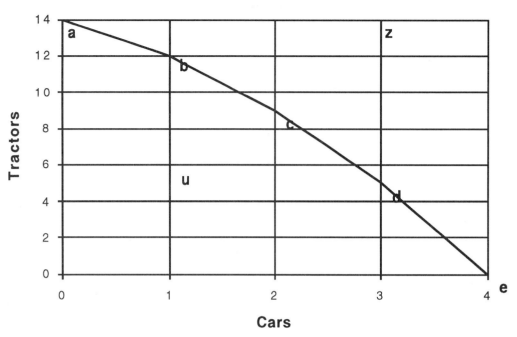

Figure 3.1

Refer to Figure 3.1 for questions 1-7.

1. Which of the following represent efficient points of production?
    a. Points "a" and "b"
    b. Point "z"
    c. Points "c", "d" and "e"
    d. Point "u"
    e. Both Answers a and c.

2. Which of the following represents an inefficient point of production?
    a. Point "a"
    b. Point "z"
    c. Point "c"
    d. Point "u"
    e. None of the above.

3. Which of the following represents an impossible point of production for this economy?
    a. Point "a"
    b. Point "z"
    c. Point "c"
    d. Point "u"
    e. None of the above.

4. What is the opportunity cost of one more car when you decide to produce four cars instead of three?
    a. Two tractors forgone.
    b. Three tractors forgone.
    c. Four tractors forgone.
    d. Five tractors forgone.
    e. Twelve tractors forgone.

5. What is the opportunity cost of one more car when you decide to produce one car instead of none?
    a. Two tractors forgone.
    b. Three tractors forgone.
    c. Four tractors forgone.
    d. Five tractors forgone.
    e. Twelve tractors forgone.

6. What is happening to the opportunity cost of cars as you produce more cars and less tractors along this Production Possibilities Frontier?
    a. The Opportunity Cost is constant, it does not change.
    b. The Opportunity Cost is increasing.
    c. The Opportunity Cost is decreasing.
    d. The Opportunity Cost decreases at first and then it increases as more cars are produced.
    e. None of the above.

7. What is happening to the slope of the Production Possibilities Frontier as you produce more cars and less tractors?
    a. The slope is constant, it does not change, the production possibilities frontier is linear.
    b. The slope is increasing, the production possibilities curve is concave.
    c. The slope is decreasing, the production possibilities curve is convex.
    d. The slope decreases at first and then it increases as more cars are produced.
    e. None of the above.

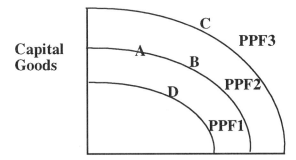

Refer to Figure 3.2 for questions 8 to 10.

8. Economic growth is shown by a movement from:
    a. Point A to B.
    b. Point B to D.
    c. Point B to C.
    d. Point C to B.
    e. None of the above.

9. When the Production Possibilities Frontier shifts inward from PPF3 to PPF1:
   a. Economic Growth has occurred.
   b. The economy has experienced a decrease in resources and an actual decline in their ability to produce.
   c. The economy has gained a Comparative Advantage.
   d. All of the above.
   e. None of the above.

10. When the Economy moves from point A to point B along PPF2:
    a. inefficient production occurs.
    b. the opportunity cost of consumer goods has increased.
    c. the opportunity cost of consumer goods has decreased.
    d. the economy has decided to produce less consumer goods and more capital goods.
    e. All of the above.

Chapter Review (Fill in the Blanks)

1. Economics deals with _____ _____ (statements of fact).

2. Economics doesn't say anything about _____, which could refer to _____ distribution of income or perhaps _____ should apply only to _____ (such as laws).

3. When an economy moves from a(n) _____ situation to one which is now _____, everyone can _____ or at least no one will _____ and some will _____.

4. The _____ _____ _____ is a graph which shows how many goods the economy can produce with available _____ and _____.

5. _____ _____ is shown by a shift outward in the production possibilities frontier.

6. Economic growth in the U.S. averaged _____ from 1950 to present.

7. People can gain from trade by producing goods that they are able to produce at a _____ _____, that is, with a _____ opportunity cost than other people.

8. When a situation is economically _____, there is no further way to change it so that some people can gain without anyone else _____.

9. Economic efficiency is _____ in that waste is _____. There are many economically efficient situations, each with a different _____ of _____.

Priority List of Concepts

Trade: When two people exchange goods, they expect to gain.

Gains from Trade: Occurs when people have different relative abilities to produce goods.

Comparative Advantage: Exists when a person can produce a good with a lower opportunity cost than others.

Opportunity Cost: What is sacrificed to do one thing rather than another. For example if you can either paint or clean on Saturday morning and you decide to paint your apartment; how much cleaning do you give up? Could you have cleaned two apartments in the time that it took you to paint one apartment. Then two cleaned apartments is the opportunity cost to you of painting one apartment.

Productivity: How much can each person produce in a certain time period.

Zero Sum Game: An environment in which one person's gain is another person's loss.

Positive Sum Game: An environment in which everyone can gain at the same time.

Economically Efficient: A situation that can't be changed so that everyone gains or so that some gain while no one loses.

Economically Inefficient: A situation that can be changed so that everyone gains or so that someone gains but no one loses.

Distribution of Income: Who gets what is produced in the economy.

Equity: fair, equal shares

Production Possibilities Frontier: shows all the possible combinations of goods that the economy can produce if it uses its resources and technology efficiently.

Economic Growth: An increase in the economy's output of goods and services per person. Shown by a shift outward of the Production Possibilities Frontier.

Technical Efficiency: A situation in which an economy cannot produce more of one good without producing less of something else. The economy is at a point on the Production Possibilities Frontier

Technical Inefficiency: A situation in which an economy could alter its use of resources so that it produces more output of some good without producing less of anything else. The economy is producing somewhere inside the Production Possibilities Frontier.

Short Answer Questions

1.   What is an efficient trade? Why do people have the incentive to make an efficient trade?

2.   How does a tax on the purchase of a good affect the efficiency of trading that product?

Basic Problems

1. Given the following information on productivity, compute the comparative advantage of Jan and Tom. Who should mow and who should wash cars?

	Productivity per hour	
	Lawns Mowed	**Cars Washed**
Jan	5	5
Tom	4	2

2. Given the following information on costs of production, compute the comparative advantage of Jan and Tom in mowing and car washing?

Costs of Production	Minutes	
	Jan	**Tom**
Mow Lawn	12.5	15
Wash Car	12.5	30

3. Draw the Production Possibilities Frontier which represents Jan's maximum production of lawns mowed or cars washed in one hour.

4. Draw the Production Possibilities Frontier which represents Tom's maximum production of lawns mowed or cars washed in one hour.

Advanced Problem

1.   Using the information given in the Basic Problems 1 and 2 about Jan and Tom, calculate the gain in leisure time for both Jan and Tom if Jan trades one car wash for one mowed lawn? Tom mows her lawn and Jan washes Tom's car. Is this trade efficient?

Chapter 4

Supply and Demand

Learning Goals

1. Draw a demand curve and a supply curve from information provided by a demand schedule and a supply schedule, respectively.

2. Determine equilibrium price and quantity given a graph of a demand and supply curve.

3. Explain the theory behind the slope of the supply and demand curves.

4. Distinguish between a shift and a movement along a demand or supply curve.

5. Explain the conditions which cause a shift in the demand or supply curves.

6. Explain and graphically illustrate an excess supply or excess demand situation in a market.

7. Draw a supply or demand curve using information provided in an equation.

8. Solve for equilibrium price and equilibrium quantity algebraically.

Key Term Matching Quiz

Terms	Definitions

Terms

_____ 1. Law of Demand

_____ 2. Tastes (Preferences)

_____ 3. Normal Good

_____ 4. Wealth

_____ 5. Substitute

_____ 6. Inferior Good

_____ 7. Income

_____ 8. Complement

_____ 9. Intertemporal Substitution

_____ 10. Income Effect

_____ 11. Substitution Effect

_____ 12. Nominal Price

_____ 13. Relative Price

Definitions

a. People's underlying likes and dislikes.

b. An increase in income decreases the demand for this good.

c. A change in the expected future price of a good causes a change in the current supply or demand of that good.

d. A good whose demand increases as income rises.

e. When the price of a good increases, its opportunity cost increases, as a result you buy less.

f. Money received annually from working, interest and gifts.

g. Goods that can be used in place of each other, such as Coke and Pepsi.

h. The opportunity cost of the first good measured in units of the second good.

i. Goods which people tend to use together, such as coffee and cream.

j. When the price of a good rises, holding constant other conditions, the quantity demanded falls.

k. When the price of a good increases, people buy less because they can't afford all the goods which they were originally able to buy. Their purchasing power has decreased.

l. The money price of a good.

m. Value of accumulated past savings.

True/False Questions

_____   1. A demand schedule lists the prices buyers actually pay for a good and the person's quantity demanded at each price.

_____   2. An increase in the price of a good, with no change in the other conditions, generally reduces the quantity demanded.

_____   3. The price on a demand or supply curve is a nominal price.

_____   4. If price is set above equilibrium price a surplus will result.

_____   5. When a surplus occurs, prices will rise towards the equilibrium.

_____   6. If the nominal price of a good rises faster than the average of nominal prices of other goods, its relative price falls.

_____   7. An increase in the price of pizza causes a decrease in the quantity demanded of pizza.

_____   8. The nominal price of a good is its opportunity cost measured in units of the other good.

_____   9. A change in tastes and preferences, such as the popularity of walking for fitness, increases the demand for products related to the sport of walking.

_____ 10. If a local sports shop has a sale on walking shoes, it will increase the quantity demanded of walking shoes.

Multiple Choice Questions

1. The amount of a good you choose to buy depends on all of the following conditions except:
   (a) its price.
   (b) how useful it is.
   (c) your income.
   (d) the price of inputs.

For questions 2 through 8 use the following answers to analyze the effects on the demand for pizza of the following changes in conditions:

   (a) Demand increases, demand curve shifts right.
   (b) Demand decreases, demand curve shifts left.
   (c) No change in demand.
   (d) Movement along the demand curve.

---

2. The Surgeon General declares pizza is a nutritious food.   (a) (b) (c) (d)

3. A college is expanding its dormitory space (Students order pizza).   (a) (b) (c) (d)

4. You receive a bonus at work.   (a) (b) (c) (d)

5. You must have a beer with your pizza if you are going to eat pizza at all and the price of beer increases greatly.   (a) (b) (c) (d)

6. The price of take-out Chinese food decreases.   (a) (b) (c) (d)

7. You expect a sale on pizza next week.   (a) (b) (c) (d)

8. The population is getting older and fewer people can digest pizza.   (a) (b) (c) (d)

For questions 9 through 12 use the following answers to analyze the effects on the supply for pizza of the following changes in conditions.

   (a) Supply increases, supply curve shifts right.
   (b) Supply decreases, supply curve shifts left.
   (c) No change in supply.
   (d) Movement along the supply curve.

---

9. The price of the cheese, which is used to make pizza, increases.   (a) (b) (c) (d)

10. There is a change in the technology for baking pizza which requires the use of a safer, but more expensive, oven.   (a) (b) (c) (d)

11. The price of calzone increases. Calzone is a product which can be produced just as easily by this producer.   (a) (b) (c) (d)

12. There is an increase in the number of pizza restaurants.   (a) (b) (c) (d)

Chapter Review (Fill in the Blank)

1. A change in quantity demanded occurs when the _____ of the good changes.

2. A change in demand occurs when a change in _____ other than the price of the good in question _____ the demand curve.

3. To graph a demand schedule, put price on the _____ axis and quantity demanded on the _____ axis.

4. Quantity demanded applies to a particular _____ period.

5. The amount of a good you choose to buy depends on many _____, including its _____, your _____ (what you like or dislike), how _____ it is, your _____, the price of _____, the price of _____, and the length of _____ you have to adjust to a past _____ in price.

6. When the price of a good rises, holding constant _____, the quantity demanded _____. Economists call this the Law of _____.

7. Demand curves slope _____ and have _____ slopes.

8. When the price of a good _____, holding constant other _____, the quantity supplied usually rises. Economists call this the _____ of Supply.

9. Supply curves slope upwards and have _____ slopes because a higher price _____ the incentive to produce and sell the good.

10. A change in quantity supplied occurs when _____ changes. A change in quantity supplied is shown as a _____ _____ a supply curve.

11. A change in supply occurs when a change in _____ _____ affects the supply schedule.

12. Conditions that affect supply include _____, _____, _____, _____ and _____.

13. Market clearing refers to market _____. At _____ there is no tendency to _____ unless some underlying _____ changes. _____ occurs where supply and demand curves intersect.

14. If price is _____ equilibrium, there is a shortage of the good and price tends to _____.

15. If price is _____ equilibrium, there is a surplus of the good and price tends to _____.

Priority List of Concepts

Algebra of Equilibrium

Given a linear equation of demand
$$Q_d = 20 - P$$

Compute P and Q_d for a Demand Schedule and graph the demand curve in Figure 4.2.

Given a linear equation of Supply
$$Q_s = -10 + 2P$$

Compute P and Q_s for a Supply Schedule and graph the Supply curve on Figure 4.2.

Graphically determine equilibrium price and quantity by the intersection of the Supply and Demand Curves.

Check your equilibrium answer algebraically by setting

$$Q_s = Q_d$$
$$10 + 2P = 20 - P$$
$$3P = 30$$
$$P = 10 \text{ (Equilibrium Price)}$$

Substitute the Price of 10 into the Supply Equation

$$Q_s = -10 + 2P$$
$$Q_s = -10 + 2(10)$$
$$Q_s = -10 + 20$$
$$Q_s = 10 \text{ (Equilibrium Quantity)}$$

The same answer for equilibrium price and quantity can be determined by graphing the demand and supply equations in Figure 4.2 and reading the equilibrium price and quantity at the intersection of the supply and demand curves.

Graphing Equilibrium

Derive a Demand Schedule by:
  setting Price equal to zero and solving for Qd;
  then setting Price equal to five and solving for Qd;
  and finally setting price equal to ten and solving for Qd

Price	$Q_d=20-P$
0	20
5	10
10	0

Graph the Demand Schedule on the graph labeled Figure 4.2.

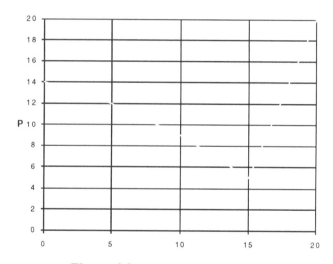

Figure 4.2

Derive a Supply Schedule by:
  setting Price equal to zero and solving for Qs;
  then setting Price equal to five and solving for Qs
  and finally setting price equal to ten and solving for Qs

Graph the supply schedule in Figure 4.2 and determine equilibrium price from the graph.

Changes in Demand: **shifts in the demand curve** caused by a change in conditions other than its own price, which affect the demand for a product.

Changes in Quantity Demanded: **movements along a demand curve** caused by a change in the price of the product.

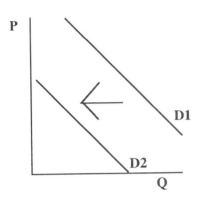

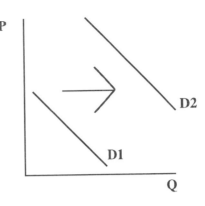

Demand Decreases

Curve Shifts Left

Less quantity demanded at every price than before the curve shifted left.

Demand Increases

Curve Shifts Right

More quantity demanded at every price than before the curve shifted right.

Conditions which can shift the Demand Curve

LEFT		RIGHT
(decrease)	Tastes and Preferences for the product	(increase)
(product becomes outdated)	Usefulness of the good	(product is a necessity)
(decreases)	Number of potential buyers	(increases)
(rises)	Price of a complement	(falls)
(falls)	Price of a substitute	(rises)
(longer)	Adjustment time after a change	(longer)
(decreases)	Income and Wealth for a Normal Good	(increases)
(increases)	Income and Wealth for an Inferior Good	(decreases)

Changes in Supply: **shifts in the supply curve** caused by a change in conditions other than its own price, which affect the supply for a product.

Changes in Quantity Supplied: **movements along a supply curve** caused by a change in the price of the product.

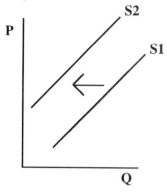
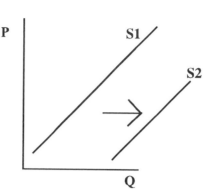

Supply Decreases	**Supply Increases**
Curve Shifts Left	Curve Shifts Right
Less quantity supplied at every price than before the curve shifted.	More quantity supplied at every price than before the curve shifted.

Conditions which can shift the Supply Curve

LEFT		RIGHT
(increase)	Costs of Production	(decrease)
(increase)	Price of Inputs	(decrease)
(increases costs)	Technology	(decreases costs)
(decrease)	Price of Other goods	(increases)
(lengthier)	Adjustment Time	(lengthier)
(decreases)	Number of Sellers	(increases)
(bad)	Weather	(good)

Relative Price of a Good: ratio of nominal prices of the goods. The relative price of a new car in terms of a new house would be equal to the Nominal Price of a new Car divided by the Nominal Price of a new House (i.e., $25,000 (car) / $250,000 (house) = 1/8 car per house.

Short Answer Questions

1. Illustrate the effects of a decrease in supply in Graph 4.4 below. Label the supply and demand curves D1, Sl, and S2. Show the beginning equilibrium as E1 and the ending equilibrium point as E2. What change takes place in price, quantity and the direction of the shift of the supply curve.

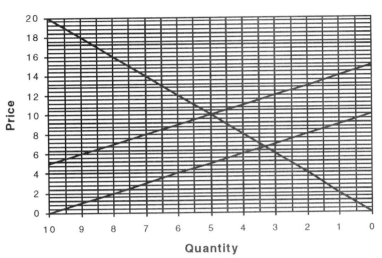

Decrease in Supply

Graph 4.4

2. Illustrate the effect of a simultaneous increase in both demand and supply on equilibrium price and quantity in Graph 4.5 below.

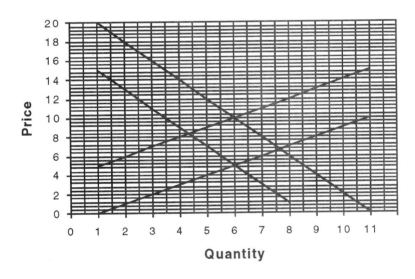

Increase in Supply and Demand

Graph 4.5

Basic Problems

1. Graph the following demand schedule for pizza as Figure 4.6.

Qd	Price
1	$4.00
2	3.50
3	3.00
4	2.50
5	2.00
6	1.50
7	1.00
8	0.50
9	0

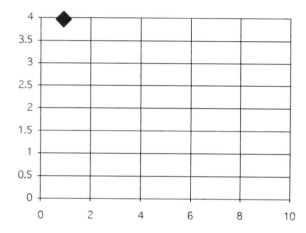

Figure 4.6.

2. Graph the following supply schedule for pizza in Figure 4.6.

Qs	Price
1	$0.00
2	0.50
3	1.00
4	1.50
5	2.00
6	2.50
7	3.00
8	3.50
9	4.00

3. What is equilibrium price and quantity? _____

4. Shade in the rectangle that represents total spending on pizza at equilibrium price.

5. Will a surplus or a shortage exist at a price of $4.00? _____

6. How much will the surplus or shortage be? _____

7. Due to this surplus or shortage that occurs at $4.00 what will happen to price to alleviate the surplus or shortage and move the economy towards equilibrium? _____

Advanced Problems

1. Using supply and demand curves, illustrate the effect of a tariff (tax) on the market for luxury Japanese cars. Explain which "other conditions" this tariff would change that would cause a shift in either the supply or demand curves or both. What is the effect on equilibrium price and quantity?

> For problems 2 and 3 below, use a supply/demand graph for each example. Illustrate the effects on equilibrium price and quantity in the following industries and identify which conditions are changing that cause the curve or curves to shift.

2. The Baby Boom population (the largest portion of the U.S. population) is aging. As a result the demand and/or supply in the following industries will be affected:
    a.   labor market
    b.   high fat, high salt, high calorie fast foods
    c.   "elder" retirement homes
    d.   college enrollment

3. Hurricane Andrew hit Southern Florida severely in 1992 destroying businesses and residential homes. How were the following industries affected?
    a.   construction
    b.   furniture
    c.   tourist, hotel/motel

Chapter 5

Elasticities of Supply and Demand

Learning Goals

1. Understand the concept of elasticity, the responsiveness of quantity demanded or quantity supplied to a change in price.

2. Calculate the percentage change in a number using the midpoint formula.

3. Interpret the relationship between elasticity and the shape of a demand or supply curve.

4. Distinguish between the elasticity and the slope of a demand or supply curve.

5. Use information about the relative elasticities of demand and supply to assess the effect of a change in demand or supply on equilibrium quantity or equilibrium price.

6. Explain the factors that can affect elasticity.

Key Term Quiz

Terms

_____ 1. Elasticity of Demand

_____ 2. Unit Elastic Demand

_____ 3. Inelastic Demand (or Supply)

_____ 4. Elastic Demand (or Supply)

_____ 5. Perfectly Elastic Demand

_____ 6. Perfectly Inelastic Demand

_____ 7. Cross Price Elasticity

_____ 8. Income Elasticity

_____ 9. Normal Good

_____ 10. Inferior Good

_____ 11. Elasticity of Supply

_____ 12. Perfectly Elastic Supply

_____ 13. Perfectly Inelastic Supply

_____ 14. Long Run Demand

Definitions

a. Horizontal demand curve. Elasticity is infinite.

b. Responsiveness of quantity demanded to a change in price.

c. Percentage change in quantity demanded of X divided by percentage change in the price of Y.

d. Negative income elasticity of demand.

e. Vertical demand curve. Elasticity is zero.

f. The absolute value of elasticity of demand is equal to one.

g. Percentage change in quantity supplied divided by percentage change in price.

h. Vertical supply curve. Elasticity is zero.

i. Positive income elasticity of demand.

j. The absolute value of elasticity of demand is greater than one.

k. Percentage change in quantity demanded of X divided by percentage change in income.

l. Horizontal supply curve. Elasticity is infinite.

m. The absolute value of elasticity of demand is less than one.

n. Shows price and quantity demanded at each price after buyers have adjusted completely to a price change.

True/False Questions

_____   1.   Elasticity of demand is the same as slope.

_____   2.   Elasticity of demand differs at different points along a straight line demand curve.

_____   3.   With unit elastic demand, total spending on a good does not change when price changes.

_____   4.   If the demand for certain Disney children's videos is inelastic, Disney would gain by having a sale (lowering the prices) on those videos.

_____   5.   With a perfectly elastic demand curve, an increase in demand means the curve shifts upward.

_____   6.   Demand for a good is more elastic if there are very few substitutes for the product.

_____   7.   A normal good has a positive elasticity of demand.

_____   8.   The larger the portion of a person's income that is spent on a good, the more elastic their demand for the good.

_____   9.   The long run refers to the time people need to fully adjust to a price change.

_____   10.   A long run demand curve is less elastic than a short run demand curve.

Multiple Choice Questions

1. An increase in supply raises total spending on a good:
    a.   if the demand curve is steep and relatively inelastic.

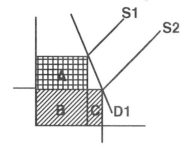

    b.   if the demand curve is flat and relatively elastic.

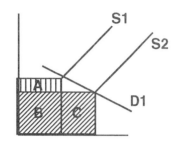

2. In question 1, total spending after supply has increased to S2 is represented by:
    a.   boxes A and B.
    b.   boxes B and C.
    c.   box C.
    d.   box B.

3. Elasticity of demand is described by all of the following except
    a.   the shape of the demand curve.
    b.   the slope of the demand curve.
    c.   the responsiveness of quantity demanded to a rise in price.
    d.   the percentage change in quantity demanded divided by the percentage change in price.

4. Elastic demand has an elasticity of demand with an absolute value:
    a.   less than one.
    b.   equal to zero.
    c.   greater than one.
    d.   equal to one.

5. Goods with elastic demands include all of the following except:
    a.   Chevy trucks.
    b.   ski lift tickets.
    c.   restaurant meals.
    d.   shoes.

6. Along the following demand curve, price increases from $4 to $6 and quantity demanded decreases from 8 to 7. What is the elasticity of demand over this range of the demand curve?

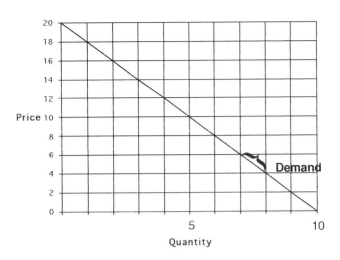

a. -3
b. -1
c. -0.5
d. -0.3

7. In question 6, the elasticity of demand over the range of price from $4 to $6 is:
a. elastic.
b. unit elastic.
c. inelastic.
d. perfectly elastic.

8. Using Graph 5.2 again, as price rises from $4 to $6, total spending:
a. rises.
b. falls.
c. remains the same.
d. cannot be determined.

9. In Graph 5.2, along the range of the demand curve from a price of 20 to a price of 18, elasticity of demand is:
a. elastic.
b. unit elastic.
c. inelastic.
d. cannot be determined.

10. Price increases by 5 percent and quantity decreases by 20 percent. What is the elasticity of demand?
a. elastic
b. unit elastic
c. inelastic
d. Cannot be determined.

Chapter Review (Fill in the Blank)

1. _____ means responsiveness to a change in conditions.

2. Elasticity of Demand refers to the responsiveness of _____ to a change in price.

3. Elasticity of demand is not the _____ of the Demand Curve.

4. Elasticity of demand _____ at different points along a straight line demand curve.

5. A vertical demand curve is _____ _____. Its elasticity is zero.

6. A horizontal demand curve is _____— _____. Its elasticity is infinite.

7. If demand is inelastic, buyers spend more on the good when price _____.

8. If demand is elastic, buyers spend _____ on the good when price rises.

9. If demand is unit elastic, buyers spend the _____ amount on a good when price rises.

10. When price decreases and demand is inelastic, buyers spend _____ on the good.

Priority List of Concepts

ELASTICITY OF DEMAND

Absolute Value of Elasticity	Elasticity	Straight Line Demand Curve	Response of Spending to a Price Increase	Response of Quantity Demanded to a Price Change
Infinite	Perfectly Elastic		Decreases to zero	Very responsive
Greater than one	Elastic		Decreases	Responsive
Equals one	Unit Elastic		Stays the same	Responds proportionately
Less than one	Inelastic		Increases	Fairly unresponsive
Zero	Perfectly Inelastic		Increases	Completely unresponsive

ELASTICITY OF SUPPLY

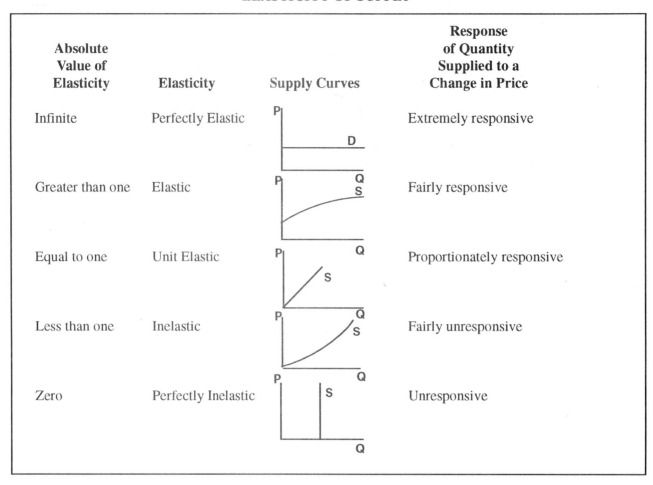

Absolute Value of Elasticity	Elasticity	Supply Curves	Response of Quantity Supplied to a Change in Price
Infinite	Perfectly Elastic		Extremely responsive
Greater than one	Elastic		Fairly responsive
Equal to one	Unit Elastic		Proportionately responsive
Less than one	Inelastic		Fairly unresponsive
Zero	Perfectly Inelastic		Unresponsive

FORMULAS:

Percentage Change in a number (Midpoint formula):

$$= (100) \times \left(\frac{\text{Change in a number}}{\text{Average of the two numbers}} \right)$$

Example: Quantity increases from a quantity of 100 to a quantity of 125. What is the percentage change?

$$= (100) \left(\frac{Q2 - Q1}{\frac{Q2 + Q1}{2}} \right) = (100) \times \left(\frac{125 - 100}{\frac{125 + 100}{2}} \right) = (100) \times \left(\frac{25}{125} \right) = 20\%$$

Elasticity of Demand $= \left(\dfrac{\text{Percentage Change in Quantity Demanded}}{\text{Percentage Change in Price}} \right)$. Elasticity of Demand is negative because an increase in price causes a decrease in quantity demanded.

Percentage Change in Price $= \left(\dfrac{\text{Percentage Change in Quantity Demanded}}{\text{Elasticity of Demand}} \right)$.

Percentage Change in Quantity Demanded = (Percentage Change in Price $\times$ Elasticity of Demand)

Elasticity of Supply $= \left(\dfrac{\text{Percentage Change in Quantity Supplied}}{\text{Percentage Change in Price}} \right)$. Elasticity of supply is positive because an increase in price raises the quantity supplied of a good.

Percentage Change in Price $= \left(\dfrac{\text{Percentage Change in Quantity Supplied}}{\text{Elasticity of Supply}} \right)$.

Percentage Change in Quantity Demanded $= \left(\text{Percentage Change in Price} \times \text{Elasticity of Supply} \right)$.

IN EQUILIBRIUM, quantity demanded equals quantity supplied. If SUPPLY SHIFTS OR CHANGES:

Percentage Change in Price $= \left(\dfrac{\text{Percentage Change in Equilibrium Quantity}}{\text{Elasticity of Demand}} \right)$.

Percentage Change in Equilibrium Quantity $= \left(\text{Percentage Change in Equilibrium Price} \times \text{Elasticity of Demand} \right)$

When supply changes the elasticity of demand measures movements along the demand curve.

IN EQUILIBRIUM, quantity demanded equals quantity supplied. IF DEMAND SHIFTS OR CHANGES:

$$\text{Percentage Change in Equilibrium Price} = \left(\frac{\text{Percentage Change in Equilibrium Quantity}}{\text{Elasticity of Supply}} \right)$$

$$\text{Percentage Change in Equilibrium Quantity} = \left(\text{Percentage Change in Equilibrium Price} \times \text{Elasticity of Supply} \right)$$

When Demand changes, the elasticity of supply measures movements along the supply curve.

$$\text{Cross Price Elasticity of Demand} = \left(\frac{\text{Percentage Change in Quantity Demanded of X}}{\text{Percentage Change in Price of Y}} \right)$$

If Cross Price Elasticity is positive, Products X and Y are substitutes. Example: If the price of Pepsi rises by 50%, and the quantity demanded of Coke rises by 100%, cross price elasticity is +2. People buy the cheaper substitute due to the price rise.

If Cross Price Elasticity is negative, Products X and Y are complements. Example: If the price of gasoline rises by 50% and the quantity of large gas guzzling cars demanded decreases by 50%, cross price elasticity is -1.

$$\text{Income Elasticity of Demand} = \left(\frac{\text{Percentage Change in Quantity Demanded}}{\text{Percentage Change in Income}} \right)$$

If Income elasticity of demand is positive, the good is a normal good. Example: If incomes rise by 20%, the quantity demanded of restaurant meals rises by 30%. Income elasticity of demand for restaurant meals is +1.5.

If income elasticity of demand is negative, the good is an inferior good. If incomes fall by 50% the quantity demanded of pasta and potatoes increases by 100%. Income elasticity of demand for starchy products like pasta and potatoes is -2.

Short Answer Questions

1. Why does the elasticity of demand differ along a straight line demand curve whereas slope remains the same?

2. What is the relationship between Total Spending on a product and the Elasticity of Demand of that product?

3. Explain the way in which the availability of substitutes, the adjustment time to a price change and the fraction of income spent on a good would have to change to increase the elasticity of demand for a product?

4. Explain how the elasticity of demand for gasoline would be affected by the invention of a cheap substitute for gasoline?

Basic Problems

1. The elasticity of demand for gasoline is -.25. By how much will quantity demanded increase if price falls by 50%?

2. If income elasticity of demand for McDonalds hamburgers is +1, by how much will quantity demanded change if income increases by 10%?

3. Price rises by 5% and quantity demanded falls by 50%. What is the elasticity of demand? Is this demand elastic or inelastic?

4. The price of beer rises by 20% and the quantity demanded of pizza falls by 50%? What is the cross price elasticity of demand? Are these products substitutes or complements?

Advanced Problems

1. An increase in the demand for cellular phones raises equilibrium quantity sold by 50%. If the elasticity of demand is -2 and the elasticity of supply is +3, by how much does the equilibrium price of cellular phones increase?

2. A firm knows that the elasticity of demand for its product is -0.5. Will its sales rise or fall if it increases prices?

3. An increase in the supply of gasoline raises the quantity sold by 50%. If the elasticity of demand is -1, what happens to the price of gasoline?

PART III

Applications of Supply and Demand

Chapter 6

Applied Price Theory

Learning Goals

1. Analyze the effects of government demand for goods and services on the total market and on private purchases.

2. Understand the time price of buying goods.

3. Analyze in economic terms the demand for health, marriage and family size and gender.

4. Explain the effect of the efficacy of the criminal justice system (Will it actually punish people who do wrong?) and the pressure of social norms on the supply and demand of a good.

Key Term Quiz

Terms

_____ 1. Private Demand

_____ 2. Market Demand

_____ 3. Government Budget Deficit

_____ 4. Time Price

_____ 5. Support Price

_____ 6. Deficiency Payments

_____ 7. Supply of Loans

_____ 8. Demand for Loans

_____ 9. "Crowding Out"

_____ 10. Non-money price

_____ 11. Expected Punishment Price

Definitions

a. Amount of money the government borrows when it spends more than it collects in taxes.

b. Borrowers need loans.

c. Government keeps milk prices high by demanding milk at this price set above equilibrium.

d. Difference between equilibrium price and target price set by the government to decrease supply.

e. Demand by people and non-governmental business.

f. The criticism that the buyer endures when he buys a good that social norms says he should not buy (i.e., cigarettes).

g. The value of the chance of being caught times the money value of the punishment given the person that is caught.

h. Sum of government demand and private demand.

i. The time necessary to buy, prepare and use a good.

j. Lenders provide this by lending money people save.

k. Refers to the reduction of private borrowing by government borrowing.

True/False Questions

_____   1.   People who are more sensitive than others to social pressures pay higher total prices for the goods than other people pay.

_____   2.   An increase in government demand for a good raises private purchases.

_____   3.   Living according to a code of honesty has an opportunity cost. People sacrifice something to be honest.

_____   4.   People with higher values of time won't pay higher prices to save time.

_____   5.   An increase in the expected bribes in an occupation increases the supply of labor and reduces the formal wage.

_____   6.   The cost of raising children on the farm years ago was more expensive than raising them in the city.

_____   7.   As women's wages have risen and as women have pursued higher levels of education, the opportunity cost of raising children has risen.

Multiple Choice Questions

1. An example of buying products at a store which charges a high time price but a low money price would be all of the following except:
    a. discount store.
    b. warehouse food store.
    c. local convenience store.
    d. department store in a fashionable mall.

2. People buy extra time when they do all of the following except:
    a) buy microwave ovens.
    b) hire someone to mow the lawn.
    c) personally grocery shop for their family every day.
    d) buy time-saving goods or services.

Use Graph 6.1 below to answer questions 3 to 7.

Increase in Government Borrowing

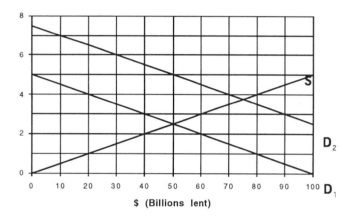

$ (Billions lent)

Graph 6.1

3. The increase in the demand for loans from D_1 to D_2 shows that the government budget deficit (as evidenced by increased government borrowing) has risen by:
    a. $50 billion.
    b. $100 billion.
    c. $25 billion.
    d. $10 billion.

4. Due to the increase in government borrowing, the interest rate:
    a. decreases from 3.75% to 2.5%.
    b. decreases from 7.5% to 5%.
    c. increases from 2.5% to 3.75%.
    d. increases from 5% to 7.5%.

5. Total lending:
    a. increases from 50 to 100 billion.
    b. decreases from 100 to 50 billion.
    c. decreases from 75 to 50 billion.
    d. increases rise from 50 to 75 billion.

6. The change in total lending is:
   a. less than the total increase in government borrowing.
   b. greater than the total increase in government borrowing.
   c. equal to the total increase in government borrowing.
   d. can't be determined from Graph 6.1.

7. Due to the increase in government borrowing, the private sector:
   a. borrows $25 billion less.
   b. borrows $30 billion less.
   c. borrows the same amount.
   d. borrows $50 billion less.

8. The private demand for loans is shown by:
   a. D_1.
   b. D_2.
   c. the horizontal distance between D_1 and D_2.
   d. S.

Using Graph 6.2, answer questions 9 to 12.

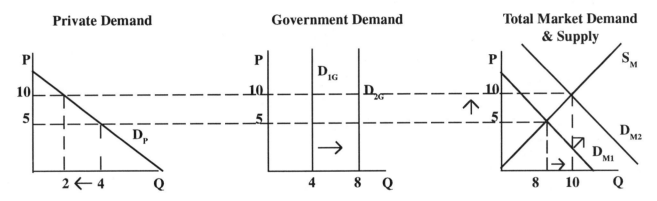

Graph 6.2

9. In Graph 6.2, government demand for healthcare has increased by a quantity of:
   a. 2.
   b. 4.
   c. 6.
   d. 8.

10. As a result of this increase in government demand for healthcare, the price of health care has:
    a. risen to 10 and private purchases of healthcare have fallen to 2
    b. risen to 5 and private purchases or healthcare have remained the same.
    c. fallen to 5 and private purchases of healthcare are equal to 4
    d. fallen to 10 and private purchases of healthcare are equal to 8.

11. The increase in the government demand for healthcare is:
    a. less than the change in total equilibrium output because the private sector buys less.
    b. greater than the change in total equilibrium output because the private sector buys more.
    c. less than the change in total equilibrium output because the private sector buys more.
    d. greater than the change in total equilibrium output because the private sector buys less.

12. As a result of increased government demand, total production of the market at equilibrium has:
    a. increased by 10.
    b. increased by 4.
    c. increased by 2.
    d. remained the same.

13. All of the following changes in conditions affecting demand would cause demand to decrease, shifting the demand curve to the left, except one.
    a. increase in the price of time
    b. increase in the expected punishment price for consuming an illegal good
    c. decrease in the probability of being caught buying an illegal good
    d. higher enjoyment opportunity costs of increased safety

Chapter Review (Fill in the Blank)

Government Spending and Borrowing

1. _____ in government demand for a good drive up its price and _____ private purchases.

2. If the government increases government spending and finances it by higher taxes, it _____ the demand for the goods the government is buying and _____ the demand for the goods which people have had to cut back their spending to pay the higher taxes.

3. The government can raise money for higher spending by _____ it. The _____ _____ _____ is the amount of money that the government borrows each _____ when it spends _____ than it collects in taxes.

4. Changes in _____-_____ affect the interest rate by changing the demand for loans.

5. Lenders _____ loans by lending the money people save. Borrowers _____ loans. The _____—_____ is the price of a loan.

6. An increase in the budget deficit _____ the market demand for loans. The _____ rises and total lending rises. The rise in total lending is less than the increase in government borrowing because the _____ _____ borrows less. The rise in the interest rate reduces the private sector's quantity demanded. Government borrowing _____ _____ (reduces) private borrowing.

7. The decrease in private borrowing reduces the _____ for goods that people would have bought with the borrowed money. This decrease in _____ reduces the equilibrium outputs of these goods. It decreases the demands for new equipment.

8. A government budget deficit can result from either of two causes: (1) _____ _____ _____ _____ _____ and (2) _____ _____ _____ _____.

Government Farm Policies

9. Governments try to keep prices of farm products _____. The U.S. government keeps milk prices high by choosing a _____ price and then buying as much milk as dairy farmers want to sell at that price. If the government did not buy milk, the price of milk would be _____ and the private sector would buy _____.

10. The U.S. government also keeps prices of farm products high by _____ their supplies. These programs reduce the supplies of farm products by _____ than they reduce total acreage planted because farmers stop producing on their least _____ land and keep farming their most _____. In administering supply-reduction programs, the government makes _____-payments to farmers.

Time Prices and Money Goods

11.   You pay two kinds of prices for many goods: a _____ price to buy, prepare and enjoy the good and the _____ price that you pay at the store. An _____ cost of time is the extra after tax income you could earn by working or the benefits you could enjoy from additional leisure time.

12.   A change in the value of _____ changes the demand for goods with high time prices such as _____ and _____.

13.   If the time price of a good decreases, the demand curve shifts _____ by the amount of the time price decrease. The market equilibrium price _____ but the total price of the good (_____ price _ + _____ price) _____.

Social Pressures, Illegal Activities and Bribes

14.   If people feel social pressure not to buy a good, they pay a _____ price and a _____ price. The _____ price is the criticism the buyer endures. An increase in social pressure not to buy a good, _____ its non money price and _____ demand for the good.

15.   The total price paid by buyers of an illegal good includes a _____ price plus an _____ _____ price that reflects the buyer's risk of being _____ and _____. If either the severity of the punishment or the risk of being caught _____, the expected punishment price will _____. A rise in the expected punishment price for buyers will _____ the demand for the illegal good. An _____ in the expected punishment price for sellers will _____ the supply of illegal goods.

16.   Safety is not _____. It has a price. You buy _____ when you drive carefully. We can measure safety as 1 minus the probability of _____, i.e., a fall in the chance of injury amounts to an increase in _____.

17.   Some people find it unfair that sellers benefit from _____ prices when a disaster occurs. Without _____ prices, sellers would lack the _____ incentive to _____ the quantity of supplies to the disaster area. The mere prospect that sellers can _____ if a disaster strikes gives these sellers the _____ to keep supplies readily available in case of a disaster.

Priority List of Concepts

An Increase Government Spending on a Good:

increases the government demand for the good from
(D1G) to (D2G),

increases the total market demand for the good from
(DM1) to (DM2)

increases the price of the good from
(P1) to (P_2),

and decreases the private purchases of the good (private demand) from
(Q1p) to (Q2p).

The private sector buys less because the increase in Qm (total amount sold in the market) is
less than the increase in Qg, the total amount sold to the government

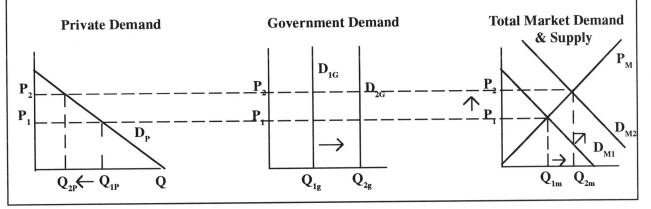

Increasing the Budget Deficit: An increase in government spending over and above the amount which the government collects in taxes:

    (Start from A in the diagram below)

    increases the government budget deficit,

    increases government borrowing,

    increases market demand for loans from D_1 to D_2,

    increases the interest rate from i_1 to i_2,

    total lending rises from Q_1 to Q_2,

    the rise in the interest rate reduces private borrowing from Q_{1p} to Q_{op}.

    Thus, government borrowing in this model has crowded out (reduced) private borrowing.

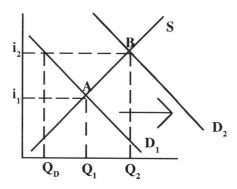

Time Price: the opportunity cost of the time it takes to buy, prepare and enjoy a good.

Total Price: the time price plus the money price you pay at the store.

Change in the price of time: shifts the demand curve of goods with high time prices (i.e., golf games, cards, etc.). If the price of time increases, the demand for the good decreases, the demand curve shifts left, equilibrium price and quantity falls.

An increase in social pressure not to buy a good (decrease in tastes and preferences) or an increase in the punishment price of an illegal activity: causes the demand for a good to decrease and the demand curve will shift left. Equilibrium price and quantity will decrease

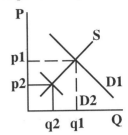

An increase in social pressure not to sell a good causes the supply for a good to decrease and the supply curve will shift left. Equilibrium price and quantity will decrease.

Bribery: partial substitute for formal wage payments. An increase in bribes increases the supply of labor, shifts the curve right and reduces the formal wage. The fall in wage, w1 to w2, is smaller than the average bribe so the worker who is bribed earns a higher total pay when you add in the bribe. Honest workers who take no bribes will earn less than those who are bribed.

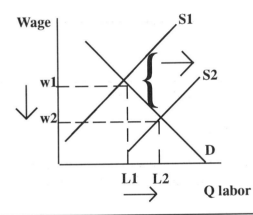

The average bribe is the vertical distance between the supply curves.

Short Answer Questions

1. Sleep takes time and, thus, has a time price. Today we earn relatively higher wages and have more wealth than our ancestors. What effect might this increase in wealth and income have on our demand for sleep? Using economic analysis, why would the demand for sleep be so affected?

Draw graphs of the supply and demand of the following products to show the effect on the money price and equilibrium quantity sold of:

2. Social pressure to buy healthy food.

3. Social pressure to sell healthy food.

4. Decision not to enforce the illegal sale of fireworks.

Basic Problems

1. Increasing the government demand for health care will have what effect on the private demand for health care? What happens to price, private purchases and total production of health care?

2. The government reduces the deficit by increasing taxes without increasing government spending. As a result people reduce spending on restaurant meals due to the increase in taxes. What effect do the aforementioned actions have on interest rates, borrowing by the private sector and the price and production of restaurant meals.

3. The government supports the price of natural gas. The supply of natural gas increases. What happens to equilibrium price, the quantity produced, the quantity consumed by government and the quantity consumed privately?

4. The money price of a concert ticket is $20. The concert will last three hours. You presently earn $5 per hour at work. If this concert is given during your afternoon work hours, what is the total price of the concert?

Advanced Problems

1. The "Big Dig" is slowing Boston traffic to a crawl. Travel time into the city has increased by at least 30 minutes. Using this chapter's exposition of the economics of time, what will this traffic disruption do to the demand for meals at Boston restaurants? Assume that the value of time is $12 an hour. How much has the time price of Boston restaurants changed and in what direction?

2. Government run state lotteries made betting on the numbers legal. In effect, this legalization decreased the expected punishment price to zero. How did this decrease in the expected punishment price affect the money price and the equilibrium quantity sold of numbers bets?

3. The Mets usher in "Pay and Usher" example in the text receives a money wage of $37.50 a game. What does the possibility of earning bribes during a game do to the supply of labor for that job and the formal wage?

4. Illustrate with a supply demand graph the effect on the demand for safety (CO_2 detectors) of two near fatalities from carbon monoxide in the home. What happens to equilibrium price and quantity as a result of this change in demand?

5. If U.S. laws, customs and social institutions have deteriorated to the point that honesty and moral lifestyles are not enforced, people who violate these codes are rarely caught and punished, what will this do to the price of expected punishment? As a result, what will have happened to the opportunity cost of living an honest life?

Chapter 7

International Trade, Arbitrage, and Speculation: Applications of Supply and Demand

Learning Goals

1. Explain the effects of international trade on equilibrium price and quantity traded.

2. Analyze the effects of a change in foreign demand or supply on equilibrium price and the quantity traded.

3. Understand the process by which arbitrage tends to eliminate price differentials (differences between the prices of identical goods in two different locations).

4. Understand the process by which speculation tends to make expected prices the same over different months or years.

5. Analyze international trade in loans using the theory developed for international trade in goods realizing that the equilibrium price is an interest rate.

6. Explain the incentive which causes people to buy and sell goods in the futures markets.

Key Term Quiz

Terms		Definitions

Terms

_____ 1. Consumption

_____ 2. Export

_____ 3. Import

_____ 4. Arbitrage

_____ 5. Price Differential

_____ 6. Arbitrage Opportunity

_____ 7. Speculation

_____ 8. Depreciation

_____ 9. Futures Market

_____ 10. Futures Price

_____ 11. Spot Price

_____ 12. Share of Stock

_____ 13. Stock Price

_____ 14. Random Walk

_____ 15. International Trade

_____ 16. Interregional Trade

Definitions

a. Sale to a buyer in another country.

b. Difference between the prices of identical goods in two different locations.

c. Buying something when its price is low and storing it to sell when its price is higher.

d. Price of a good for delivery at a future date.

e. Loss in value of goods because of spoilage or other wear and tear due to storage.

f. Amount of a good people use for their current benefit.

g. A price differential that exceeds the cost of arbitrage.

h. Trade that connects economies of regions within a country.

i. Buying goods to resell elsewhere.

j. Markets where people buy and sell goods for future delivery.

k. Links economies of different nations.

l. Legal right of ownership in business firms.

m. Prices of goods for current delivery.

n. Purchases from a seller in another country.

o. Price of a share of stock.

p. Equally likely to rise of all by the same amount, so on average it stays where it is.

True/False Questions

1. International trade is economically inefficient because it raises the price that some buyers have to pay.

2. With international trade, each country's supply and demand curves determine equilibrium price.

3. Exports will equal imports at the world equilibrium price.

4. An increase in demand in either of a pair of countries raises world equilibrium price.

5. Arbitrage prevents the prices of goods from equalizing in different locations.

6. In equilibrium there are no arbitrage opportunities.

7. When arbitrage costs nothing, the equilibrium price differential is zero.

8. With costless speculation, a good's expected future price exceeds its current price.

9. Economic conditions now depend partly on what people expect about the future.

10. The gains from speculation are larger than the losses if speculators have no costs of speculating.

Multiple Choice Questions

Given Graph 7.1, answer questions 1 to 6.

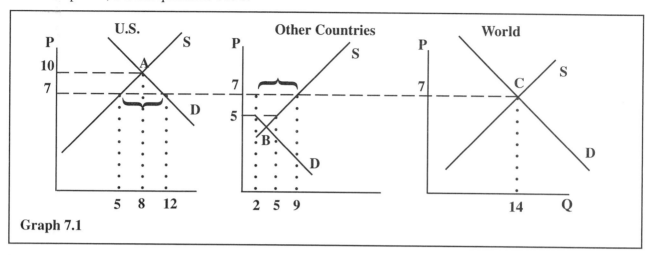

Graph 7.1

1. How much does the U.S. consume?
    a. 5
    b. 8
    c. 12
    d. 7

2. How much does the U.S. produce?
    a. 5
    b. 8
    c. 12
    d. 7

3. How much does the U.S. trade?
    a. The U.S. imports 4.
    b. The U.S. exports 4.
    c. The U.S. imports 7.
    d. The U.S. exports 7.

4. What incentive does the U.S. have to trade?
    a. The world price is above the price without trade in the U.S. so the U.S. could make a profit by exporting its goods at the world price.
    b. The world price is above the price without trade in the U.S. so the U.S. could make a profit by importing the good at the world price.
    c. The world price is below the price without trade in the U.S. so the U.S. could make a profit by exporting its goods at the world price.
    d. The world price is above the price without trade in the U.S. so the U.S. could make a profit by importing the good at the world price.

5. What represents the U.S. gain from trade?
    a. U.S. manufacturers have to sell the good at a lower price. due to the competition of foreign trade.
    b. U.S. buyers find that trade has reduced the price they have to pay for the good. Imports goods at a lower price than it could have produced the goods without foreign trade.
    c. U.S. buyers consume more.
    d. Both answers (b) and (c).

6. World production at the world price is the sum of:
    a. Equilibrium quantity supplied in each country when there is no international trade.
    b. Quantity supplied in each country with trade at the world price.
    c. Quantity demanded in each country with trade at the world price.
    d. Equilibrium quantity supplied in each country when there is no international trade.

7. Winners from international trade gain more than losers lose. As a result, international trade is:
    a. unfair.
    b. economically inefficient.
    c. economically efficient.
    d. equitable.

8. A rise in foreign supply:
    a. increases world equilibrium price and raises world quantity traded.
    b. decreases world equilibrium price and raises world quantity traded.
    c. decreases world equilibrium price and reduces world quantity traded.
    d. increases world equilibrium price and reduces world quantity traded.

9. The costs of speculation include:
    a. the cost of buying the good now rather than in the future.
    b. the risk that the future price will not be what you expect.
    c. the storage costs of the good from now into the future.
    d. All of the above.

10. The costs of arbitrage include all of the following except:
    a. identifying price differentials and traveling to the low cost location.
    b. buying the goods and finding a buyer.
    c. shipping the goods to the higher price location.
    d. profits.

11. You have an arbitrage opportunity if:
    a. the equilibrium price differential is zero.
    b. the price differential exceeds your costs of arbitrage.
    c. the price differential equals your costs of arbitrage.
    d. the price differential is less than your costs of arbitrage.

12. An increase in government borrowing:
    a. increases the interest rate by increasing the supply of loans.
    b. increases the interest rate by increasing the demand for loans.
    c. decreases the interest rate by decreasing the supply of loans.
    d. increases the interest rate by decreasing the demand for loans.

Chapter Review (Fill in the Blanks)

International Trade

1. Each year, people in the U.S. export _____ of total U.S. output and import even more. This international trade has been _____. In 1970, the U.S. exported only _____ of its total output. Just as _____ trade links the economies of different nations, _____ trade between cities and states connects the economies of regions within a country. _____ creates economic links across time.

2. Without international trade, _____ _____ supply and demand curves determine its equilibrium price and quantity traded. With international trade, _____ supply and demand determine equilibrium price. The quantity supplied in each U.S. the equilibrium price shows the amount that each country _____. The quantity demanded in each country at the world equilibrium price shows the amount that each country _____.

3. A country _____ a good if it produces more of that good than it consumes (if quantity supplied exceeds quantity demanded). A country _____ a good if it consumes more of that good than it produces (if quantity supplied is less than quantity demanded).

4. Only at _____ price does one country's exports equal its foreign imports.

5. Winners from international trade include buyers who pay a price that is _____ with international trade and sellers who sell at a world equilibrium price that is _____ than it would have been without trade. Losers from international trade include buyers who pay a price that is _____ than the price that would have prevailed without trade and sellers who sell at a world equilibrium price that is _____ than it would have been without trade.

6. Because winners from international trade gain more than losers lose, international trade is _____-_____.

7. Arbitrage means buying a good at a place where its price is _____ and selling it where its price is _____. Like international trade, arbitrage tends to _____ price differentials.

8. Speculation is the process of buying something at a _____ when its price is low and storing it to sell _____ when its price might be higher. Speculation differs from international trade and arbitrage in that the future is _____. Speculators _____ the chance that the future price might be _____ rather than higher. Speculators expect to _____. However, with costless speculation, a good's expected future price cannot _____ its current price. Like arbitrageurs, speculators earn _____ expected profits in equilibrium.

9. International trade in loans resembles international trade in _____. People supply loans when they _____ money. People demand loans when they _____ money. The price of a loan is the _____ _____. An increase in a country's demand for loans _____ the world interest rate and _____ the amount that the country borrows on world markets.

10. Futures markets are markets in which people buy and sell goods for _____ delivery. _____ Prices are the prices of goods for current delivery. The equilibrium futures price equals the expected _____ spot price.

Priority List of Concepts

Equilibrium with International Trade: World supply and demand determine world equilibrium price (PW) and the equilibrium price in each country at which goods are traded both domestically and internationally.. Only at this equilibrium price do the exports of the good equal the foreign imports.

Production: The quantity supplied in each country at the world equilibrium price. (In Graph 7.1, (U.S. q1 + Other Countries q3) = Production.)

Consumption: The quantity demanded in each country at the world equilibrium price. (In Graph 7.1, (U.S. q3 + Other Countries q1) = Consumption.)

Exports: A country produces more of that good than it consumes. The horizontal distance between the supply and demand curves of a country when quantity supplied exceeds quantity demanded. (In Graph 7.1, Other Countries, (q3-q1) = Exports.)

Imports: A country consumes more of that good than it produces. The horizontal distance between the supply and demand curves of a country when quantity supplied is less than quantity demanded. (In Graph 7.1, U. S. (q3-q1) = Imports.)

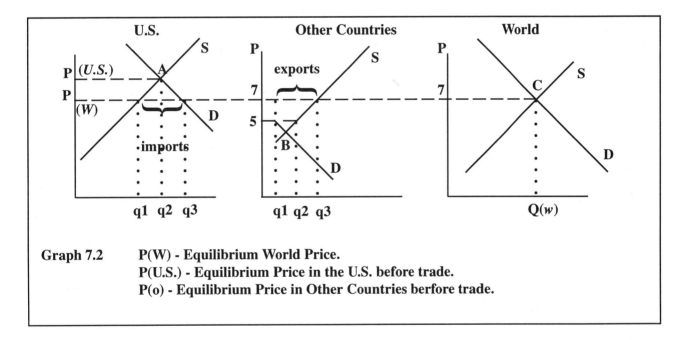

Graph 7.2   P(W) - Equilibrium World Price.
P(U.S.) - Equilibrium Price in the U.S. before trade.
P(o) - Equilibrium Price in Other Countries berfore trade.

Changes in Supply and Demand in International Trade:

Rise in Foreign Demand:

Foreign demand curve shifts right, (D_1 to D_2)

World demand rises, world demand curve shifts right, (D_{1W} to D_{2W})

This causes a rise in equilibrium price (P_{W1} to P_{W2}) and quantity (Q_{W1} to Q_{W2}).

Output rises in each country because the price increase raises quantity supplied (q_1 to q_2).

Consumption equals the quantity demanded at world equilibrium price.

Foreign consumption rises and U.S. consumption decreases.

U.S. imports decrease.

Foreign exports decrease.

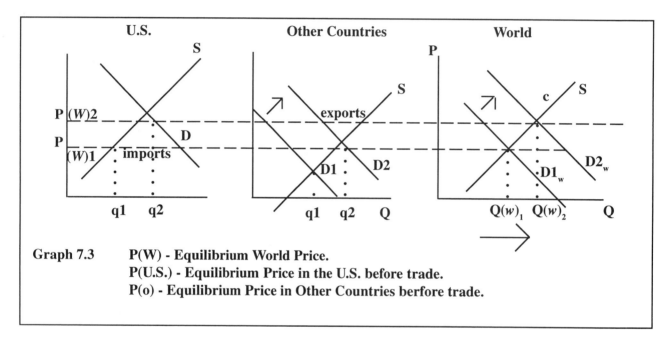

Graph 7.3   **P(W) - Equilibrium World Price.**
P(U.S.) - Equilibrium Price in the U.S. before trade.
P(o) - Equilibrium Price in Other Countries berfore trade.

Arbitrage: The process of buying something at a place where it's price is low, and selling it where its price is higher. Arbitrage tends to eliminate price differentials.

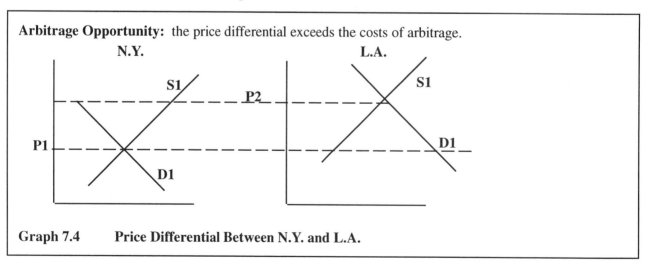

Arbitrage Opportunity: the price differential exceeds the costs of arbitrage.

Graph 7.4   Price Differential Between N.Y. and L.A.

Arbitrage reduces the price differential as shown in Graph 7.5. People buy goods at a low price in N.Y. and resell them at a high price in L.A. The demand for goods rises in N.Y., the supply of goods rises in L.A. This additional arbitrage reduces the price differential until the arbitrage opportunity disappears and the price differential is equal to the arbitrage costs.

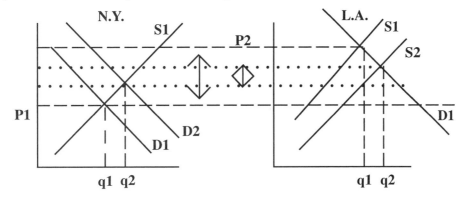

Graph 7.5   Price Differential between L.A. and N.Y. decreases.

Costless Arbitrage: Price differential at equilibrium disappears. Equilibrium price (P3) is determined by the supply and demand everywhere.

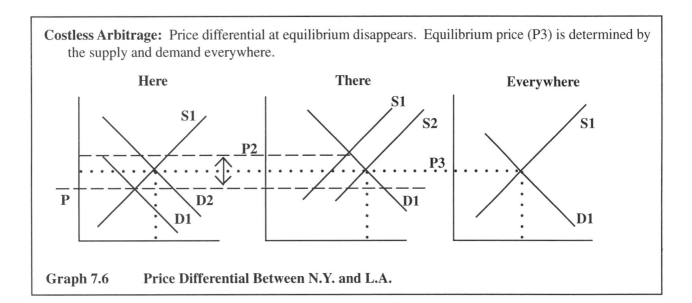

Graph 7.6   Price Differential Between N.Y. and L.A.

Speculation: Buying something at a time when its price is low and storing it to sell later when its price might be higher. Speculation differs from international trade and arbitrage in that the future is uncertain. Speculators risk the chance that the future price might be lower rather than higher. Speculators expect to profit.

Costless speculation: A good's expected future price cannot exceed its current price. Speculators earn zero expected profits in equilibrium.

International Borrowing and Lending: International trade in loans. Effects of Lower U.S. Borrowing, Graph 7.7 (i.e., the government budget deficit decreases):

  decrease the U.S. demand for loans (D_1 to D_2)

  decreases the world demand for loans, (D_1 to D_2)

  decreases the world interest rate, (6 to 5.5%)

  the interest rate decrease

    decreases U.S. lending (q_2 to q_1)

    decreases U.S. borrowing (q_4 to q_3)

    decreases foreign lending (q_4 to q_3)

    increases foreign borrowing (q_1 to q_2)

Lower government budget deficits decrease equilibrium borrowing from foreign countries.

  Total borrowing falls, but total borrowing by the private sector increases.

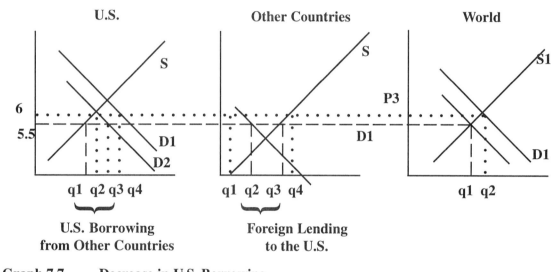

Graph 7.7   Decrease in U.S. Borrowing

Short Answer Questions

1. What would happen to U.S. interest rates if foreign countries could not lend to the U.S.?

Basic Problems

1. Illustrate graphically the effects of a decrease in the foreign supply of oil on the U.S. and the World. What happens to equilibrium price, quantity, consumption, production, imports and exports in the World as a whole, the U.S. and the other countries?

2. Illustrate graphically the effects of a decrease in foreign demand for U.S. steel. What happens to equilibrium price, quantity, consumption, production, imports and exports in the World as a whole, the U.S. and the other countries?

Chapter 8

Price Controls and Taxes

Learning Goals

1. Explain the intended as well as the unintended effects of the imposition of a legal price.

2. Understand the types of rationing that are used to alleviate a shortage when price is legally set and not able to rise.

3. Analyze the effects of taxes and subsidies on equilibrium price and quantity traded.

4. Explain the effects of restrictions on international trade on equilibrium price and quantity traded of both U. S. and foreign goods.

5. Using the theory of minimum legal prices set above equilibrium, be able to present a case against the imposition of a minimum wage.

Key Term Quiz

Terms

_____ 1. Maximum Legal Price

_____ 2. Shortage

_____ 3. Nonprice Rationing

_____ 4. Tie-in Sale

_____ 5. Black Market

_____ 6. Minimum Legal Price

_____ 7. Surplus

_____ 8. Tax Rate

_____ 9. Tariff

_____ 10. Import Quota

_____ 11. Queuing

_____ 12. Laffer Curve

Definitions

a. Price floor, lowest price at which the government allows people to buy or sell a good.

b. Sale only to a buyer who also agrees to buy some other product.

c. Tax on imports.

d. The buying or selling of an illegal good.

e. Quantity demanded is less than the quantity supplied at the current price.

f. Limit on the quantity of imports.

g. System for choosing who gets how many goods when there is a shortage.

h. Price ceiling, highest price at which the government allows people to buy or sell a good.

i. Per unit tax expressed as a percentage of its price.

j. Rationing by waiting.

k. Quantity demanded exceeds quantity supplied at the current price.

l. Graphically illustrates the concept that above certain tax rates, a rise in tax rates lowers income tax payments.

True/False Questions

_____ 1. Rationing by waiting lets the buyer pay less than the money price.

_____ 2. The government tries to keep prices low by setting minimum legal prices.

_____ 3. Black markets are common wherever the government imposes price controls or tries to limit trade.

_____ 4. With a tax imposed on the product, the price to buyers rises by a large percentage of the tax if demand is very inelastic.

_____ 5. An increase in the tax rate will always increase total tax payments.

_____ 6. Some evidence indicates that the tax payments in the U.S. increased as a result of the tax rate cuts in the 1980's.

_____ 7. A quota on imports raises the price that U.S. buyers pay and the extra money goes to the U. S. Government.

_____ 8. It is estimated that government programs which support the price of milk at a minimum legal price have doubled the price of milk.

_____ 9. Due to the imposition of import quotas and minimum legal prices, sugar costs less in the U.S. than in the rest of the world.

_____ 10. A subsidy is a negative tax.

Multiple Choice Questions

1. A maximum legal price:
   a. is a price ceiling that is set above equilibrium price and will cause a surplus.
   b. is a price floor that is set above equilibrium price and will cause a shortage.
   c. is a price ceiling that is set below equilibrium price that will cause a shortage and reduce production.
   d. is a price floor that is set below equilibrium price and will cause a surplus.

2. All of the following are means of nonprice rationing except:
   a. queuing.
   b. taxes.
   c. coupons which grant the legal price to buy a good.
   d. bribery.

3. The maximum legal price with rationing by sellable coupons:
   a. decreases the costs to buyers.
   b. rations the available supply with no change in costs.
   c. raises the cost to buyers.
   d. is more costly to consumers than giving them the coupons.

4. The long run effects of rent control include all of the items below except:
   a. it creates no change in the number of apartments because their supply is inelastic in the long run.
   b. it reduces the incentives to build new or repair old apartments.
   c. it creates incentives for landlords to convert to condos.
   d. it decreases the quality of the available apartments.

Using Graph 8.1, answer questions 5 through 7.

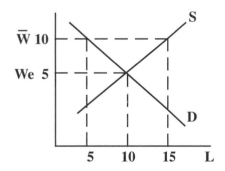

Graph 8.1

5. When minimum wage is set at $10, what is the effect on employment?
   a. Employment falls to zero.
   b. Employment falls to 5.
   c. Employment remains at 10.
   d. Employment rises to 15.

6. When minimum wage is set at $10, what is the effect on unemployment?
    a. Unemployment remains at zero.
    b. Unemployment rises to 5.
    c. Unemployment rises to 10.
    d. Unemployment rises to 15.

7. When the minimum wage is set above equilibrium wage,
    a. the quantity of labor demanded is equal to the quantity supplied of labor.
    b. an excess demand for labor occurs.
    c. an excess supply of labor occurs.
    d. a shortage of labor occurs.

8. In Graph 8.2 below, the government sets a maximum legal price at $5. This legal price creates:
    a. a shortage of 10.
    b. a surplus of 10.
    c. a shortage of 20.
    d. a shortage of 25.

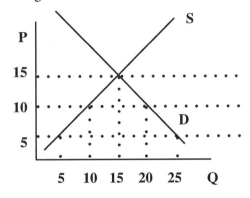

Graph 8.2

9. Sellers try to avoid maximum legal prices by engaging in:
    a. tie in sales.
    b. bribery.
    c. queuing.
    d. Both a and b.

10. Refer to Graph 8.3 (a, b, and c). In which graph will the price to the buyer rise the least if a tax of $1.00 is imposed?
    a. Graph 8.3(a)
    b. Graph 8.3(b)
    c. Graph 8.3(c)
    d. The price to the buyer falls in all three cases.

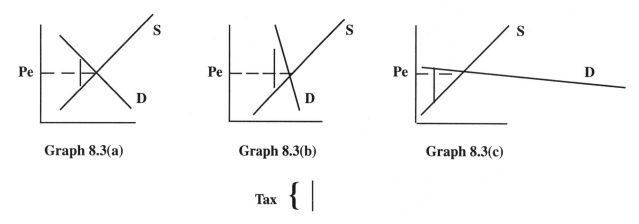

Graph 8.3(a)   **Graph 8.3(b)**   **Graph 8.3(c)**

Tax {

11. In Graph 8.4, a an excise tax is imposed on the product. Who pays the tax?
    a. The buyer pays the whole tax.
    b. The seller pays the whole tax.
    c. Both buyer and seller pay equal shares of the tax.
    d. Neither pay any of the tax because the demand for the product in perfectly inelastic.

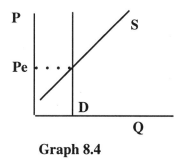

Graph 8.4

Chapter Review (Fill in the Blanks)

Maximum Legal Prices

1. Governments throughout history have tried to keep prices _____ by making it illegal to charge prices _____ some level. But laws cannot repeal the forces of _____ and demand, so price controls in the form of price ceilings, _____- _____ _____ set below equilibrium price, cause _____ _____ and _____ and reduce _____.

2. A shortage is a situation in which the quantity _____ exceeds the quantity _____ at the current price. When there is a shortage at a legal price, _____ rationing is a system for choosing who gets how many goods. Types of rationing include: _____, _____, and _____.

Minimum Legal Prices

3. Governments sometimes impose price controls to keep prices high. Today, the best known minimum legal price is the _____ _____. This _____ _____ is a _____ _____ _____, the lowest price at which the government allows people to buy or sell a good. Assume this _____- _____ exceeds the equilibrium price. This causes a _____ and reduces _____ of the good. A surplus situation occurs when quantity _____ exceeds quantity _____. Sellers cannot _____ all the goods they would like to _____ at the _____ legal price.

4. Minimum wage causes a _____ of labor services, _____, when it exceeds the equilibrium wage. Minimum wage lowers the quantity _____ of labor services and thereby, _____ employment. The minimum wage has a stronger effect on the employment of _____ than on the employment of _____.

5. The government sets _____ legal prices above equilibrium (called _____ prices) on three grades of milk and buys all the _____ milk at those prices. The milk _____ price exceeds the world equilibrium price, so foreign producers try to _____ their milk to the U. S. To prevent imports, the U.S. imposes _____- _____. The government programs have _____ the price of milk which benefits _____.

Taxes

6. A tax on a good creates a _____ between the price that buyers pay including the tax and the price that sellers receive net of the tax, the difference is the _____ _____ _____. A tax _____ the price to the buyers (Pb) and _____ the price to the sellers (Ps) and _____ the quantity traded.

7. Neither the _____ buyers pay nor the _____ sellers receive depends on who is legally responsible for paying the tax to the government.

Tariffs (Tax on Imports)

8. A tariff _____ the price of a good to the importing country and _____ the price to the exporting country; the difference is the _____. The tariff _____ output and _____ consumption in the importing country and _____ output and _____ consumption in the exporting country. It also _____ international trade. A _____ on imports has the same effects, except that the _____ collects _____ from a tariff but _____ from a quota. The quota _____ the price that foreign exporters receive, so they get the _____ that the government would have collected with a _____.

Priority List of Concepts

Price Controls

Maximum Legal Price (Graph 8.5):
highest price at which the government allows people to buy or sell a good.
price ceiling.
usually set below equilibrium price.
causes shortages (Qd-Qs), long lines and a decrease in production from Qe to Qs
the legal price control prevents price from rising due to the shortage, thus the shortage will
persist.

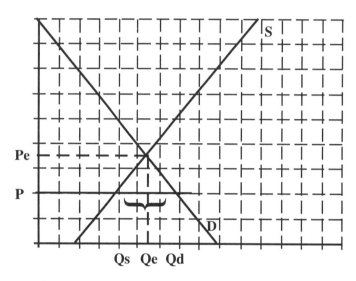

Graph 8.5

Nonprice Rationing: a system for choosing who gets how many goods when there is a shortage.
Rationing by Waiting: queuing, goods are allocated on a first come, first served basis.
forces buyers to pay a time price in addition to the money price.
Rationing by Coupons: government provides certain buyers with legal rights to buy a good. Usually the government does not sell the coupons.
Sellable Coupons: raises the cost to buyers. In Graph 8.6(a), the price ceiling decreases available
quantity supplied to Qs. This represents the inelastic supply of coupons provided for sale by the
government. The coupons will sell for Pc. in Graph 8.6(b). People will pay a total price of the
legal price plus the coupon price, $\overline{P} + P_c$ = Total Price.

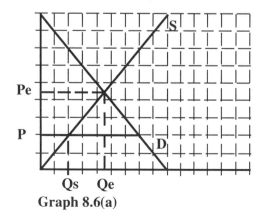

Graph 8.6(a)

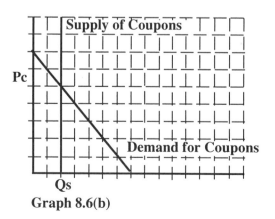

Graph 8.6(b)

Bribery: Buyers pay a money price plus a bribe.

Legal Price set at zero: causes a shortage and the development of indirect ways of paying for the product. Graph 8.6

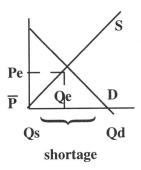

Graph 8.6

Black Market: market for illegal goods or a market where goods are sold at illegal prices.

Price Controls
    Minimum Legal Price (Graph 8.7):
        lowest price at which government allows people to buy or sell a good.
        price floor.
        usually set above equilibrium price.
        causes a surplus (Qs-Qd), Quantity supplied is greater than quantity demanded.
        reduces the quantity demanded and increases the quantity supplied.
        the legal price control prevents price from falling due to the surplus, thus the surplus will persist.

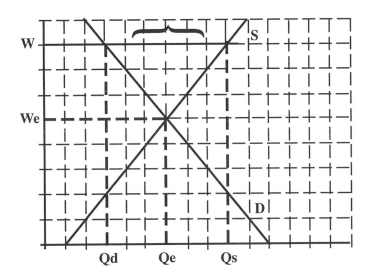

Graph 8.7

Tax rate: per unit tax expressed as a percentage of its price.
    Per unit tax: creates a gap between the price the buyer pays and the price that sellers receive.

Equilibrium with a tax: Price that buyers pay (Pb) exceeds the price that sellers receive (Ps) minus the tax. by the per unit tax (T). Pb - Ps = T

In Graph 8.8 equilibrium quantity traded before the tax was Qe. The imposition of a per unit tax equal to T causes equilibrium quantity to fall from Qe to Q1, the price to buyers (Pb) rises and the price to sellers (Ps) falls.

Graphical analysis of a per unit tax: (Graph 8.8) Fit a line with a height equal to the per unit tax into the Supply/Demand diagram until the top of the tax line (T) touches the demand curve and the bottom of the tax line (T) touches the supply curve.

Proportion of the tax paid by buyers vs. sellers:

Buyers pay (Pb-Pe) more due to the tax.

Sellers receive (Pe-Ps) less due to the tax.

Sellers pass some of the tax on to the consumer (Pb-Pe) but they pay the rest (Pe-Ps)

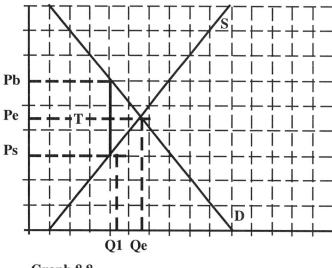

Graph 8.8

Taxes and elasticities of demand and supply: relative elasticities determines who pays the tax. Whomever has the relatively more inelastic (steeper sloped) demand or supply will pay more of the tax. For example, in Graph 8.8 above, both demand and supply curves are similarly sloped and have the same elasticity, thus buyer and seller share the tax. In Graph 8.9 below, the demand is perfectly inelastic while the supply curve is relatively elastic. In this case the buyer pays all of the tax.

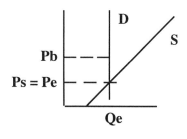

Graph 8.9

Tax Payment: per unit tax rate multiplied times the quantity traded (Qd). In Graph 8.9 this would equal
(Q1 * T)

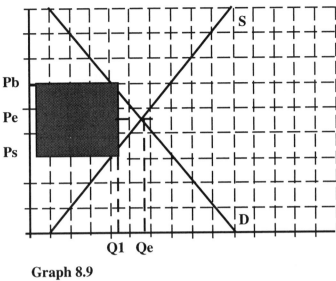

Graph 8.9

Subsidies: negative taxes. Graph 8.10
the price to the buyer net of subsidy (Pb) will be less than the price to the seller (Ps) plus the subsidy
(Y).
the subsidy (Y):
raises the price to the seller (Ps)
decreases the price to the buyer (Pb)
increases the quantity traded from Qo to Q1
costs are equal to Y multiplied times Q1 (Y*Q1) shown as a shaded rectangle in Graph 8.11

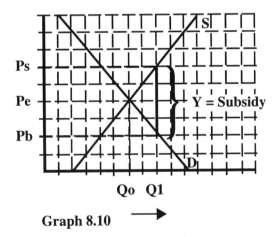

Graph 8.10

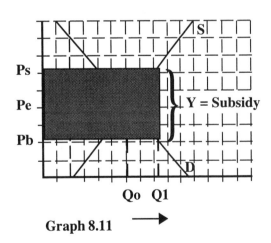

Graph 8.11

Tariff: tax on imports
 tariff works like a cost of arbitrage.
 without trade, U.S. price =$300 and Foreign price = $200.
 with trade the World price equals $260 and the U.S. imports the product.
 the U.S. imposes a tariff of $50 which raises the price U.S. suppliers receive to $280 and decrease
  price foreigners receive to $230.
 both buyers and sellers are affected by the tariff.
  hurts U.S. buyers, they pay more.
  hurts foreign sellers, they receive a lower price.
  helps foreign buyers, they pay less.
  helps U.S. government with increased tax revenue

Quota: a quantity limit on imports.
 similar to a tariff, it raises the price U.S. buyers pay.
 different from a tariff in that the extra money goes to foreign sellers, not the U.S. government.

Short Answer Questions

1. The legal price for organ transplants is set at zero.   This means that people can't receive payments for donating organs. How does this price ceiling affect the market for organs?

2. Present an argument against the imposition of a minimum wage if that minimum wage will be a minimum legal price set above equilibrium price.

3. The government wants to penalize a producer for pollution. It levies a tax on the producer. Under what conditions of elasticity of supply and demand will this producer pay none of the tax.

Basic Problems

1. Given the following demand and supply curves in Graph 8.12, a legal price of $3 is imposed. Will this cause a surplus or a shortage? What is the size of the surplus or shortage? At the legal price of $3, what quantity will be available for sale?

If rationing is accomplished by selling coupons, trace out on the Graph 8.13 the demand for coupons. How many coupons will be sold and how much will they be sold for? Would it make any difference as to who finally bought the merchandise if you had given away the coupons rather than sold them?

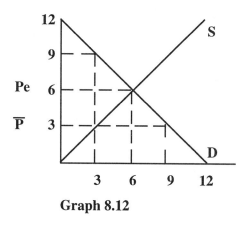

Graph 8.12

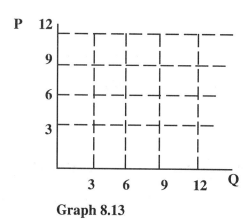

Graph 8.13

2. Given the supply demand curves in Graph 8.14, a tax of $2 is imposed on the producer. Graphically levy the tax. Who will pay the greatest portion of the tax? How much tax revenue will the government receive? Show Pb, Ps and T on the graph. Darken in the rectangle representing tax revenue. Which curve, supply or demand, is relatively inelastic?

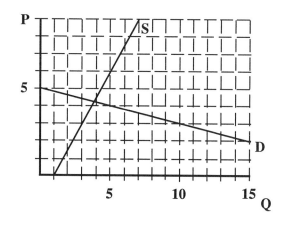

PART IV

Choices and Their Implications

Chapter 9

Choices and Demand

Learning Goals

1. Graph a consumer's budget line from information on the price of goods and the consumer's income.

2. Determine consumer surplus given graphical or numerical information on the Demand Curve and equilibrium price.

3. Explain the theory of a rational choice by a consumer.

4. Distinguish between value and price.

5. Discuss the implications of the subjective nature of utility.

6. Explain the theory of utility maximization.

7. Maximize Net Benefit using the logic of rational choice.

8. Solve for Consumer Surplus mathematically.

Key Term Matching Quiz

Terms

____ 1. Consumer Surplus

____ 2. Willingness to Pay

____ 3. Budget Line

____ 4. Marginal Benefit

____ 5. Marginal Cost

____ 6. Net Benefit

____ 7. Sunk Costs

____ 8. Indifferent

____ 9. Marginal Rate of Substitution of Y for X

____ 10. Marginal Utility

____ 11. Utility

____ 12. Utils

____ 13. Maximize Utility

____ 14. Indifference Curve

Definitions

a. Height of the demand curve.

b. The increase in total benefit from doing something once more.

c. Costs you have already paid and cannot recover.

d. Graph of a person's feasible choices, what the person can afford.

e. Represents combinations of goods between which a consumer does not care which combination he consumes.

f. Benefit people get from consuming goods and services.

g. The increase in total cost from doing something once more.

h. Increase in total utility gained from an additional unit of the good.

i. When the marginal rates of substitution between any pair of goods equals their relative price.

j. Total benefit minus total cost.

k. Slope of the Indifference Curve.

l. Units of utility.

m. Benefit to a consumer of being able to buy a good at the equilibrium price.

n. A person does not care which combination of goods he consumes.

True/False Questions

_____ 1. Consumer surplus is based on each person's own tastes and values.

_____ 2. Willingness to pay does not depend on the ability to pay.

_____ 3. Consumer surplus measures the happiness and enjoyment that consumers get from goods.

_____ 4. The equilibrium price of a good measures its value to people.

_____ 5. It is rational to do something until its marginal benefit equals its marginal cost.

_____ 6. Marginal benefit is the total benefit from doing something.

_____ 7. If the price of good X increases relative to good Y, the budget line will shift outward along both horizontal and vertical axes.

_____ 8. Indifference curves cross or intersect when the two goods being consumed are complements.

_____ 9. The logic of rational choice always reaffirms that notion that "Anything worth doing, is worth doing well."

_____ 10. The rational consumer prefers points on higher indifference curves to points on lower indifference curves.

Multiple Choice Questions

1. Consumer surplus is a measure of all listed below except:
    a. the benefit consumers get when they buy at the equilibrium price.
    b. your benefit from buying the good.
    c. your income.
    d. happiness or enjoyment that consumers get from goods.

Using Graph 9.1 below, answer questions 2 to 6.

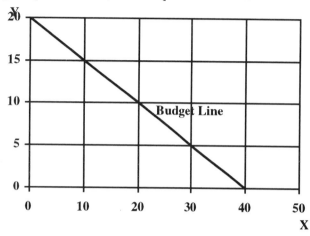

Graph 9.1

2. The slope of the budget line represents:
    a. the price of X divided by the price of Y.
    b. the relative price of X in terms of Y.
    c. the opportunity cost of good X measured in units of Y.
    d. All of the above.

3. The slope of the budget line equals:
    a. -2.
    b. -0.5.
    c. -4.
    d. -0.25.

4. If the price of X equals $2, what is this person's income?
    a. $20
    b. $40
    c. $60
    d. $80

5. This person can afford to buy
    a. 10Y and 40X.
    b. 5 Y and 40X.
    c. 10Y and 20X.
    d. 20Y and 10X.

6. Where a person chooses to buy along the budget line depends on:
   a. that person's income.
   b. the price of goods X and Y.
   c. that person's tastes and preferences.
   d. All of the above.

7. Rational choices:
   a. include all costs, opportunity costs as well as sunk costs, in their decision making.
   b. are more likely to be talked about than performed. Most people will talk rationally but when it comes to action, they act irrationally more often than not.
   c. reflect the fact that people learn from repeated decision making.
   d. All of the above.

Using Graph 9.2, answer questions 8 to 10.

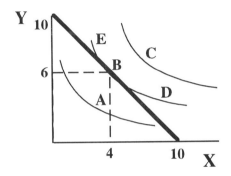

Graph 9.2

8. The following point or points are feasible (affordable) for this consumer:
   a. A.
   b. E, B and D.
   c. C.
   d. A and B.

9. A rational choice by the consumer would be to consume at point:
   a. A.
   b. B.
   c. C.
   d. None of the above.

10. Which of the following changes in conditions might allow this consumer to consume at point C?
   a. an increase in the price of
   b. an increase in both the price of X and the price of Y
   c. an increase in his income
   d. None of the above.

Chapter Review (Fill in the Blanks)

1. _____ _____ measures a buyer's gain from a trade. It is represented by the triangular area under the _____ _____ and above the _____ _____.

2. A _____ _____ shows a person's opportunities (feasible choices).

3. The absolute value of the budget line's slope equals the _____ price of the good on the _____ axis in terms of the good on the _____ axis.

4. Changes in _____ shift the budget line without changing its _____.

5. Changes in relative _____ _____ the budget line and can change its _____.

6. Rational choice occurs when you do something until its marginal _____ equals its marginal _____ so as to maximize _____-_____.

7. Considerable evidence indicates that people make most economic decisions _____.

8. People sometimes make irrational decisions by ignoring _____ costs or not ignoring _____-costs which are costs that have already been paid and cannot be _____. The evidence also shows that people learn from repeated situations, so their decisions become more _____.

9. Economists graph people's _____ with indifference curves.

10. Rational choice means reaching the _____ possible indifference curve.

Priority List of Concepts

Consumer Surplus: measures a buyer's gains from trade. Graphically measured by the triangular area under a demand curve but above equilibrium price.

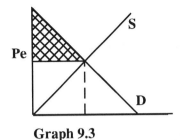

Graph 9.3

Willingness to Pay of the Consumer: measured by the height of the demand curve. The demand curve shows the highest price that buyers would pay, if they had to, for each unit.

Computation of Consumer Surplus on Each Unit Purchased: [Height of Demand Curve for the unit (Willingness to Pay)] minus [Equilibrium Price] equals [Consumer Surplus on the unit].

In Graph 9.4 below, Consumer Surplus on the 5th unit = [$14 - $10] = $4.

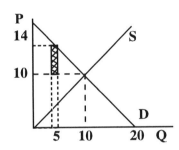

Graph 9.4

Budget Line : Shows affordable consumption opportunities.

Illustrated by a graph of a budget line.

The consumer can afford to buy at any point on or below his budget line.

Graphed by using information on the consumers income and the price of the consumption goods, X and Y.

The vertical intercept equals income divided by Price of Y.

The horizontal intercept equals income divided by Price of X.

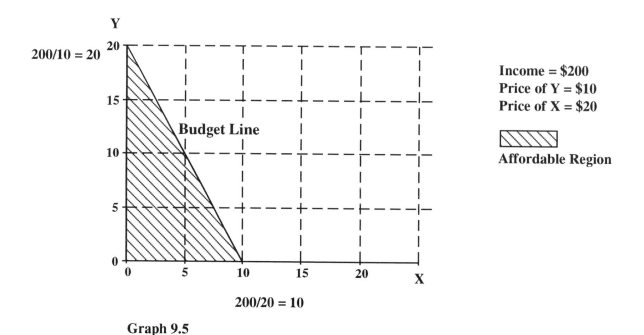

Graph 9.5

Slope of the Budget Line: (Absolute value) equals the price of the good on the horizontal axis (X) divided by the price of the good on the vertical axis (Y).

Changes in Opportunities

Change in Income: shifts the entire budget line outward if income increases, inward if income decreases.

Change in Price: rotates the budget line inward on the axis of the good whose price has increased, outward on the axis of the good whose price has decreased.

Rational Choice: is the choice in your budget set that the consumer prefers based on his own tastes.

Logic of Rational Choice: Do something until its marginal benefit equals its marginal cost. Q* in Graph 9.6 (B).

When marginal benefit equals marginal cost, net benefit if maximized.

Net benefit or profit from doing something is the total benefit minus the total cost of doing it. Shaded area in Graph 9.6(A)

Graph 9.6(A)

Graph 9.6(B)

Indifference Curves: Graph 9.7

    Show combinations of goods between which a person is indifferent, and does not care which combinations of goods is received.

    In Graph 9.7, the person would be indifferent as to whether he consumed at point E, B or D because they are all on the same indifference curve.

    Graphs of peoples tastes and preferences.

    The consumer prefers higher indifference curves to points on lower indifference curves. In Graph 9.7, the person prefers point C which is on the highest indifference curve to any of the other points.

    Can't cross if the person always prefers more to less.

    Slopes downward due to the diminishing rate of marginal substitution of Y for X as a person gets more and more X.

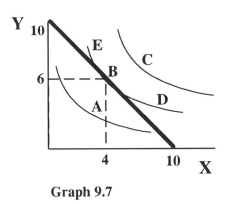

Graph 9.7

Rational Choice means:

- Reaching the highest possible indifference curve that a budget line could reach, Point B in Graph 9.7.
- Buying quantities of products that set your marginal rate of substitution between X and Y equal to their relative price.

    Thus, at Point B in Graph 9.7:

    the slope of the indifference curve equals the slope of the budget line.

    the marginal rate of substitution of Y for X equals the slope of the budget line.

    the change in Y divided by the change in X equals the Price of X divided by the Price of Y.

$$\left(\frac{\Delta Y}{\Delta X}\right) = \left(\frac{Px}{Py}\right)$$

    the marginal rate of substitution equals the relative price of X in terms of Y.

Utility: benefit people get from consuming goods.

Measured subjectively, depends on peoples tastes.

Rational people maximize utility by choosing the quantities of goods that give you the same marginal utility per dollar spent on each good you buy. This will also occur at point B in Graph 9.7

$$\left(\frac{MU(x)}{Px}\right) = \left(\frac{MU(y)}{Py}\right) \text{ or another way to state this condition is: } \left(\frac{MU(x)}{MU(y)}\right) = \left(\frac{Px}{Py}\right) \text{ and the}$$

$$\left(\frac{MU(x)}{MU(y)}\right) = \text{ Marginal Rate of Substitution between X and Y.}$$

Computation of Consumer Surplus: The base of the Consumer Surplus triangle is equilibrium quantity, so the area of the triangle consumer surplus, is 1/2 the area of the base times the height.

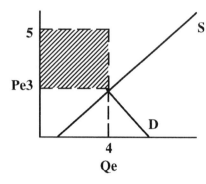

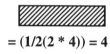

Consumer Surplus is 1/2 the area of this rectangle

= (1/2(2 * 4)) = 4

Graph 9.8

Rational Choice: To maximize net benefit, take its derivative with respect to Q and set the derivative equal to zero. Thus set MB = MC.

Short Answer Question

1. The price of a barrel of water is much less expensive than the price of a barrel of oil. Explain the concepts of value and price as they apply to these goods. Which good is most valuable, such that we can't exist without it?

Basic Problems

1. Given an income of $100, the price of X = $10 and the Price of Y = $25, graph the budget line with Y on the vertical axis and X on the horizontal axis. Label this budget line B.

2. The income in problem 1 increases to $200. Draw the new budget line and label it C. What has happened to this person's opportunities due to this budget increase?

3. Given the information in problem 1, assume that the price of X rises to $20. Draw the new budget line as a dotted line and label it D.

4. Given Graph 9.9 below, what happens to consumer surplus if the demand curve shifts from D2 to D1? Shade in the new consumer surplus. Did the consumer surplus increase or decrease?

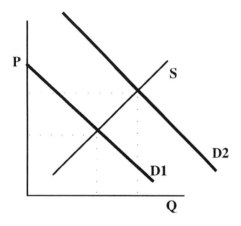

Graph 9.9

5. Given the following information on what people will pay for pizza, compute the consumer surplus if the equilibrium price of pizza is $2.50.

Qd	Price
1	$4.00
2	3.50
3	3.00
4	2.50
5	2.00
6	1.50
7	1.00
8	0.50
9	0

6. Given the following information on the Total Cost and the Total Benefit of doing something, compute the Marginal Cost and the Marginal Benefit and determine the number of times that activity should be engaged in to maximize net benefit.

Number of Times 1	Total Benefit	Marginal Benefit	Total Cost	Marginal Cost	Net Benefit
1	20		1		
2	38		3		
3	54		6		
4	68		13		
5	78		23		
6	85		37		
7	91		56		
8	96		81		
9	100		113		
10	103		153		
11	105		203		
12	106		268		

Advanced Problems

1. Suppose the demand curve is $Q^d = 10 - 2P$ and the supply curve is $Q^s = p + 2$.
    a.   Calculate equilibrium quantity and price.
    b.   Show equilibrium on a graph of supply and demand.
    c.   Calculate Consumer Surplus. Use your graph and compute the area of the triangle.

Chapter 10

Business Decisions and Supply

Learning Goals

1. Explain the procedure to determine how much and how to produce in the short run.

2. Apply the logic of rational choice to a producer's decision to produce.

3. Explain the procedure, step by step, to determine how much to produce in the the short run.

4. Calculate, graph and explain short run total and average costs.

5. Distinguish between long run and short run production decisions.

6. Estimate the value of the firm by discounting expected future profits.

7. Explain and graphically illustrate the seller's gain from trade.

Key Term Matching Quiz

Terms

_____ 1. Firm

_____ 2. Technical Efficiency

_____ 3. Economic Efficiency

_____ 4. Total Revenue

_____ 5. Profit

_____ 6. Long Run

_____ 7. Short Run

_____ 8. Fixed Input

_____ 9. Variable Input

_____ 10. Average Revenue

_____ 11. Total Cost

_____ 12. Average Variable Cost

_____ 13. Capacity Output

_____ 14. Value of a Firm

_____ 15. Price Taker

_____ 16. Producer Surplus

Definitions

a. Period of time over which people cannot vary the quantities of all inputs.

b. Total receipts from selling a good.

c. A period of time over which people fully adjust to changes in conditions.

d. Total Variable Cost divided by the quantity produced.

e. A production method that does not waste inputs.

f. Area above the supply curve and below the price.

g. Quantity at which average cost reaches its lowest point.

h. Inputs whose quantities can be changed.

i. Total Revenue minus Total Cost.

j. A firm that faces a perfectly elastic demand for its product.

k. Inputs whose quantities can't be changes.

l. Production that is technically efficient and least cost.

m. An organization that coordinates the activities of workers, owners, etc., to produce and sell a good or service.

n. Total Fixed Cost (Overhead Cost) plus Total Variable Cost.

o. Total Revenue/Quantity

p. Discounted present value of its expected future profits.

True/False Questions

_____ 1. Three fourths of all U.S. firms are sole proprietorships with a single owner responsible for all its debts.

_____ 2. A method of production is technically efficient if the firm could produce the same amount using less of any one input without using more of another input.

_____ 3. A production function summarizes the technically efficient methods of production.

_____ 4. All technically efficient methods of production are economically efficient.

_____ 5. The value of the firm will increase if the discount rate rises.

_____ 6. Short run costs differ from long run costs due to the fact that some inputs are fixed in the short run.

_____ 7. A firm can produce at the same cost or at a lower cost in the long run.

_____ 8. Average variable and average total cost are the same in the short run.

_____ 9. Producer surplus is equal to the firm's profit.

_____ 10. When marginal cost is greater than average cost, average cost is falling as output rises.

Multiple Choice Questions

1. This type of firm has two or more people sharing ownership who are responsible for all the firm's debts.
   a. a corporation
   b. a sole proprietorship
   c. a partnership
   d. a mutual fund

2. This type of firm is treated as an artificial person by the law. It owners, stockholders, have limited liability that shields them from personal liability for the firm's debts.
   a. a corporation
   b. a sole proprietorship
   c. partnership
   d. a mutual fund

3. The corporation, the sole proprietorship and the partnership:
   a. have their corporate income taxed twice.
   b. pay differing amounts of taxes. The corporation pays corporate tax on its income and other taxes on its dividends and capital gains. Sole proprietorships and partnerships pay personal income taxes only.
   c. pay differing rates of personal income taxes.
   d. pay no corporate income tax.

4. Which of the following types of business firms pay personal income taxes but no corporate income tax.:
   a. a corporation
   b. a sole proprietorship
   c. a partnership
   d. Both b and c.

5. Which type of firm can borrow directly from investors by selling bonds?
   a. a corporation
   b. a sole proprietorship
   c. a partnership
   d. Both b and c.

6. The economically efficient method of production:
   a. may depend on how much the firm produces.
   b. is the technically efficient method with the lowest cost.
   c. is summarized by the production function.
   d. answers (a) and (b).

7. The basic rule of rational behavior states that if a firm produces at all, it maximizes profit by making sure the following conditions hold:
   a. marginal cost equals marginal revenue.
   b. marginal cost is stable or rising.
   c. Answers a and b.
   d. All of the above.

Given the information in Table 10.1 below, answer questions 8 and 9.

Q	P	TR $(P*Q)$	MR $\left(\dfrac{\Delta TR}{\Delta Q}\right)$	TC	MC $\dfrac{\Delta TC}{\Delta Q}$	Profit $TR-TC$
1	60	60	60	50	50	10
2	55	110	50	90	40	20
3	50	150	40	120	30	30
4	45	180	30	160	40	20
5	40	200	20	210	50	-10
6	35	210	10	270	60	-60
7	30	210	0	340	70	-130

8. Given the revenue and cost information in Table 10.1 above, using the basic logic of rational choice behavior, how much would this firm produce and sell?
   a. Quantity of 1.
   b. Quantity of 2 or 4.
   c. Quantity of 3.
   d. Any quantity above 4.

9. In Table 10.1, profit maximization occurs:
   a. where Marginal Revenue is equal to but not less than Marginal Cost.
   b. where Total Revenue less Total Cost produces the greatest net benefit.
   c. where Total Revenue is maximized.
   d. answers (a) and (b).

10. In Graph 10.1 below, the firm is presently producing 10 units.
    a. This firm is producing the profit maximizing output.
    b. To profit maximize, this firm needs to reduce its output.
    c. To profit maximize, this firm needs to increase its output.
    d. This firm will maximize profits at any output above a quantity of 10.

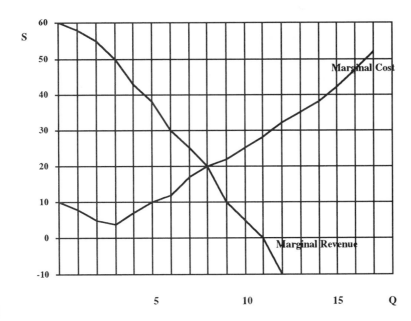

Graph 10.1

Refer to Graph 10.2 for questions 11 to 13.

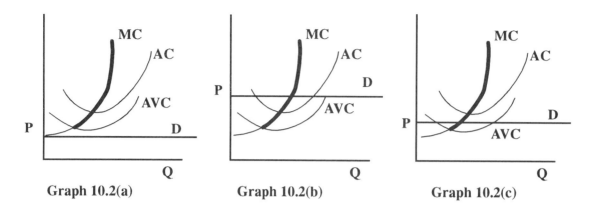

Graph 10.2(a)   **Graph 10.2(b)**   **Graph 10.2(c)**

11. To profit maximize in the short run, these firms will produce:
    a. Firm (a) and (b).
    b. Firm (b) and (c).
    c. Firm (a) and (c).
    d. All the firms shown in Graph 10.2 above.

12. In the short run, this firm will make a profit:
    a. Firm (a).
    b. Firm (b).
    c. Firm (c).
    d. Firm (d).

13. In the long run, these firms would shut down.
    a. Firm (a) and (b).
    b. Firm (b) and (c).
    c. Firm (a) and (c).
    d. All the firms shown in Graph 10.2 above.

14. If Marginal Cost is less than Average Cost:
    a. Average Cost is rising as output increases.
    b. Average Cost is falling as output increases.
    c. Average Cost is at a minimum.
    d. All of the above.

15. To profit maximize in the long run, if Total Revenue is less than Total Cost:
    a. a firm will shut down.
    b. a firm will produce and make a loss equal to Total Cost minus Total Revenue.
    c. a firm will produce and make a profit equal to Total Revenue minus Total Cost.
    d. All of the above.

Chapter Review (Fill in the Blanks)

1. A _____ consists of a network of _____ between owners, workers and others that state each party's _____, _____ and payoffs in various situations.

2. A sole proprietorship is a firm owned by _____ person. The owner pays _____ income tax on the firm's revenue. The owner is _____ responsible for _____ the debts of the _____ _____. _____ of all U.S. firms are sole proprietorships. They receive _____ of the total revenue of all U.S. firms.

3. A partnership is _____ or more people sharing _____ through a _____ _____. _____ partners bear _____ responsibility for the firms _____. _____ percent of U.S. firms are partnerships. They account for _____ of the total revenue of U.S. firms.

4. A _____ is a firm with special legal rights. The law treats it as an _____ person that lives on even if its _____ change. The owners, _____, pay tax on dividends and capital gains. _____ percent of U.S. firms are corporations. They receive _____ of the total revenue of all U.S. firms.

5. Every producer must make two critical decisions: _____ to produce and _____ _____ to produce.

6. A firm's decision of how to produce includes:
   a. choosing a hypothetical _____ to produce and listing all the _____ efficient ways of producing. _____ efficient methods are methods that do not waste inputs.
   b. choosing the _____ efficient (least cost) method of producing that quantity.

7. A firm maximizes profit, finding the level of output where _____ _____ equals _____-_____ while marginal cost is _____ or _____.
   <u>In the long run</u>, the firm produces this quantity if _____ _____ exceeds _____ _____. The firm shuts down in the long run if _____ _____ is less than _____ _____.
   <u>In the short run</u>, the firm produces this quantity if _____ _____ exceeds _____ _____. The firm shuts down in the long run if _____ _____ is less than _____ _____._____ _____.
   Using average costs, the firm produces this quantity if _____ _____ (_____) exceeds _____ _____. The firm shuts down if _____ _____ (_____) is less than _____ _____.

8. When marginal cost exceeds average cost, average cost is _____ as output increases. When marginal cost is less than average cost, average cost is _____ as output increases.

9. To maximize its value, the firm maximizes the _____ _____ _____ of its expected future profits.

10. A firm is a price taker if it faces a _____ _____ demand curve.

Priority List of Concepts

How to Produce: Choose the least cost (economically efficient) method of production from an array of all the possible technically efficient methods of producing the quantity you decide to produce.

How Much to Produce: Apply the logic of rational choice and maximize net benefit (profit) by producing where Marginal Cost is equal to Marginal Benefit (Marginal Revenue).

> **Net Benefit:** Profit and Non-monetary rewards.
> > **Profit:** Total Revenue minus Total Costs.
> > **Non-monetary rewards:** Benefits other than profit from producing and selling a good (i.e., a sense of accomplishment, a feeling of power, etc.)

> **Marginal Revenue:** the change in total revenue that occurs when you produce one more unit of the good.

$$Marginal\ Revenue = \left(\frac{\Delta TR}{\Delta Q}\right)$$

> Marginal Revenue is the derivative of TR with respect to Q.
> $MR = f'(Q)$

Long Run: A period of time over which a firm can change the quantities of all its inputs.

Steps to Achieve Profit Maximization in the Long Run:
1.   Determine the level of output where Marginal Revenue equals Marginal Cost when Marginal Cost is either rising or constant.
2.   Calculate Total Revenue and Total Cost at the level of output determined in Step (1).
3.   Produce the level of output determined in Step (1).
     If Total Revenue equals or exceeds Total Cost.
     Total Revenue minus Total Cost will equal zero or a positive number. A breakeven situation or a profit will occur respectively.
     Shut down (do not produce) if Total Revenue is less than Total Cost. Total Revenue minus Total Cost equals a negative number. A Loss will occur. By shutting down the firm avoids the Loss.

Marginal Revenue (MR) equals Marginal Cost (MC):
Profit Maximization Rule.
If MR exceeds MC (i.e., at Q_1), the firm will raise its profit by producing more, moving towards Q* in the diagram below.
Conversely, if MR is less than MC (i.e., at Q_2), the firm will raise its profit by producing less and moving towards Q*.

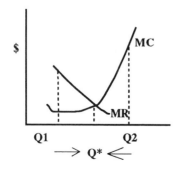

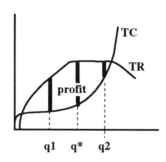

Short Run: a period of time over which the firm can't vary the quantity of all of its inputs. At least one input is fixed in size.

Steps to Achieve Profit Maximization in the Short Run:
1. Determine the level of output where Marginal Revenue equals Marginal Cost when Marginal Cost is either rising or constant.
2. Calculate Total Revenue and Total Variable Cost at the level of output determined in Step (1).
3. Produce if Total Revenue equals or exceeds Total Variable Cost.
   Produce if TR = or is > TVC, Graphs (a) (b) and (d) below [Profit (+) or Loss (-) = TR-TC]
   Shutdown if Total Revenue is less than Total Variable Cost.
   Shutdown if TR < TVC, Graph (c) below.
   [Loss = Total Fixed Costs]

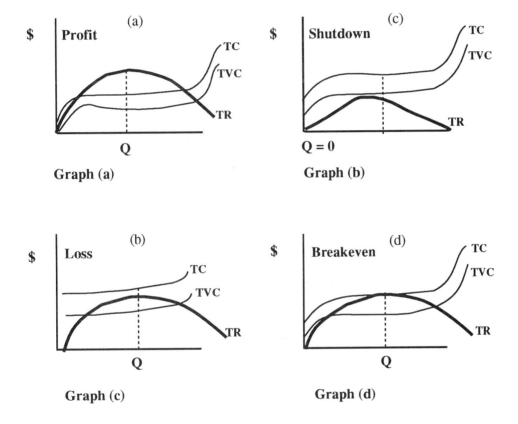

Graph (a)   Graph (b)

Graph (c)   Graph (d)

Fixed Inputs: Inputs whose quantities can't change in the short run.

Variable Inputs: Inputs whose quantities can be varied.

Fixed costs: Costs of fixed inputs. Overhead costs, already paid for, unavoidable in the short run.

Variable costs: Costs of variable inputs. These costs can be avoided in the short run by producing less.

Steps to achieve Profit Maximization in the Short Run using average costs:
1. Determine the level of output where MC = MR and MC is rising or constant.
2. Calculate Average Revenue and Average Variable Cost at this Output.
   Average Revenue equals Total Revenue divided by Quantity. (AR = TR/Q).
   Average Variable Cost equals Total Variable Cost divided by Quantity. (AVC = TVC/Q)

3.   Produce if Average Revenue is greater than Average Variable Cost. Produce if (AR > AVC)
      [Profit (+) or Loss (-) equals AR-AC].
     Shutdown if Average Revenue is less than Average Variable Cost. Shutdown if (AR<AVC)
      Loss equals Average Fixed Cost. [Loss = AFC]

Marginal Pulls Average Along:

When MC is greater than AC, MC pulls AC upward. When MC is greater than AC, AC is rising as output
increases.
[When MC > AC, as output ↑, AC is ↑].
When MC is less than AC, MC pulls AC downward. When MC is less than AC, AC is falling as output
increases.
[When MC < AC, as output ↑, AC is ↓].
When MC = AC, Average cost does not change and is at a minimum. [When MC = AC, AC is at a
minimum.]

Capacity Output: the quantity at which average cost reaches its minimum.

Long Run	Short Run
No fixed costs because all inputs are variable.	Fixed costs occur due to the fact that in the short run some inputs are fixed in size.
Average Cost and Average Variable Cost are the same	Average Variable Cost differs from Average Cost due to the existence of Fixed Costs in the short run. AC = AVC + AFC
A firm can produce at the same or at a lower cost in the long run than in the short run.	Short run cost curves lie above or at the same level as long run cost curves.

Long Run Average Cost Curve: just touches each of the short run Average Cost curves. Along a U-shaped
long run Average Cost curves, at low levels of output there are decreasing costs, and at high levels of
output there are increasing costs, and for a period at a middle level of production there are constant
costs.

Constant Costs: Long run Marginal Cost and long run Average Cost are the same and equal for all
levels of output.
Increasing Costs: Long run Marginal Cost and long run Average Cost rise at with increases in output.
Decreasing Costs: Long run Marginal Cost and long run Average Cost fall with increases in output.

Value of the Firm: discounted present value of its expected future profits.
Example: If you expect $100 profit in years 1, 2, 3 and 4, the value of that stream of future profits must
be discounted to today's present value. Using a time line:

	Year 1	Year 2	Year 3	Year 4
Profits	$100	$100	$100	$100

Discounted Present Value of the Future Stream of Profits equals the sum

$$(\$100/1+i) \quad + \quad \$100/1+i)^2 \quad + \quad (\$100/1+i)^3 \quad + \quad (\$100/1+i)^4$$

Assume the discount rate is 10%. Use the decimal equivalent (0.1) in the formula , ($100/1.1), where n is the year you receive each profit stream. The result is:

Discounted Present Value	Year 1	Year 2	Year 3	Year 4
$316.99	$90.91	82.64	$75.13	$68.30

Present Value of the Firm's stream of profits equals $316.99. This discounted present value is the amount you would need to save and invest today to amass the future stream of profits.

Supply Decisions: supply curves

> **Price Takers:** a firm which faces a perfectly elastic demand for its product. If the price taker raises its price, it loses all its customers. Price is something it cannot affect.

> **Supply Curve:** that portion of its Marginal Cost curve that lies above its Average Variable Cost curve. (Heavy dark curve in Graph 10.4.)

Average Revenue equals Price equals Marginal Revenue along the horizontal demand curve.
To profit maximize the price taker follows three steps:
  1. Determine where Marginal Revenue = Marginal Cost
  2. Produce at this quantity if Price is greater than Average Variable Cost.
  3. Profit (+) or Loss (-) per unit equals price less average cost.

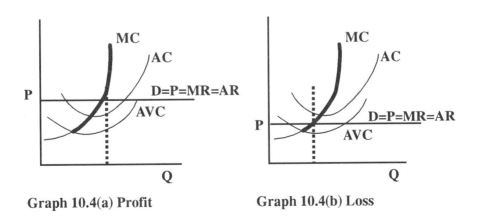

Graph 10.4(a) Profit   **Graph 10.4(b) Loss**

4.   Shutdown if Price is less than Average Variable Cost. Loss will equal Total Fixed Costs.

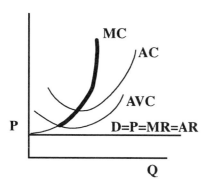

Graph 10.4(c) Shutdown

Producer Surplus: Benefit to the producer of selling goods at the equilibrium price rather than being unable to sell them at all. Equals the firm's profit plus its fixed cost in the short run. (In the long run, producer surplus is the firm's profit.) In Graph 10.5(a), the area above the supply surve and below the price, between quantity zero and the quantity the firm produces.

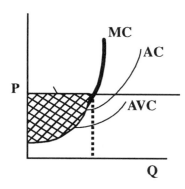

Graph 10.5(a) Producer Surplus

Total revenue appears in Graph 10.5(b) as the area of a rectangle with its height equaling price and its base equaling quantity produced.

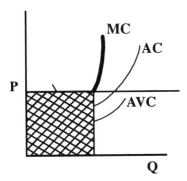

Graph 10.5(b) Total Revenue

Short Answswer Questions

1. How can it be assumed that firms maximize their value when you see many firms making irrational decisions at times?

Basic Problems

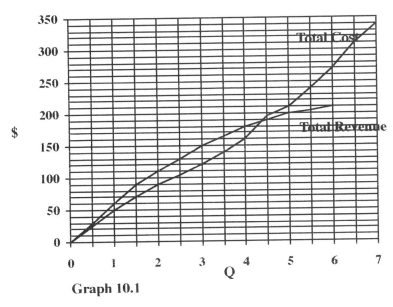

Graph 10.1

1. In Graph 10.1 above, shade in the area of profit and place a dark horizontal line where the area of maximum profit occurs. At what quantity does this take place?

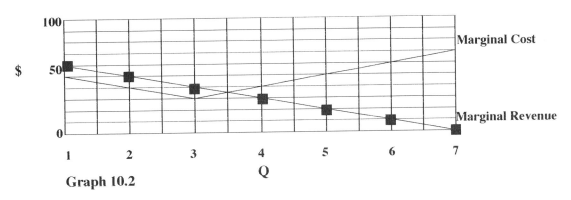

Graph 10.2

2. In Graph 10.2 above, determine profit maximizing quantity using the logic of rational choice. State the rule. Circle the quantity.

3. Given the following information on Total Cost and Total Revenue, fill in the blanks.

Q	TR	AR	MR	TC	TFC	TVC	AC	AVC	AFC	MC	Profit
0	0			13							
1	20			26							
2	38			38							
3	54			49							
4	68			58							
5	80			65							
6	90			74							
7	98			84							
8	104			95							
9	108			107							
10	110			120							

Determine the profit maximizing output using the MC = MR rule. Graph MC and MR.

4. If the interest rate is 5%, what is the discounted present value of $100 to be paid each year over the next four years? What would happen to your answer if the discount rate fell to 2%?

Advanced Problems

1. The firm is a price taker, able to sell its product at a price of $24. Given the firm's Total Costs listed below, determine the profit maximizing output in the short run using the average cost method. Graph profit maximization and shade in producer surplus. Estimate the value of producer surplus.

Q	TC	TFC	TVC	AFC	AVC	ATC	MC
0	50						
1	65						
2	75						
3	84						
4	92						
5	102						
6	114						
7	129						
8	148						
9	172						
10	202						
11	252						

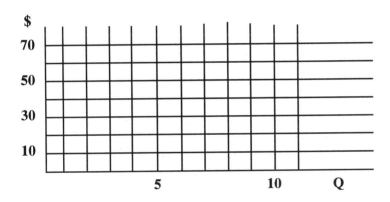

Chapter 11

Economic Efficiency and the Gains From Trade

Learning Goals

1. Identify deadweight social loss on a graph from information provided.

2. Determine who gains and who loses from international trade, taxes, subsidies and price controls.

3. Explain the theory behind argument for free trade.

4. Distinguish between a Pareto improvement and a potential pareto improvement.

5. Explain the conditions which cause economic inefficiency.

6. Explain and graphically illustrate whether there is a gain or loss to efficiency from a tax on a product with an inelastic supply.

7. Graph and compute the effect of a tax on efficiency using information provided in an equation.

8. Solve for the price paid for consumers after a tax is imposed on a product.

Key Term Matching Quiz

Terms

_____ 1. Total Gain From Trade

_____ 2. Pareto Improvement

_____ 3. Potential Pareto Improvement

_____ 4. Increase in Economic Efficiency

_____ 5. Economically Efficient Situation

_____ 6. Economically Inefficient Situation

_____ 7. Deadweight Social Loss

Definitions

a. Pareto efficient situation, there is no possibility for Pareto improving change.

b. A change in the economy that promotes a large enough gain to allow winners to compensate the losers for their loss.

c. Sum of the producer and consumer surplus.

d. Pareto inefficient situation, there are potentially Pareto improving changes that could be made in the economy.

e. A loss to some people that is not a gain to anyone else. It is the amount that people would be willing to pay to eliminate the inefficiency.

f. A change in the economy in which one person gains and no one loses.

g. Potential Pareto improvement.

True/False Questions

_____ 1. Consumer Surplus is smaller when demand is more elastic.

_____ 2. Producer Surplus is larger when supply is more elastic.

_____ 3. All potential Pareto improvements are actual Pareto improvements.

_____ 4. If winners gain more than the losers lose, the change in the economy is termed a potential Pareto improvement.

_____ 5. The existence of a potential Pareto improvement means the economy is inefficient.

_____ 6. The loss from an economic inefficiency is measured by the difference between consumer surplus and producer surplus at the new equilibrium.

_____ 7. An advance in technology that increases the supply of the product is a Pareto improvement.

_____ 8. International trade is a potential Pareto improvement because the producers' gains exceed the consumers' losses.

_____ 9. International trade is economically efficient.

_____ 10. Subsidies, unlike taxes, are economically efficient.

144 Study Guide Microeconomics

Multiple Choice Questions

1. The total gain from international trade is equal to:
   a. consumer surplus minus producer surplus.
   b. total benefit to buyers from the good minus the total variable cost of producing it.
   c. the area above the demand curve.
   d. All of the above.

2. If there are potential Pareto improvements in the economy, then enacting these improvements:
   a. increases the efficiency of the economy because winners could compensate the losers.
   b. increases the efficiency of the economy because some people gain but no one loses.
   c. will allow the winners to gain more than the losers lose.
   d. Both answers a and c.

3. An economy will experience an increase in economic efficiency if:
   a. a potential Pareto improvement is enacted.
   b. a Pareto improvement is enacted.
   c. no potential Pareto improvement exists.
   d. Both answers a and b.

4. Deadweight loss from a maximum legal price:
   a. is lower for rationing by sellable coupons than for rationing by waiting.
   b. is higher for rationing by sellable coupons than for rationing by waiting.
   c. is lower for rationing by sellable coupons thus increasing inefficiency.
   d. Both answers a and c.

5. Which of the following situations improves economic efficiency, and is a Pareto improvement?
   a. A decision to subsidize the production of a good.
   b. The repeal of an excise tax.
   c. The imposition of a trade embargo.
   d. All of the above.

6. Which of the following situations causes economic inefficiency?
   a. An excise tax on gasoline.
   b. A restraint on foreign trade.
   c. A maximum legal price.
   d. All of the above.

Refer to Graph 11.1 for questions 7 to 11. Graph 11.1 shows the effects of rationing by sellable coupons at a maximum legal price of P*.

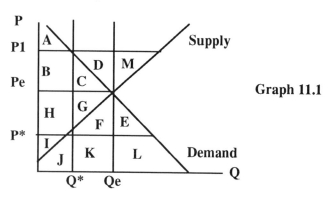

7. Producer Surplus at the original equilibrium price and quantity, Pe and Qe is equal to:
   a. (H + G + I + F + E).
   b. (H + G + I +F + J + K).
   c. (H + G + I).
   d. the price of inputs.

8. As a result of the imposition of a maximum legal price, P*, with sellable coupons, producer surplus:
   a. falls from (H + G + I) to (I).
   b. rises from (I) to (H + G + I).
   c. rises from (H + G + I) to (H + G + I+ F + E).
   d. falls from (B + C +H + G + I) to (H + G + I).

9. Consumer Surplus at equilibrium price and quantity, Pe and Qe is equal to:
   a. (A).
   b. (A + B + C).
   c. (A + B + C + H + G + F + E).
   d. (A + B + H).

10. As a result of the imposition of a maximum legal price, P*, with sellable coupons, consumer surplus now equals:
   a. (A).
   b. (A + B + C).
   c. (A + B + C + H + G + F + E).
   d. (A + B + H).

11. The deadweight social loss due to the legal maximum price with sellable coupons equals the triangle:
   a. (F + E).
   b. (C + G).
   c. (D + M).
   d. (G + F).

Chapter Review (Fill in the Blanks)

1. The total gain from trade in some good is the sum of _____ and _____ _____ . This sum equals the _____ _____ to buyers minus the _____ _____ cost of production.

2. A change in the economy is a Pareto improvement if at least one person _____ and no one _____. A change is a _____ _____ improvement if the _____ gain more than the losers lose.

3. A situation is _____ _____ if there is no potentially Pareto-improving change that could be made.

4. _____ _____ _____ measures the size of the loss from an economic inefficiency.

5. International trade is a _____ _____ improvement over a situation without trade. International trade _____ consumers and _____ producers in the country where the price would have been _____ without international trade, however, consumers _____ _____ than producers _____ in that country. International trade hurts _____ and helps _____ in the country where the price would have been lower without international trade, however, producer's _____ exceed the consumers _____ in that country. After international trade takes place, the winners can _____ the losers, thus, international trade is _____ _____. Arbitrage and speculation are also _____ _____ for the same reason.

6. Taxes cause _____. The government revenue from a tax is _____ than the losses that it causes in _____ and _____ _____ (except when either supply or demand is _____ _____). The difference is the _____ _____ _____ from the tax.

7. Subsidies are also _____ _____. The cost of the subsidy to the government _____ the gains to _____ and _____, and the difference is a _____ _____ _____.

Priority List of Concepts

Gains from Trade: Sum of the producer and consumer surplus that buyers and sellers receive from trading the good.

Share of the Gains from Trade: Can be measured by the relative magnitude of Consumer vs. Producer Surplus.
Consumer Surplus is larger when demand is less elastic.
Producer Surplus is larger when supply is less elastic.

Pareto Improvement: a change in the economy that makes at least one person better and and no one loses.

Potential Pareto Improvement: A change in the economy that allows winners to compensate the losers. (Winners gain more than the losers lose.)

Economic Efficiency: No Pareto improving change exists.
Competitive Equilibrium is Economically Efficient. In Graph 11.2 at equilibrium quantity, Q_1, the Marginal Benefit to buyers (willingness to pay) is equal to the Marginal Cost to firms of producing and these are also equal to the equilibrium price. At Q_1, MC = MC = Pe. Total gains from trade are maximized.

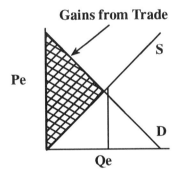

Gains from Trade

Graph 11.2

Economic Inefficiency: Pareto improving changes exist in the economy.
Deadweight Social Loss:
Loss from the situation at Q_1 that is not a gain to anyone.
Occurs because quantity is restrained below equilibrium Qe.
Evidence of economic inefficiency.

Q1 Economically Inefficient Quantity

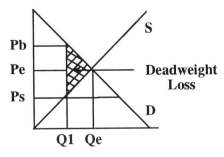

Graph 11.3

Analyzing the Effects of a Change in Economic Conditions:

(i.e., an improvement in technology causing an increase in supply, Graph 11.4)

Measure the change in the sum of producer and consumer surplus.

If the total gains from trade increased, this is at least a potential Pareto improvement, if not a Pareto improvement. For it to be a Pareto improvement, no one could lose.

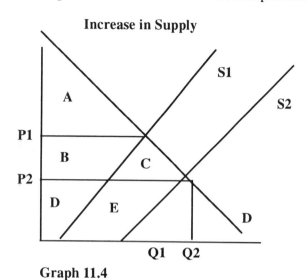

Graph 11.4

Due to the increase in supply, total gains from trade increased from (A + B + D) to (A + B + D+ E + C). This change was a potential Pareto improvement because although total gains increased, consumers gained B + C and producers gained E but lost B + C. Consumers gained, producers lost, but consumers gained more than producers lost.

International trade, taxes, government subsidies and price controls can be analyzed using the measurement of the changes in producer and consumer surplus.

Short Answer Questions

1. Why is it easy to convince people to enact Pareto improving changes in the economy but harder to convince people to enact potentially Pareto improving changes?

2. Give an example of a recent government policy on the environment that was a potential Pareto improvement but caused great controversy between the winners and the losers?

3. How could the distribution of wealth be affected by a technological innovation that is potentially Pareto improving?

Basic Problems

1. In Graph 11.5 below, show and compute the deadweight loss of producing 5 units at a price of $5 rather than the equilibrium quantity of 10 at a price of $10.

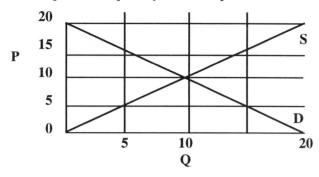

Graph 11.5

2. Graph 11.6 in the text illustrates the Pareto improvement from international trade. Does this improvement involve a redistribution of income between producer and consumer? Explain in terms of the situation after trade in the U.S., in the foreign country and between the two countries?

3. Illustrate the deadweight loss of a $1 tax in the following diagram.

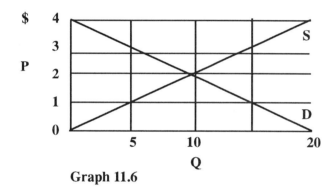

Graph 11.6

Advanced Problems

1. Using graphs, analyze the effect of prohibiting trade between the U.S. and Japan if without trade Japan produces at a higher price than the U.S.

2. Given the following equations for demand and supply, determine equilibrium price and quantity. Then assume that a tax of \$1 is imposed on the supplier. What is equilibrium price and quantity after a tax is imposed? What is the deadweight loss of the tax?

$$Q_D = 10 - P_B$$

$$Q_S = 2P_S$$

PART V

Competition and Strategic Interactions

Chapter 12

Perfect Competition

Learning Goals

1. Understand the process of competition which channels buyers and sellers towards equilibrium.

2. Using elasticities, determine the effect of a change in a firm's output on equilibrium price in the market as a whole.

3. Identify on a graph the short run equilibrium price and quantity produced of a perfectly competitive firm.

4. Distinguish between Accounting and Economic Costs. Distinguish between Accounting and Economic Profits.

5. Explain the effect of free entry and free exit on long run equilibrium of the industry and the firm.

6. Describe the effect of the cost assumptions on the slope of the long run supply curve and on changes in long run equilibrium of the industry.

7. Explain the conditions which make equilibrium under perfect competition economically efficient.

Key Term Matching Quiz

Terms

_____ 1.   Perfect Competition

_____ 2.   Profit Margin

_____ 3.   Entrepreneur

_____ 4.   Historical Cost

_____ 5.   Inventories

_____ 6.   Capital Goods

_____ 7.   Implicit Rental Rate

_____ 8.   Depreciation

_____ 9.   Implicit Costs

_____ 10. Explicit Costs

_____ 11. Economic Costs

_____ 12. Economic Profit

_____ 13   Accounting Profit

_____ 14. Free Entry

_____ 15. Free Exit

_____ 16. Long Run Equilibrium

_____ 17. Normal Accounting Profit

_____ 18. Economic Rent

_____ 19. Constant Cost Industry

_____ 20. Increasing Cost Industry

Definitions

a.   Price paid for an input in the past.

b.   (Total revenue - total economic cost)

c.   Implicit cost of the special input that enables the firm to produce more efficiently than other firms.

d.   Inputs the firm can use repeatedly to produce other goods.

e.   All costs, explicit and implicit.

f.   Upward sloping LR supply curve.

g.   The fall in the value of the capital good due to age and accumulated use.

h.   No legal barriers prevent a firm from entering an industry.

i.   Markup, (P - AC).

j.   Costs that require direct payment.

k.   Goods the firm owns that are unsold.

l.   Total Revenue minus Total Costs as measured on accounting statements.

m.   Perfectly elastic LR supply curve.

n.   Cost of owning and using a capital good over some period of time.

o.   Level of accounting profit required for a zero economic profit.

p.   Competition among price taking sellers.

q.   Costs that do not require direct payments, solely opportunity costs.

r.   No legal barriers prevent a firm from exiting the industry.

s.   A person who acts on a new business idea and takes the risk of failure.

t.   Entry or exit adjusts the market until each firm earns zero economic profit.

True/False Questions

_____ 1. In short run equilibrium, the number of firms is fixed, but a firm may shut down.

_____ 2. Historical costs measure implicit rental rates on capital goods.

_____ 3. FIFO (first-in, first out) method, values inventory at historical costs.

_____ 4. Depreciation of an intangible asset is an explicit cost.

_____ 5. In return for their work and the risks they take, entrepreneurs always receive profits.

_____ 6. In the short run, a firm's profit is its Total Revenue minus its Total Variable Cost.

_____ 7. Depreciation is the interest cost of owning the capital good.

_____ 8. Total Economic Costs are only explicit costs.

_____ 9. Implicit costs do not require direct payments.

_____ 10. In long run equilibrium for the perfectly competitive firm, each firms earns zero economic profits.

Multiple Choice

1. A price taker is a firm that:
   a. faces a perfectly elastic demand curve.
   b. can sell as much as it wants above the equilibrium price.
   c. has a supply curve equal to its marginal cost curve.
   d. Answers a and b.

2. A good measure of depreciation from the point of view of economics would:
   a. reflect the original price of the capital good.
   b. measure the historical cost of the capital good.
   c. measure the fall in value of the capital good, its resale price.
   d. measure depreciation so that it meets the requirements of tax laws.

3. The historical cost of an input:
   a. equals the firms cost of using the input now.
   b. measures how useful it is.
   c. is used to measure accounting costs.
   d. is used to measure economic costs.

4. Accounting measures of costs:
   a. measure both implicit and explicit costs.
   b. omit implicit costs.
   c. differ from economic costs.
   d. Both b and c.

5. Entrepreneurial services to the firm refer to all of the following except:
   a. implementing new ideas.
   b. explicit costs.
   c. providing money to buy the firm's capital goods.
   d. taking risk.

6. Implicit costs include:
   a. intangible assets such as brand names and trademarks.
   b. the nonuse of its intangible assets, how useful it is.
   c. depreciation of intangible assets.
   d. All of the above.

7. The rate of return on equity:
   a. is a measure of accounting profit.
   b. is the same as economic profit.
   c. includes costs associated with intangible assets.
   d. Both answers a and c.

8. A normal profit:
   a. results when Total Revenue minus Total Economic Costs is equal to zero.
   b. is the level of accounting profit required for zero economic profit.
   c. occurs in long run equilibrium under perfect competition.
   d. All of the above.

9. An economic rent is:
    a. an explicit cost of production.
    b. the cost of a special input that enables the firm to produce more efficiently than any other firm.
    c. is an accounting measure of costs.
    d. Does not affect the calculation of economic profits.

10. In long run equilibrium:
    a. a firm can increase its profit by increasing its output.
    b. firms have an incentive to enter the industry.
    c. every firm can earn an economic profit.
    d. None of the above.

Chapter Review (Fill in the Blanks)

Competition

1. The firms that best anticipate and satisfy the _____ of customers at the _____ cost can earn _____ and survive the process of _____; other firms suffer _____ and may go _____ _____ _____.

2. _____ gives sellers an incentive to _____ with buyers by providing the products that buyers _____ at the _____ possible prices.

3. Perfect competition is competition between _____ _____ firms.

Economic Costs and Accounting Measures

4. The cost of any decision is its _____ cost.

5. Accounting measures of cost do not necessarily measure _____ _____ _____ because they measure the costs of inventories and inputs at their _____ cost rather than their current _____ costs and because accounting measures do not include _____ costs. _____ _____ are the correct measure of costs for a firm's decisions.

6. In long run equilibrium, economic profits are _____.

Conditions for Perfect Competition to be Economically Efficient

7. If there are no _____, in equilibrium with perfect competition, the economy makes the tradeoffs that consumers _____ to make, as revealed by their _____ _____ _____ for various goods. No externalities means that the producer of a good pays _____ the costs of producing it and the people who buy the good receive _____ of its benefits.

8. In equilibrium with perfect competition, the relative price of each good equals the _____ that consumers are willing to make to buy the good. The relative price of each good also equals the tradeoff in _____, that is the _____ _____ of producing the good, measured in terms of other goods.

9. The tradeoff that consumers _____ to make equals the tradeoff that the economy _____ make to produce the goods.

10. Whenever the tradeoff that the economy _____ make does not equal the tradeoff that consumers _____ to make, there are _____ _____ _____ changes that could be made in the economy. Equilibrium with perfect competition is economically efficient because it sets these _____ tradeoffs _____ equal to each other.

Priority List of Concepts

Short-Run Equilibrium with Perfect Competition: Each firm is a price taker facing a perfectly elastic demand curve along which price equals marginal revenue. Graph 12.1.

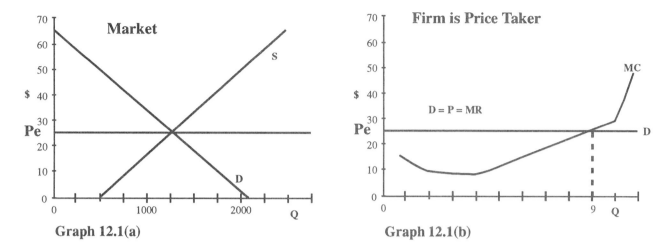

Graph 12.1(a)   Graph 12.1(b)

To profit maximize in the short run under perfect competition:
1. determine the quantity at which MC = MR = P with MC rising or constant. (Refer to dotted perpendicular line drawn in Graph 12.2(a) or (b) to determine quantity)
2. Produce this quantity if Price is greater than Average Variable Cost. Graph 12.2(a) or (b).
    Profit (+) [Graph 12.2(a)] or Loss (-) [Graph 12.2(b)] per unit is equal to Price less average cost. (Refer to dark perpendicular line in Graphs 12.2 (a) or (b)
    [Profit (+) or Loss(-) = P - AC]. Average Cost is equal to Average Fixed Cost plus Average Variable Cost.
3. Shut down if Price is less than Average Variable Cost.
    Graph 12.2(c). Firm produces zero output
    Loss equals fixed costs.

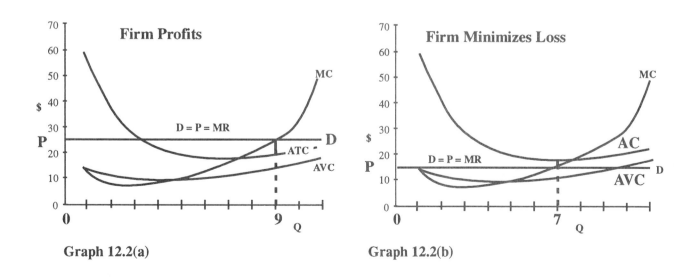

Graph 12.2(a)   Graph 12.2(b)

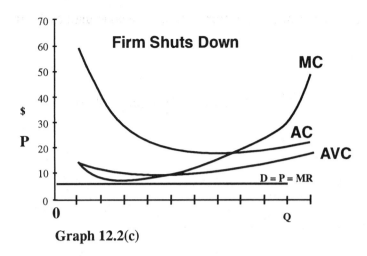

Graph 12.2(c)

Costs

Economic Costs: opportunity costs, the value of what you sacrifice.
      all costs, explicit and implicit.
      the correct measure of costs for a firm's decisions.

      Explicit Costs: require direct payment (i.e., wages).
      Implicit Costs: do not require direct payment (i.e., costs of entrepreneurial services or intangible assets).

Accounting Costs Differ from Economic Costs: use historical costs to measure the costs of inputs and omit implicit costs, opportunity costs that are not direct payments.

      Historical Cost of an Input: fails to measure the economic cost of an input due to price changes of inventory over time and the implicit rental rate on capital.

      Implicit Rental Rate on Capital: cost of owning and using the capital good over a period of time. It is the sum of depreciation and the interest cost of owning the capital good.

      Depreciation: Fall in the value of the capital good due to age or accumulated use.

      Interest Cost of Capital: Interest the firm would have paid to borrow money to buy the capital good.

Profit

Economic Profit: Total Revenue minus Total Economic Cost.

Accounting Profit: Total Revenue minus Accounting measures of Total Cost.
      Accounting profit is not equal to economic profit because accounting statements do not measure economic costs.

Long Run Equilibrium with Perfect Competition: Entry and exit of firms adjust the market until each firm earns zero economic profit.

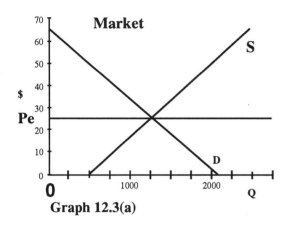

Graph 12.3(a)

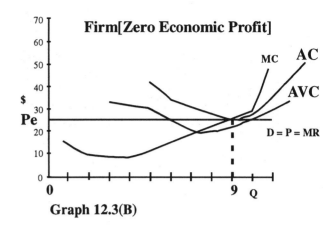

Graph 12.3(B)

Firms with <u>losses exit</u> the industry. Graph 12.4(b)
  Market supply curve shifts left, Graph 12.4 (a)
  Equilibrium price rises increasing the profits of the firms remaining in the industry. Graph 12.4(c)

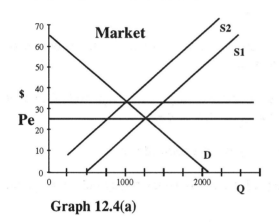

Graph 12.4(a)

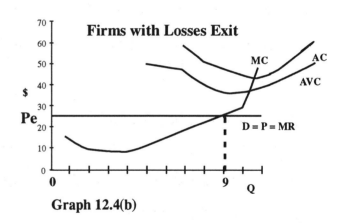

Graph 12.4(b)

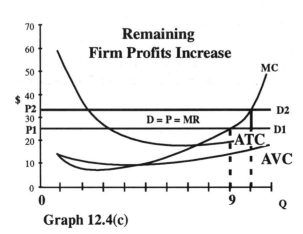

Graph 12.4(c)

New firms <u>enter</u> the industry to capture potential <u>profits</u>.
>   Market supply curve shifts right, Graph 12.5(a)
>   Equilibrium price decreases, decreasing the profits of the firms remaining in the industry to zero. Graph
>   12.5(b)

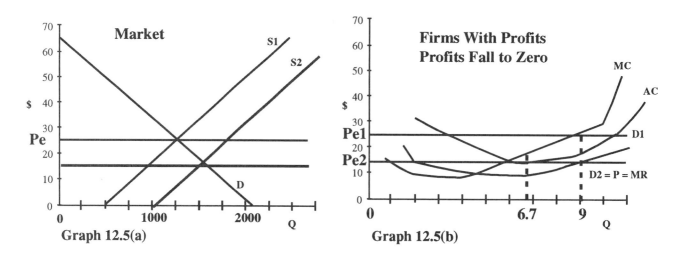

Graph 12.5(a)

Graph 12.5(b)

Long Run Supply Curves
>   **Perfectly Elastic:** Constant Cost Industry.
>>   Many firms have the same cost of producing the good in the long run and their costs do not
>>   depend on the total output of the industry.

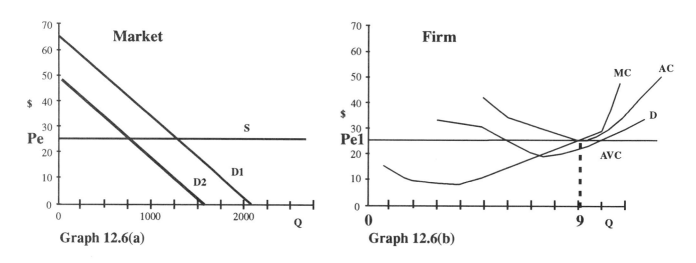

Graph 12.6(a)

Graph 12.6(b)

With a constant cost industry, a change in demand does not affect the price of the good or the quantity
each firm produces. It changes the number of firms in the industry.
Graphs 12.6 (a) and(b). A decrease in demand decreases the number of firms in the industry.

Long Run Supply Curves

Upward Sloping: Increasing Cost Industry

A firm's average cost rises with total output in the industry or some firms may operate more efficiently than others.

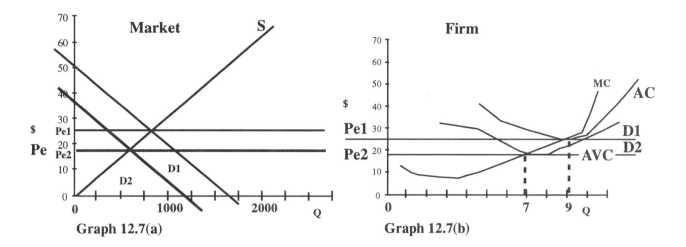

Graph 12.7(a)

Graph 12.7(b)

With an increasing cost industry, a change in demand changes the price of the good, the quantity each firm produces and the number of firms in the industry.

When Demand decreases from D1 to D2, Price decreases, quantity produced by the firm decreases and the number of firms in the industry decreases.

Short Answer Questions

1. Explain the conditions under which a firm, which faces a demand core that is more elastic than the market demand curve, can be termed a price taker?

2. Why do accountants measure costs differently from economists?

3. Why would a firm stay in business in the long run under perfect competition? It earns zero economic profits.

4. Why would an industry have increasing long run costs? What would the shape of the Long Run supply curve be?

5. Under what conditions is equilibrium quantity under perfect competition economically efficient?

Basic Problems

1. The elasticity of market demand for corn is -1/2. World output is 100,000,000 tons. Farmer Brown decides to double his output of corn from one ton to two tons per year. Using the midpoint formula for percentage change from Chapter 5, this change represents a (1/1.5) or 67% change in Farmer Brown's output. What effect does the increase in Farmer Browns output have on the world output and equilibrium price in the market?

Advanced Problems

1. Technical change for safety reasons requires a firm to produce an existing product, i.e. a car at a higher cost. Average cost and marginal cost rise (curves shift upwards). Using graphs, illustrate and analyze what will happen to market supply, equilibrium price and quantity, the short run profits or losses of existing firms, long run exit or entry into the industry and the effect of that exit or entry on long run equilibrium price and quantity.

Chapter 13

Monopoly

Learning Goals

1. Explain how a monopolist can profit by restricting the size of its output and sales.

2. Determine profit maximizing price and quantity under monopoly conditions.

3. Illustrate the goal of firms or countries that collude to raise prices and explain why this collusion often fails.

4. Describe the conditions which are required for price discrimination to take place.

5. Identify the deadweight loss of monopoly. Describe conditions under which a monopoly would be termed economically efficient.

Key Term Matching Quiz

Terms

_____   1. Monopoly

_____   2. Barrier to Entry

_____   3. Increasing Returns to Scale

_____   4. Natural Monopoly

_____   5. Multipart Price

_____   6. Cartel

_____   7. Antitrust Law

_____   8. Predatory Pricing

_____   9. Price Discrimination

_____   10. Perfect Price Discrimination

_____   11. Rent Seeking

_____   12. Monopsony

Definitions

a.   Charging different prices to different buyers for the same good.

b.   A price composed of several parts, such as a startup fee, a monthly fee and a per-use fee.

c.   The only seller of some product.

d.   A group of firms collude to act like a monopoly and share the monopoly profit.

e.   Competition for favors from the government.

f.   An industry with increasing returns to scale over sufficiently large quantities.

g.   A seller charges each customer the highest price she is willing to pay.

h.   Costs high enough to prevent potential competitors from entering an industry.

i.   Monopoly buyer of some product.

j.   Laws that prohibit monopolies and cartels or monopoly-like behaviors.

k.   Average cost of production decreases with higher output.

l.   A seller charges less than its average cost to try to drive a competitor out of business.

True/False Questions

_____ 1. A monopoly produces the economically efficient quantity and charges a price equal to marginal cost.

_____ 2. Laws or government regulations can serve as a barrier to entry for a firm into a profitable industry.

_____ 3. A natural monopoly is an industry with decreasing returns to scale over sufficiently large quantities.

_____ 4. Predatory pricing, charging less than average cost to drive a competitor out of business, is a rare occurrence because the predator loses money.

_____ 5. Monopolies charge prices above their marginal costs and fully pass on all cost increases to their customers.

_____ 6. License requirements to do business are illegal and a restraint of trade.

_____ 7. Though a natural monopoly makes it efficient to have a single producer, the monopoly level of output is not economically efficient.

_____ 8. Tie-in sales were made illegal by the Clayton Act.

_____ 9. Selling two goods at the same price even if their costs of production differ is price discrimination.

_____ 10. Free agency increased the monopsony power of baseball owners.

Multiple Choice Questions

1. A monopoly:
    a. must reduce its price to sell more.
    b. can't raise price without losing its customers.
    c. is one of many sellers of a product that has many substitutes
    d. None of the above.

Table 13.1

Price	Quantity Sold	Total Revenue	Marginal Revenue
$10	1	10	
9	2	18	
8	3	24	
7	4	28	
6	5	30	
5	6	30	
4	7	28	
3	8	24	
2	9	18	
1	10	10	

2. Table 13.1 shows the price, amount sold and total revenue for a monopolist selling his product. If the monopolist's marginal cost of selling each extra unit of product is $2, at what quantity sold will he maximize profit?
    a. 5.
    b. 4.
    c. 3.
    d. Because the monopolist is the sole seller, he can maximize his profit at any of the quantities given in answers a, b or c.

3. In Table 13.1, what is the marginal revenue from selling 3 units of product?
    a. 2
    b. 4
    c. 6
    d. 8

4. Marginal Revenue differs from the Demand Curve:
    a. of a monopoly because the monopoly can always sell one more unit of the good at a higher price.
    b. of a monopoly because to sell one more unit of the good, the monopoly has to lower its price to all customers.
    c. of a price taker because they do not have to reduce their price to sell more.
    d. Answers b and c.

5. Monopoly Profit equals:
    a. Total Revenue minus Total Variable Cost.
    b. [Price minus Average Cost] multiplied by the quantity sold.
    c. Markup multiplied by the quantity sold.
    d. All of the above.

6. A monopoly's supply curve:
   a. is the portion of the Marginal Cost curve that lies above average variable cost.
   b. is impossible to define because the quantity supplied at any one price depends on demand.
   c. is equal to its average variable cost curve.
   d. None of the above.

7. The deadweight social loss of a monopoly:
   a. occurs because the monopoly charges a price above its marginal cost.
   b. occurs because the monopoly does not produce the economically efficient quantity.
   c. represents the potential gains from the trades that do not occur because of the monopoly.
   d. All of the above.

8. Compared to perfect competition, consumer surplus with a monopoly which has the same costs of production as the perfect competitor:
   a. is larger because buyers pay more for each good and they buy more.
   b. is smaller because buyers pay more for each good and they buy less.
   c. is equal to consumer surplus with a perfectly competitive firm because their marginal cost curves are the same.
   d. Answers b and c.

9. Cartels are unstable and do not last long because:
   a. the cartel members cheat on the price they charge.
   b. the cartel members cheat on the quantity they sell.
   c. it is difficult to assign and enforce quotas on the cartel members.
   d. Answers b and c.

10. To price discriminate the monopolist must be able to:
    a. sell the same product at different prices to different buyers.
    b. be able to prevent the buyer from reselling the product.
    c. discern the highest price that each buyer is willing to pay.
    d. All of the above.

Chapter Review (Fill in the Blanks)

1. A monopoly, the _____ seller of a product, faces a _____ sloping demand curve for its product and makes its decisions _____ of the reactions of other firms. A monopoly has _____ supply curve. It chooses the price-quantity combination along its _____ curve that maximizes _____. The monopoly maximizes profit by choosing the quantity that sets _____ _____ equal to _____ _____. Monopoly profit equals its _____ times the quantity sold.

2. Monopolies cause economic _____ because they sell _____ than the economically efficient quantity. Deadweight social loss represents the potential gains from the trades that do _____ occur because of the monopoly. Monopoly _____ output below the _____ _____ _____ and charges a price _____ marginal cost.

Barriers to entry

3. Monopoly profits tempt other firms to _____ the industry. A firm can _____ a monopoly in the long run only if some _____ _____ _____ keep other firms _____. Example of barriers to entry include: _____ costs of production at the monopoly firm, _____ or copyrights, _____ _____ requirements.

4. _____ laws. such as the Sherman Act of 1890 made _____ _____ in restraint of trade or monopolizing an industry illegal. The Clayton Act of 1914 made _____ _____ sales, _____ and _____ _____ illegal.

5. Price Discrimination occurs when a seller charges _____ prices to _____ buyers for the _____ good. Sellers can _____ profits by price-discriminating.

6. Although monopolies create _____ _____, they have no incentive to produce _____ products or products that become _____.

7. A _____ is a monopoly buyer, a buyer that faces an _____ sloping supply curve and makes decisions _____ of the reactions of their buyers. A monopsony chooses a quantity to buy that sets its _____ _____ equal to its _____ _____; then the monopsony pays the _____ price at which it can buy that quantity. Monopsonies cause _____ _____ by reducing or restricting the quantity traded.

Priority List of Concepts

Monopoly: Single seller that faces a downward sloping demand curve. Has no supply curve. It chooses the price quantity combination along its demand curve that maximizes profit.

Profit Maximization: Chooses quantity at which marginal cost equals marginal revenue, and sells at the price on the demand curve at that quantity.

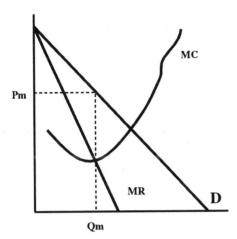

Figure 13.1

Monopoly Profit for a Monopoly without Fixed Costs: can be measured in two different ways:
1. Total Revenue (Price times Quantity) minus Total Variable Costs (area under the MC curve).

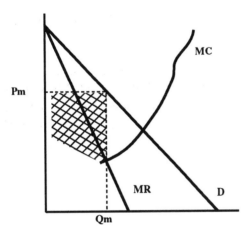

Figure 13.2

2. Markup (Price minus Average Cost) multiplied by the number of goods it sells.

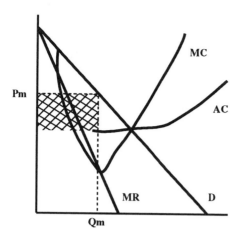

Figure 13.3

Deadweight Social Loss From a Monopoly: Potential gains from trade that do not occur because of the monopoly (Graph 13.4).

Monopoly sells less than the economically efficient quantity, *Qe*. *Qe* occurs at the quantity where MC and Demand curve intersect.

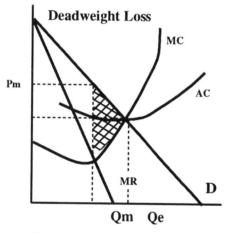

Figure 13.4

Barriers to Entry: A firm can remain a monopoly in the long run only if there are high costs that prevent potential competitors from entering the industry (i.e., government regulations, patents, copyrights, or natural cost advantages).

Table 13.2
Comparison of Monopoly and Perfect Competition*

Monopoly	Perfect Competition
Restricts output below the economically efficient quantity.	produces the economically efficient quantity.
P > MC	P = MC
Producer surplus is larger.	
Consumer surplus is smaller. Buyers must pay more for the good and they buy less.	
Deadweight social loss.	
Has no supply curve.	Supply is the MC curve above AVC.

*assuming they both have the same costs of production.

Cartels: A group of firms collude to act like a monopoly and share the monopoly profit. To charge the high monopoly price, the cartel must restrict the output of its members to individual quotas that sum to the monopoly output. Each member of the cartel has an incentive to cheat on the quantity sold. This cheating eventually destabilizes the cartel by lowering the price of the product.

Natural Monopoly: a natural barrier to entry results when the average cost of producing a good falls with quantity over a large range of possible outputs. The are increasing returns to scale as evidenced by the downward slope of the average total cost curve, AC. A natural monopoly occurs when it is more efficient for one firm to produce all units of the good.

Monopoly output (Qm), where MC = MC, is not economically efficient. A monopoly profit of {(Pm-ACm) * Q} would be made.

The economically efficient quantity, $Qe,$ occurs where Demand intersects MC. However, at this price, Pc, a loss equal to [Pc - ACe] would occur.

To get the firm to produce the economically efficient quantity, $Qe,$ would require multipart pricing. The firm would charge Pc per unit sold plus a monthly fee that would cover the loss.

Another possibility for the regulator is to make the firm charge P_{ac}, the price that would let the firm cover his average costs. and produce Q_{ac} This price lets the natural monopoly cover its costs, but it still produces less than $Qe.$

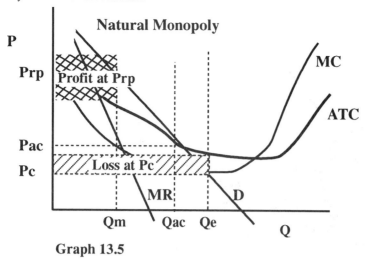

Graph 13.5

Price Discrimination: a monopolist can raise its profit by charging different prices to different buyers for the same good.

Perfect Price Discrimination: a seller charges each customer the highest price that she is willing to pay. The monopoly captures all the gains from trade; consumer surplus is zero and producer surplus is the shaded area. The Monopoly seller produces the economically efficient quantity, *Qe*, and creates no deadweight loss.

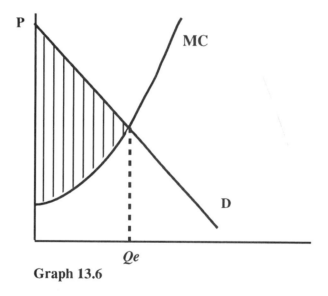

Graph 13.6

Rent Seeking: firms compete for rights to a legal monopoly.
   These actions, which spend time and other resources, can create economic inefficiency.

Monopsony: A single buyer that reduces purchases to keep the price low. A monopsony faces an upward sloping supply curve and decides without considering the reactions of other buyers. Buys a quantity that sets its marginal benefit equal to its marginal cost and pays a price on the supply curve at that quantity. The monopsony buys less than the Economically efficient quantity and creates a deadweight social loss.

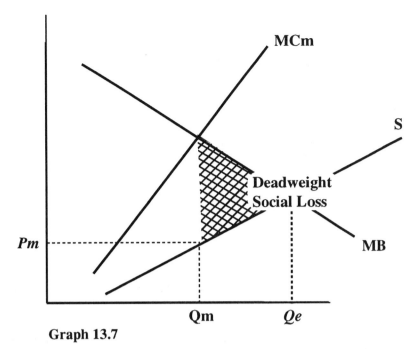

Graph 13.7

Short Answer Questions

1. Why would the monopolist restrict the output it sells whereas the price taker sells everything they have?

2. Compare the gains from trade under monopoly vs. perfect competition. Comment on the relative magnitudes of consumer surplus, producer surplus and deadweight social loss.

3. How much would a firm be willing to pay to become a monopoly?

Basic Problems

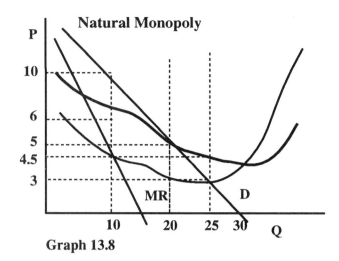

Graph 13.8

1. Given Graph 13.8 on an industry which will foster the development of a natural monopoly, identify and illustrate with the appropriate abbreviations on the graph provided and the numerical answer in the spaces provided below:

Monopoly Output Qm_____
Monopoly Price Pm_____
Profit _____

If the firm is regulated to sell the Economically Efficient Quantity?

Economically Efficient Quantity Qe_____
Perfectly Competitive Price Pc_____
Profit or Loss at Pc paid and Qe sold _____

If the firm is regulated to sell at its Average Cost, Q_{ac} _____

Price = Ac, P_{ac} _____

Would there be profit or loss at P_{ac}?

At P_{ac} would the firm be producing the economically efficient quantity.

How could the firm produce the economically efficient quantity and not suffer a loss?

Chapter 14

Monopolistic Competition and Oligopoly

Learning Goals

1. Describe the conditions that define monopolistic competition and oligopoly.

2. Compare and contrast the market structures.

3. Explain the presence of non-price competition and advertising.

4. Use marginal cost and marginal revenue to determine equilibrium in these market structures.

5. Explain the tradeoff between production efficiency and product variety.

6. Measure the degree of competition in an industry.

7. How strategic interaction affects the profit maximizing decision of the firm.

Key Term Matching Quiz

Terms

_____ 1. Differentiated Product

_____ 2. Monopolistic Competition

_____ 3. Excess Capacity

_____ 4. Non-price Competition

_____ 5. Oligopoly

_____ 6. Concentration Ratio

_____ 7. Price Rigidity

_____ 8. Rate of Return on Investment

_____ 9. Best Response

_____ 10. Nash Equilibrium

_____ 11. Bertrand Model

_____ 12. Cournot Model

Definitions

a. There is a differentiated product, free entry and the industry has enough firms that when one cuts its price, the others lose only a small quantity of sales.

b. Accounting profit per dollar of its previous investments, expressed as a percentage per year.

c. Firms compete by providing better quality products or product characteristics designed to match the preferences of specific groups of consumers.

d. Each firm believes that other firms will react to its decisions by changing their _prices_ to maintain their levels of output.

e. Each firm makes its best response.

f. These firms face a downward sloping demand curve and interact strategically.

g. Each firm believes that other firms will react to its decisions by changing the _quantities_ they sell to keep their prices fixed.

h. Exists when a firm can reduce its average cost by raising its output.

i. Total sales of the largest _n_ firms as a percentage of total industry sales.

j. The action that maximizes its profit, given the action of its rivals.

k. Buyers consider the products to be good but not perfect substitutes.

l. Slow adjustments of prices to changes in costs or demand.

True/False Questions

_____   1.   Advertising may differentiate products by creating a unique image for each one.

_____   2.   Flexible technologies can deter entry and help a cartel prevent cheating on quotas.

_____   3.   Concentration ratios are closely related to costs of production and economic efficiency.

_____   4.   Oligopolies can use large inventories to deter entry by threatening to sell them and thus decrease prices if a new competitor enters.

_____   5.   A duopoly under Cournot oligopoly model assumptions will charge a price equal to marginal cost.

_____   6.   The cartel (monopoly price) is a Nash equilibrium for the Bertrand model of oligopoly.

_____   7.   Even in an industry with many firms, if only a few sell close substitutes, those firms may strategically interact with each other.

_____   8.   Short run profits in monopolistically competitive firms will provide an incentive for new firms to enter the industry.

_____   9.   The difference between Monopolistic Competition and Perfect Competition vanishes as demand becomes large enough to accommodate many firms in one industry in long run equilibrium.

_____   10.   Firms in an industry with monopolistic competition at long run equilibrium would be able to reduce their average costs if they produced more.

Multiple Choice Questions

1. The existence of free entry into an industry:
   a. fosters the entry of new firms in the long run if its offers positive economic profits.
   b. fosters the exit of new firms in the long run if it offers positive economic profits.
   c. generates profits in the long run.
   d. All of the above.

2. Under the structure of monopolistic competition, the condition that each firms sells a differentiated product means:
   a. that each firm faces a perfectly elastic demand.
   b. that each firm is a price taker.
   c. that each firm faces a downward sloping demand curve.
   d. Answers b and c.

3. An example of a monopolistically competitive industry is:
   a. the airline industry.
   b. the video game industry.
   c. the credit card industry.
   d. the soft drink industry.

4. Excess Capacity, which occurs in equilibrium under monopolistic competition:
   a. is economically efficient.
   b. implies that average cost is higher with a larger quantity produced.
   c. is the price people pay for more product diversity and choice.
   d. Answers a and c.

5. Concentrated industries:
   a. have high three or four firm concentration ratios.
   b. have more price rigidity.
   c. earn higher profits on average.
   d. All of the above.

6. Dominant firms arise in an industry due to all of the following except:
   a. patents.
   b. high average costs.
   c. charging a price equal to average cost on leftover demand.
   d. Answers a and c.

Answer questions 6 to 11 based on the following diagrams which represent firms in either perfect competition or monopolistic competition.

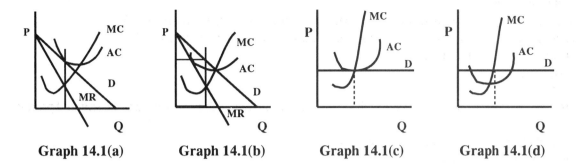

Graph 14.1(a)   **Graph 14.1(b)**   **Graph 14.1(c)**   **Graph 14.1(d)**

7. Which graphs illustrate a firm producing with excess capacity?
   a. Graphs a and b.
   b. Graphs b and d.
   c. Graph c.
   d. Graphs a and c.

8. Which graphs illustrate a firm producing where P = MC?
   a. Graphs a, b and d.
   b. Graphs b and d.
   c. Graph c.
   d. All of the graphs.

9. Which graph illustrates a firm producing at capacity, where AC is at a minimum?
   a. Graph a.
   b. Graph b.
   c. Graph c.
   d. Graph d.

10. Which graphs illustrate a firm in long run equilibrium with no long run profits, where price is equal to average cost?
    a. Graph a.
    b. Graph b and d
    c. Graph c.
    d. Graph a and c.

11. Which graphs illustrate a firm making a short run profit, where price is greater than average cost?
    a. Graphs a, b and d.
    b. Graphs b and d.
    c. Graphs c and d.
    d. All of the Graphs.

12. Which graphs refer to a monopolistic competitor?
    a. Graphs a and b.
    b. Graphs c and d.
    c. Graphs a and c.
    d. All of the Graphs.

Chapter Review (Fill in the Blanks)

1. In monopolistic competition, _____ firms in an industry produce _____ products and act _____. _____ entry guarantees that firms earn _____ economic profits in _____ _____ equilibrium.

2. Monopolistically competitive firms have _____ _____ demand curves, so its marginal revenue curve lies _____ its demand curve. It maximizes _____ by choosing a _____ where MC = MR and charging the _____ price at which it can sell that quantity along its _____ _____.

3. Monopolistically competitive firms have _____ capacity in long run equilibrium.

4. _____ _____ Competition occurs when firms compete by producing _____ quality products.

5. In the long run, economic _____ induce new firms to _____. As more firms share the industry, customers _____ for each firm _____, the demand curve and the marginal revenue curves shift _____. Long run equilibrium occurs when economic profits equal _____ and _____ firms have _____ further incentive to _____ the industry. At long run equilibrium, price equals _____ _____, so each firms earns _____ economic profit.

6. Monopolistic Competition resembles Perfect Competition in two ways: first, each firm _____ _____ without regard to the response of competitors; and second, _____ _____ guarantees that firms earn zero economic profits in long run equilibrium.

7. Monopolistic Competition differs from Perfect Competition in two ways: first, each Monopolistically Competitive firm faces a _____ _____ demand curve because each firm produces a _____ product; and second, monopolistically competitive firms are _____ price takers. The monopolistically competitive firm's price _____ marginal cost and firms have _____ _____ in the long run.

8. The main difference between Monopolistic Competition and Monopoly is that Monopolistic Competition applies to situations with _____ _____ in the long run. Free entry guarantees that _____ profits in the long run are _____.

9. Oligopoly occurs when firms are _____ price takers and each firm acts _____. In strategic interaction, each firm's _____ take into account the _____ of other firms and the _____ of those reactions.

10. Short run equilibrium under oligopoly may result in _____, but new firms enter in the long run and reduce _____ _____ to zero unless there are _____ _____ _____.

11. Equilibrium with an oligopoly is a _____ equilibrium. Each firm follows its _____ response, maximizes _____, given the actions of rival firms.

12. Different beliefs by the oligopoly firms as to the reactions of their _____ lead to _____ models of oligopoly.

13. In the Bertrand model, a firm believes other firms will keep their _____ fixed. In the Cournot model a firm believes other firms will keep their _____ fixed.

14. In a dominant firm situation, the firm acts like a _____, charging the _____ for _____ demand, that is, the demand leftover after other, _____ firms have sold their outputs.

15. The _____ model applies when one firm operates an industry. The _____ model applies when two firms compete and _____ _____ is a good model when _____ firms compete. When the _____ firms act _____ in an industry with only a _____ firms, the _____ (cartel) model applies best.

Priority List of Concepts

Monopolistic Competition: many firms in an industry produce differentiated products. It has many characteristics of both perfect competition and monopoly.

Perfect Competition	Monopolistic Competition	Monopoly
	Differentiated Product	
	Downward Sloping Demand Curve	⇐⇐⇐⇐⇐
⇒⇒⇒⇒⇒⇒	Many Firms	
⇒⇒⇒⇒⇒⇒	Each firm acts independently	
⇒⇒⇒⇒⇒⇒	Free entry and exit	
⇒⇒⇒⇒⇒⇒	Zero Economic Profits in the Long Run	
⇒⇒⇒⇒⇒⇒	Profit Maximize where MC = MR so long as P > AVC	⇐⇐⇐⇐⇐
	P > MR	⇐⇐⇐⇐⇐
	P > MC	⇐⇐⇐⇐⇐
	Excess Capacity	
	Non Price Competition	

Differentiated Products: good but not perfect substitutes. Products differ in appearance, design, quality, location, usage, etc. Difference can be real or perceived.

Monopolistic Competition requires the existence of three conditions:
1. The firm sells a differentiated product, thus it is not a price taker and faces a downward sloping demand curve.
2. Many firms in the industry so that one firm's actions have only a slight effect on the sales of others.
3. Free entry and exit. Generates zero economic profits in the long run. Positive economic profit causes firms to enter the industry. Negative economic profits causes firms to exit the industry.

Equilibrium with Monopolistic Competition:
Short Run: MC = MR as long as Price >AVC. If short run profits occur, new firms enter the industry, the demand for each firm shifts left as it has to share the market with more producers. The price at which the firm can sell the product falls and profits dissipate.
Long Run: Zero economic profits. No incentives for firms to either exit or enter the industry.

Excess Capacity: occurs at equilibrium in Monopolistic Competition. In Graph 14.2, if the firm increased its output, its average cost would decrease. The monopolistically competitive firm would not take this action, because it would have to lower its price and in long run equilibrium, it would incur a loss.

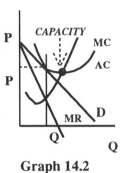

Graph 14.2

Capacity: occurs at minimum average cost.

Inefficiency of Monopolistic Competition: Price is greater than Marginal Cost and Average cost is greater than minimum average cost, but monopolistic competition provides buyers with product variety.

Non Price Competition: firms compete by providing better quality products or product characteristics designed to match the preferences of specific groups of consumers (i.e., the characteristic of location, a nearby convenient store).

Oligopoly: competition among a small group of sellers who interact and have a downsloping demand curve.

Strategic Interaction: Each firm anticipates its competitors reaction to its own actions when it decides what to produce.

Barriers to Entry: costs high enough to prevent new firms from entering an industry. Protects oligopolies from competition and allows oligopolies to earn positive long run economic profits.

Concentration Ratios: measures the level of competition in an industry. Total sales of the largest n firms expressed as a percentage of total industry sales. Ignores foreign competition.

Concentrated Industries: have high three or four firm concentration ratios. Have more price rigidity. Earn higher profits on average.

Nash Equilibrium: Each firm makes its best response, maximizes profits, given the actions of its rivals.

Equilibrium under Oligopoly: depends on *what firms believe* about the likely reaction of their competitors.

Bertrand Model   **Cournot Model**   **Oligopoly Models Compared**

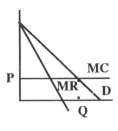   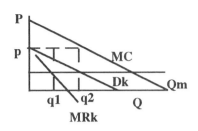   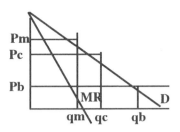

Graph 14.3(a)   **Graph 14.3(b)**   **Graph 14.3(c)**

Bertrand Model: Each *firm believes that the other firms will keep prices fixed*. That is, the other firms will react to its decisions by changing quantity sold but keeping price fixed.
In the long run, the Nash equilibrium will be where Price equals Marginal Cost. (P = MC). Graph 14.3(a) This model assumes no product differentiation, capacity constraints or steep MC curves.

Cournot Model: Each *firm believes that the other firms will keep their levels of sales fixed*. That is, the other firms will react to its decisions by changing price but keeping quantity sold fixed. The Nash Equilibrium under the Cournot model will be where each firms price (Pc) is less than the monopoly price (Pm) but greater than marginal cost. Graph 14.3(c). In the duopoly shown in the Graph 14.3(b) above, firm 1 produces q1, and firm 2 produces the same amount, q2-q1, price charged is p.

Oligopoly model equilibrium results are compared in Graph 14.3(c). Cournot Model, Pc, qc; Monopoly Model, Pm, qm; Bertrand Model, Pb, Qb.

Other Strategies in Oligopoly Decision Making:

Flexible technologies: allow the oligopoly to increase or decrease quantities in response to the actions of another firm. Inflexible technologies: can deter entry if increasing output by just a little cause average costs to rise precipitously. This cost situation would help a cartel to maintain output quotas and discourage firms from cheating on the cartel agreement and increasing the quantity sold.

Inventories: holding large stocks and threatening to sell them and decrease prices if new competitor enters.

Industrial Secrecy: try to keep costs secret and make your competitors believe you are a low cost producer.

Investment in Experience: Learning by doing and thereby decreasing costs. Trade off lower price and short run loss for lower costs, less competition and higher profits in the long run.

Dominant Firm: arises in an industry due to early entry, low average costs and patents or prior patents which have since expired. Charges the monopoly price for quantity sold at MC = MR on the leftover demand curve, that is demand for what is left over after the smaller firms have sold their output.

Short Answer Questions

1. At long run equilibrium with Monopolistic Competition, there is excess capacity. Why doesn't the firm produce more to reduce average cost and move to capacity output?

2. Why doesn't a Bertrand model of oligopoly predict that the producer will charge a price greater than marginal cost?

3. Why doesn't a Cournot model of oligopoly charge the monopoly (cartel) price?

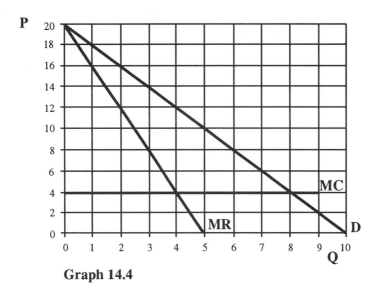

Graph 14.4

1. Assuming a Cournot Duopoly model of oligopoly, the market demand curve is shown above in Graph 14.4. There are two companies, A and B. Company A decides to produce 4 units of the product and sell it at a price of $12. According to the Cournot model, how will Company B respond in its production and pricing decisions? Show the demand that Company B thinks it faces and the amount that Company B will produce when it first enters the market after A has decided to produce 4 units. In the long run, what price will each firm charge and how much will they produce? If there were no fixed costs, would these firms be making a profit in the long run? Why don' t these firms and charge the monopoly price and act as a cartel?

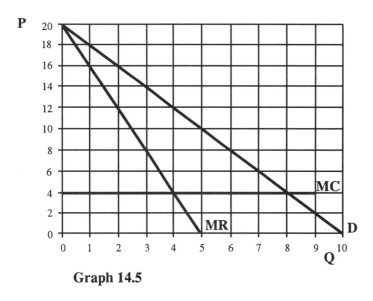

Graph 14.5

2. Given the above model of a oligopoly market (Graph 14.5), how much quantity and what price would a firm operating on the Bertrand theory of oligopoly produce and charge? Assuming no fixed costs, would firms in the market make a profit? Is this output efficient?

Advanced Problems

1. Assume your company wishes to enter the laundry detergent business. Two products in particular are very successful. How will you differentiate your product in a way that will maximize the number of your customers?

2. The Monopolistic Competition that occurred among cities for the U.S. Summer Olympics in 1996 was intense. Use the logic of monopolistic competition to predict Atlanta's profit in the long run from winning the competition to host the 1996 Olympics.

3. Should advertising be banned if it creates a perceived, as opposed to a real, difference in competing products? Could the perceived effect be viewed just as likely to be beneficial as harmful to the consumer? Give some examples of advertising that give a perceived rather than a real differentiation to a product.

Chapter 15

Game Theory

Learning Goals

1. Describe examples of strategic interaction between people, firms and nations in everyday life.

2. Explain the strategy of decision making using Game theory.

3. Explain the connections between individual incentives and socially desirable outcomes.

4. Explain the market signals given by commitments and reputations.

6. Distinguish between a Nash Equilibrium and a Dominant Strategy.

7. Apply the Prisoners Dilemma theory to the pricing decisions of firms in an oligopoly market structure.

Key Term Matching Quiz

Terms

_____   1. Game Theory

_____   2. Rules of a Game

_____   3. Strategy

_____   4. Payoff

_____   5. Dominant Strategy

_____   6. Sequential Game

_____   7. Subgame Perfect Nash Equilibrium

_____   8. Commitment to a Future Action

_____   9. Repeated Game

_____   10. Tit for Tat

_____   11. Prisoner's Dilemma

_____   12. Credible Strategy

_____   13. Decision Tree

_____   14. Payoff Matrix

Definitions

a. Amount a player wins or loses in a particular situation.

b. Does something now to limit her future options or change her future incentives so that she will have an incentive to take that action in the future.

c. Summarizes the possible outcomes of the game.

d. A player has an incentive to carry out that strategy.

e. Players make some of their decisions at different times.

f. Who can do what and when can they do it.

g. Each firm makes its best response given the action of its competitors. The firms are prevented from cooperating. The dilemma is that both firms would be better off if they could cooperate but they lack the proper incentives to achieve this better outcome.

h. "Doing to others what they did to you."

i. Players best strategy does not depend on what others do.

j. Plan for action in each possible situation.

k. Every player's strategy is credible.

l. Show possible choices of firm 1 and then possible responses of firm 2 for each of these choices. The resulting payoffs are given at the end of each branch.

m. Study of strategic behavior in decision making.

True/False Questions

_____   1. In the Prisoner's Dilemma, if one prisoner commits to keep quiet, both prisoners have the incentive to keep quiet.

_____   2. By limiting their capacity to produce, firms may commit not to cheat on a cartel.

_____   3. Equilibrium in an oligopoly tends to be closer to the monopoly (cartel) solution if the same firms compete repeatedly than if they compete only once.

_____   4. Repeated games tend to discourage cooperative behavior.

_____   5. A Nash equilibrium is always economically efficient because both parties have made their best response.

_____   6. To measure the payoff from a tariff, measure the change in the taxing country's producer and consumer surplus.

_____   7. In deciding between multiple equilibria, the economist needs information that is not part of the game to predict what will happen (i.e., information on the culture of the people involved).

_____   8. A subgame perfect Nash equilibrium is economically efficient.

_____   9. In the prisoner's dilemma, if one prisoner could commit not to confess, both would have the incentive not to confess.

_____   10. By limiting their capacity to produce, firms may commit not to cheat on a cartel.

Multiple Choice Questions

1. A firm can commit to future actions by all of the following except:
   a. using the legal system by getting the government to regulate them.
   b. limiting their capacity to produce.
   c. investing in excess capacity.
   d. expanding its future choices.

2. Game Theory was first developed by the mathematician:
   a. John von Neumann.
   b. Robert Axelrod.
   c. Oskar Morgenstern.
   d. Alfred Marshall.

3. In the book, *Evolution of Cooperation*, after repeating a prisoner's dilemma game many times, the winning strategy was:
   a. cooperate, never be the first to cheat.
   b. aggressive competition.
   c. punish with an "eye for an eye," then cooperate again.
   d. Answers a and c.

4. When economists analyze an economic situation with game theory, the plan for actions in each possible situation is known as:
   a. the player's payoff.
   b. the player's strategy.
   c. a Nash equilibrium.
   d. the rules of the game.

5. In Game theory, a player's best strategy:
   a. often depends on what others will do.
   b. is always a dominant strategy.
   c. does not depend on what others will do.
   d. Answers b and c.

6. A dominant strategy:
   a. depends on what others do.
   b. does not depend on what others do.
   c. creates multiple Nash equilibria.
   d. is any situation in which a player makes her best response.

7. In the article, *Ad Spending, Growing Market Share*, a competitor, who is a market leader with an aggressive ad spending strategy will:
   a. keep up the advertising attack as long as it adds to market share.
   b. have a share of advertising spending that will be greater than its share of the market.
   c. have no scale advantage, even though it outspends its followers and is spending at a higher unit cost.
   d. keep spending even when its ads cease to produce gains in market share.

8. Which of the following behaviors is consistent with subgame perfect Nash equilibrium?
   a. A player maximizes his payoff.
   b. A player makes the best response given the strategies of other players.
   c. Every player's strategy is credible.
   d. All of the above.

Use the information provided in the Payoff Matrix, Table 15.1 below to answer questions 9 to 12.

Table 15.1   Player B

		Advertise	*Don't Advertise*
Player A	*Advertise*	A: +$2 B: +$2	A: +$10 B: -$10
	Don't Advertise	A: -$10 B: +$10	A: +$3 B: +$3

9. Given the Payoff Matrix, find firm B's payoffs from advertising:
   a. sum the column titled *Advertise* for player B.
   b. read across the row titled *Advertise*.
   c. read down the column titled *Advertise* for player B's payoffs based on player A's response.
   d) sum the row titled *Advertise* for player B.

10. In the Payoff Matrix of Table 15.1 there:
    a. is a Dominant strategy.
    b. are multiple equilibria.
    c. is a Nash equilibria
    d. Both answers a and c.

11. If player B advertises, what is player A's best response and payoff?
    a. Advertise, payoff equals $2.
    b. Don't advertise, payoff equals -$10
    c. Advertise, payoff equals $10.
    d. Don't advertise, payoff equals $3.

12. If Player A advertises, what is player B's best response and payoff?
    a. Advertise, payoff equals $2.
    b. Don't advertise, payoff equals -$10
    c. Advertise, payoff equals $10.
    d. Don't advertise, payoff equals $3.

Chapter Review (Fill in the Blanks)

1. Game theory is the general theory of _____ _____. A game is described by its _____, _____ and _____.

2. A _____ equilibrium of a game in a situation in which each player's strategy is a _____ _____ to the other players' strategies.

3. In the _____ dilemma, each player gains by _____ from the cooperative solution regardless of what the other player does, do both plays deviate and end up receiving _____ payoffs than they would with the _____ solution. The _____ dilemma applies to many situations such as _____ on a cartel, _____ wars between countries and _____ wars.

4. A player has a _____ strategy when that player's _____ strategy does not depend on other players' actions.

5. The _____ game is an example of a game with multiple Nash equilibria.

6. Players make decisions at different times in a _____ game. A _____ _____ _____ _____ is a Nash equilibrium in which every player's strategy is _____; that is, when players have incentives to carry out their strategies.

7. A person _____ to a future action by Doing something to limit his future options or change his future incentive to take that action. People can _____ from future commitments, even though they _____ their future choices.

8. A _____ game is a game that the same players play more than once. In a _____ game, players' actions can depend on past behavior of other players, so they can _____ other players for _____ behavior in the past. Players can also learn from _____.

9. One strategy of _____ games is _____. In this strategy players _____ unless one of them fails to _____ in some round of the game, in which case the others _____ in the next round whatever the _____ player did in the current round, and then return to _____.

Priority List of Concepts

Game Theory: study of strategic behavior, decision making, considering the likely reactions of competitors. To analyze an economic situation with game theory, economists must determine:
1. **Rules of the Game:** who can do what and when can they do it.
2. **Players' Strategy:** a plan for actions in each possible situation.
3. **Players' Payoff:** amount player wins or loses.
4. **Best Response or Best Strategy:** may depend on what others do.

Dominant Strategy: Player's best strategy does not depend on what others do.

Nash Equilibrium: Each player makes his best response.

Prisoner's Dilemma: Two people are held prisoner with no communication or cooperation permitted between them. Each must decide whether to confess or keep quiet without knowing what the other prisoner will do. The confess strategy dominates for both prisoners. The dilemma is that each prisoner is faced with the uncertainty of whether the other will confess and is led to adopt a course of action that is less beneficial to both prisoners (2 years if they both confess) than if they were able to cooperate and keep quiet. (1 year if they both keep quiet). The payoff matrix (Table 15.2) presented by the jailer provides a strong incentive for one prisoner to squeal on the other.

Table 15.2

		Prisoner B	
		Confess	*Keep Quiet*
Prisoner A	*Confess*	A: 2 years B: 2 years	A: 6 months B: 20 years
	Keep Quiet	A: 20 years B: 6 months	A: 1 year B: 1 year

To read the payoff matrix for Prisoner A, read across each row. To read the payoff matrix for Prisoner B, read down each column.

Decision Tree: shows the possible choices of Prisoner B, then the possible responses of Prisoner A for each of Prisoner B's choices. The resulting payoffs are given at the end of each branch. To find the solution, work backwards from the end of each branch.

Decision Tree for Prisoner A from Table 15.1

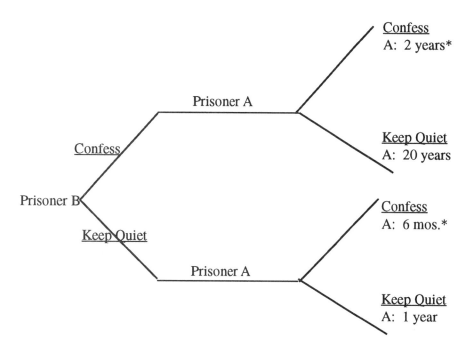

No matter what strategy Prisoner B decides, confess or keep quiet, A's best strategy is to confess. A has a dominant strategy, confess.

Decision Tree for Prisoner B from Table 15.1

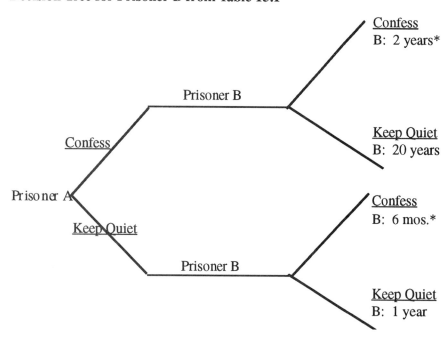

Prisoner B's best strategy is also to confess. If they both confess they get 2 years in prison. Both Prisoner A and Prisoner B would fare better if they did not confess (1 year in prison) but they have no incentive to do so.

Applications of Prisoner's Dilemma

Cartel: Firms have an incentive to cheat on the cartel agreement and increase profits by charging a lower price and taking away others market share.

Table 15.3   Company B

Cartel

		Low Price	Monopoly Price
Company A	**Low Price**	A: $1 B: $1	A: $6 B: $0.5
	Monopoly Price	A: $0.5 B: $6	A: $4 B: $4

A Nash equilibrium takes place, both firms charge the low price, which is also a dominant strategy.

Other applications of the Prisoner's Dilemma include trade wars between countries. The efficient solution is free trade. Tariffs always cause some deadweight loss. However, game theory directs the economic situation to a Nash equilibrium that is economically inefficient because, if there was free trade, both countries would gain. For an example, see Advanced Problem #1.

No Dominant Strategy: One company's response depends on what the other company does.

Multiple equilibria: Two best responses to one economic situation. In this case the game theorist would need information outside of the game to predict what will happen (i.e., knowledge of the culture, etc.).

Subgame perfect Nash equilibrium: Every player's strategy is credible (i.e., there are no unbelievable threats).

Commitments: People and firms can benefit by committing to a future action that limits their future options.
>   For example, in wartime, if you burn the bridges behind you, the soldiers can't retreat, so they must fight to stay alive. Retreat is not an option.
>   A business example would be health care companies that charge a flat upfront fee to cover your health care over the year. They are committed to keeping you healthy so that your premium will cover your health care needs. To a certain extent, product service warranties also provide the same commitment.
>   Excess Capacity is an example of the use of commitment to make a threat credible. A monopoly invests in excess capacity to make its threat to lower price and flood the market with product if a new competitor enters.

Sequential game: Players make some of their decisions at different times.

Repeated Game: a game the same players play more than once.
>   Encourages cooperative behavior. Players can learn from experience about what other players will do.

>   **Tit for Tat:** In a repeated game, players cooperate unless one of them fails to cooperate in some round of the game, in which case the others do in the next round what the uncooperative player did in the current round.

Short Answer Question

1. How can a company employ commitment to deter new entrants?

Basic Problems

1. Find the Nash equilibrium in the following situation. Is there a dominant strategy for both parties?

This is a classic case of the Prisoner's Dilemma. The names are fictitious. Any similarity to actual people is coincidence.

Table 15.4

		Gilooley *Confess*	*Keep Quiet*
Harding	*Confess*	H: 5 years G: 5 years	H: 2 years G: 10 years
	Keep Quiet	H: 10 years G: 2 years	H: 3 years G: 3 years

Advanced Problem

1. Two countries, the U.S. and Japan, engage in foreign trade. The U.S. produces only food and Japan produces only televisions. Japan exports televisions and imports food. The U.S. exports food and imports televisions. The food and television industries are assumed to be perfectly competitive. A $2 tariff on imports is being considered by both Japan and the U.S.

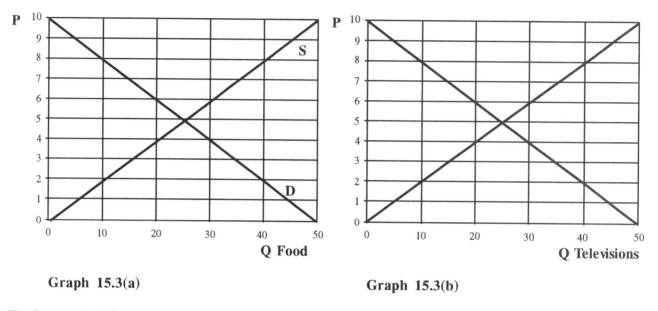

Graph 15.3(a)   **Graph 15.3(b)**

The Demand and Supply curves for these products are shown in Graphs 15.3 (a) and (b) above.
   a. Graphically analyze the effect of the tariff on the U.S. and Japanese consumers and producers, the U.S. government, and efficiency.
   b. Numerically compute the changes in producer and consumer surplus for the Japanese and the U.S. traders.
   c. Construct a payoff matrix for Japan and the U.S. to show the effects of a Tariff vs. no Tariff.
   d. Construct decision trees for both the U.S. and the Japanese.
   e. What strategy will the two countries adopt? Is it a dominant strategy? Is it an optimal strategy?

PART VI

Inputs and Their Earnings

Chapter 16

Economics of Input Markets

Learning Goals

1. Compute and graph the average product and the marginal product of an input in the short run from information on input usage and total product.

2. Determine the Demand for an input given information on productivity and the price of the final good.

3. Explain the theory behind the Law of Diminishing Returns.

4. Distinguish between a durable and a nondurable input.

5. Explain the conditions which cause the demand for an input to rise.

6. Explain the relation between input prices and the distribution of income in an economy.

7. Describe the scope of a firm.

8. Solve for least cost production graphically in the long run using isoquants and a budget line.

Key Term Matching Quiz

Terms

_____ 1. Average Product of an Input

_____ 2. Marginal Product of an Input

_____ 3. Law of Diminishing Returns

_____ 4. Value of Marginal Product of an Input

_____ 5. Nondurable Input

_____ 6. Price Taker in Input Market

_____ 7. Complementary Inputs

_____ 8. Substitute Inputs

_____ 9. Durable Input

_____10. Net Present Value (NPV) of a Durable Input

_____11. Capital Stock

_____12. Investment

_____13. Economic Rent

_____14. Transactions Costs

_____15. Isoquant

_____16. Marginal Rate of Substitution in Production.

Definitions

a. Increase in output when firm adds one more unit of input holding all other inputs fixed in size.

b. An increase in the price of one input raises the demand for the other.

c. Costs of finding people with whom to trade and the costs of buying, selling or negotiating agreements, paying for products or services, etc.

d. Change in money value of a firm's output when it adds one more unit of input.

e. Discounted Present Value of the Future Value of its marginal product minus the discounted Present Value of its Cost.

f. Slope of an isoquant.

g. Faces a perfectly elastic input supply.

h. Increase in the capital stock.

i. Total Output divided by the quantity of the input employed.

j. Increase in the price of one input lowers demand for the other.

k. Price of a resource minus its opportunity cost.

l. Increase in the quantity of inputs employed in the short run eventually decreases their marginal product.

m. Input that a firm buys for future use or one that the firm can use repeatedly.

n. Graph of technically efficient combinations of inputs that give the same amount of output.

o. An input a firm uses soon after acquiring it and can use only once.

p. Quantity of durable goods at a firm or in an economy at a point in time.

True/False Questions

_____ 1. The cost of producing a product is determined by the prices of its inputs.

_____ 2. The demand for inputs is more elastic in the short run than in the long run.

_____ 3. Marginal Cost and Marginal Product are related because of the Law of Diminishing Returns.

_____ 4. The value of marginal product is determined by the total output of the firm multiplied by the price of the input.

_____ 5. An increase in the demand for the final product will decrease the demand for the inputs used to produce that final product.

_____ 6. To maximize the value of a firm, the firm will buy a durable input with a future cash flow.

_____ 7. Leasing a durable input is like buying a nondurable input in that you use the rule, lease as long as the value of marginal product is equal to the price of the lease.

_____ 8   Economic rent is the sum of producer surplus and variable cost.

_____ 9. If markets coordinate all inputs, no firms would operate.

_____ 10. Isoquants with perfect substitution among inputs are drawn as right angles.

Multiple Choice Questions

Answer Questions 1 and 2 based on Table 16.1 below.

Labor	Output	MPP	APP
1	5	_____	_____
2	15	_____	_____
3	27	_____	_____
4	35	_____	_____
5	42	_____	_____
6	48	_____	_____
7	53	_____	_____
8	57	_____	_____
9	60	_____	_____

1. The Marginal Product of the sixth unit of labor is :
    a. 8.
    b. 6.
    c. 4.
    d. 2.

2. Diminishing returns sets in when this firm hires the :
    a. first unit of labor.
    b. the second unit of labor.
    c. the third unit of labor.
    d. the fourth unit of labor.

3. The average product of labor:
    a. falls when average product is less than marginal product.
    b. rises when average product is less than marginal product.
    c. rises when marginal product is less than average product.
    d. None of the above.

4. When total product is at a maximum:
    a. average product is positive.
    b. marginal product is positive.
    c. marginal product is equal to zero.
    d. All of the above.

5. In perfect competition, the demand for labor:
    a. a horizontal line at the prevailing wage.
    b. slopes downward due to the law of diminishing returns.
    c. is equal to the marginal physical products of labor.
    d. will shift to the right if more labor is hired.

6. According to the Law of Diminishing Returns, employing more inputs to produce more output:
   a. always causes marginal product to increase.
   b. always causes marginal product to increase at a rate proportionate to the rate of increase in input use.
   c. has no effect on the marginal product after a certain point.
   d. causes marginal product to decrease after a certain point if the quantity of at least one other input is fixed in size in the short run.

7. An increase in the demand for a final product:
   a. decreases the price of the final product.
   b. decreases the value of the marginal product of each input employed in its production.
   c. increases the demand for the inputs to produce the final product.
   d. All of the above.

8. A firm maximizes its value by choosing a quantity of each input that:
   a. equates value of marginal product with the price of the input.
   b. maximizes total output.
   c. equates marginal benefit with marginal cost.
   d. Answers a and c.

9. A price taker in an input market:
   a. faces a horizontal perfectly elastic demand curve.
   b. faces a vertical perfectly elastic demand curve.
   c. hires the input where the value of marginal product is equal to average cost.
   d. Answers a and c.

10. An increase in the price of a substitute input:
   a. lowers demand for the other input.
   b. raises demand for the other input.
   c. causes the firm to switch to the substitute input.
   d. Answers a and c.

11. A nondurable input:
   a. can be used only once.
   b. is an input that can be used repeatedly.
   c. is an input a firm buys for future use.
   d. All of the above.

12. The amount of a durable input that a firm buys is determined by:
   a. the use of the logical rule, MC = MB.
   b. the net present value of the durable input.
   c. the discounted present value of its cost.
   d. All of the above.

13. An economic rent refers to all of the following except:
   a. a resource with a perfectly inelastic supply that earns a profit.
   b. the price of leasing an input.
   c. the difference between the price of a resource input and its opportunity cost.
   d. None of the above.

14. If the supply of an input increases, it causes:
    a. the price of the input to rise.
    b. the marginal cost of the final product to rise.
    c. an increase in the supply of the final good.
    d. an increase in the price of the final good.

Chapter Review (Fill in the Blanks)

1. Machines have replaced _____ _____ _____ as _____ _____ has reduced the cost of equipment. This _____ _____ is the one reason why U. S. manufacturing output has increased by _____ _____ since 1980 while employment has decreased about _____ _____.

2. Firms buy _____, factors of production, to produce _____ products. The demand for _____ is related to their _____ and the _____ of the final good that they produce.

3. The _____ _____ of an input is the increase in a firm's _____ _____ when it adds _____ _____ unit of the input, keeping the quantities of other inputs _____.

4. The _____ _____ _____ states that raising the quantity of an input eventually reduces its _____ _____, if the quantity of some other input remains _____. _____ _____ imply that short run marginal cost and average variable cost _____ with _____ output.

5. A firm's demand curve for a nondurable input shows the _____ _____ _____ _____ of that input. According to the rule for rational decisions, in perfect competition, a firm chooses a quantity of each nondurable input so that the value of each input's _____ _____ is equal to the _____ of the input.

6. In perfect competition, the value of marginal product of an input is determined by multiplying the _____ _____ of the input by the price of the _____ _____. Thus, anything that increases the marginal product of the _____ or the price of the _____ _____, increases the _____ for the input. An increase in technology by raising the _____ _____ of the input, will increase the _____ for the input. An increase in demand for the final good, by increasing the _____ of the final good, will increase the _____ for the input.

7. Capital is a _____ input that can be used _____ or _____ for future use. A firm maximizes the _____ _____ _____ by buying any _____ input that has a _____ net present value.

8. A(n) _____ _____ is the price of a resource minus its _____ _____.

9. Input markets affect _____ markets and vice versa. A decrease in the supply of an input _____ the prices of final goods that use the input in their _____. An increase in the demand for a final good _____ the prices of inputs that the firms use to produce it.

10. Input prices _____ resources by ensuring that inputs go to their most _____ _____ _____. and by providing _____ for firms to create more inputs when the benefits _____ the costs. Input prices also _____ income which raises issues of _____.

11. Inputs can be coordinated by the _____ or by _____ within firms. People establish firms to _____ inputs when doing so reduces _____.

Priority List of Concepts

Demand for inputs: related to productivity.

Productivity: measured by average product and marginal product.

Average product of an input = Output divided by the quantity of that input employed in production. Marginal product of an input = Change in the firms total output when it adds one more unit of the input while keeping quantities of other inputs fixed.

Law of Diminishing Returns: If at least one input is fixed in size (i.e., capital), as you increase the use of another input (i.e., labor), eventually the marginal product of labor will fall. In Table 16.2 below, diminishing returns set in when marginal product falls with the hiring of 3 units of labor.

Table 16.2

Labor (L)	Output (Q)	Marginal Product $(MPP_l) = Q/L$	Average Product of Labor $(APP_l) = Q/L$
0	0	0	0.0
1	10	10	10.0
2	25	15	12.5
3	35	10	11.7
4	44	9	11.0
5	52	8	10.4
6	59	7	9.9
7	65	6	9.4
8	70	5	8.8
9	74	4	8.2
10	77	3	7.7

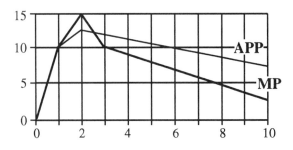

Graph 16.2 (a)

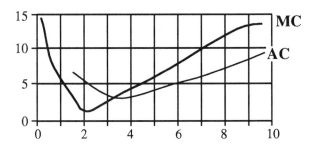

Graph 16.2 (b)

Relation Between Average Product of an Input and Marginal Product of an Input: marginal pulls average along.

If the $MPP_1 > APP_1$, then the APP_1 is rising.
If the $MPP_1 < APP_1$, then the APP_1 is falling.
If the $MPP_1 = APP_1$, then the APP_1 is at a maximum.

Relation between the Average Product Curves in Graph 16.2(a) and the Average Cost Curves in Graph 16.2(b): The cost curves begin sloping upward in Graph 16.2(b) when diminishing returns sets in with the hiring of the third unit of labor, in Graph 16.2(a) (i.e., the MPP_1 starts to fall in Graph 16.2 (a)).
Marginal Cost = Price of labor/ MPP_1.
Average Cost = Price of labor/ APP_1.

Relation between Average Cost and Marginal Cost: marginal pulls average along. If the MC > AC, then the AC is rising.

If the MC < AC, then the AC is falling.
If the MC = AC, then the AC is at a minimum.

Demand for Nondurable Inputs (i.e., labor)

Value of Marginal Product: the demand for labor in an industry with perfect competition, equals the MPP_1 multiplied by the price of the firm's final product. (Pq). The demand curve for an input slopes downward due to the law of diminishing returns. The height of the demand curve shows the VMP of the input. See Graph 16.3.

Profit Maximization in the Input Market: hire inputs where the marginal cost of the input is equal to its marginal benefit. (MC = MB). For a nondurable input, hire where the price of labor is equal to its VMP. See Graph 16.3.

Price Taker in an Input Market: faces a perfectly elastic (horizontal) supply curve, can buy the input at the going price, hires labor where the marginal cost of labor is equal to its price. Graph 16.3.

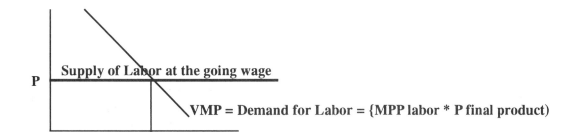

Changes in Input Demand: an increase in input demand can be caused by an increase in the demand for the final good, an increase in technology, an increase in the price of a substitute input, a decrease in the price of a complementary input or the passage of period of time.

Chronology of a Increase in the Demand for an Input: Graph 16.4.
1.   Demand for the final good increases. (D1 to D2).
2.   The price of the final good increases. (Pq1 to Pq2).
3.   The value of the marginal product increases, increasing the demand for labor. (VMP1 to VMP2).
4.   More labor is hired, (L1 to L2).

Graph 16.4 Final Good   **Input**

Demand for Durable Inputs (Capital): Choose the quantity of each input so that its marginal benefit equals its marginal cost.

Optimal Investment Decisions for Durable Goods:
    Buy any durable input with a positive net present value. The net present value of a durable input is the discounted present value of the future value of its marginal product minus the discounted present value of its cost.
    Lease durable inputs at the quantity where the VMP = Price of the lease.

Equilibrium across Input and Output Markets: input and output markets affect each other. Prices of an input and a final product are jointly determined by supply and demand in each market. Both markets respond to changes in the supply of inputs, technology and the demand for final products.

Inputs Go to Their Most Highly Valued Uses: The highest price that a firm is willing to pay for an input is the value of the input's marginal product to the firm. For example, if a developer values land for a subdivision of houses more than the farmer values the land for farming, the land will be used for houses, not farming.

Economic Rent: the difference between the price of a resource minus its opportunity cost. When a resource has a perfectly inelastic supply, its opportunity cost is zero, and the producer surplus is a pure economic rent.

Prices of Inputs:
    Allocate Resources: inputs go to their most highly valued uses.
    Distribute Income: inputs receive a price for their services.
        Workers receive wages and owners of capital and land receive an income from selling the services of these inputs.
    Owners of inputs must receive the income from those inputs to assure that they will be allocated to their most highly valued uses, except in the case of economic rents.
    Exception: a tax that reduced the economic rent of an input, would not affect the allocation of the input to its most valued use.
    Inputs go to their most valued uses even when their owners do not receive the economic rents.

Economic Efficiency and the Distribution of Income by Input Prices: for the economy to use inputs efficiently, input prices must affect the distribution of income.

Is it fair that the firm makes a profit after it has paid labor the value of its marginal product?

Has the worker been exploited so that the firm can make a profit?

Each worker receives all the extra money that the firm earns by employing him (VMP). Workers and firms share the gains from trade.

A machine used in production is valuable because the worker would have produced less without it. The owner should receive the opportunity cost of the machine to give them the incentive to provide the machine to the firm. The owner of the machine may in addition, receive an economic rent for the use of the machine. This economic rent won't last in the long run unless the machine can't be replicated. Otherwise, new firms will enter and the economic rent will decrease to zero in the long run.

Firms Coordinate the Use of Inputs:

through markets by hiring independent contractors; and through its use of inputs by a command system within the firm. Inputs are employees.

People form firms to reduce transactions costs. It is sometimes less costly to organize inputs within a firm than through markets.

If markets coordinated all inputs, no firms would operate.

Short Answer Questions

1. Discuss the similarities between the optimal investment decision rule for durable inputs and the profit maximizing rule for hiring nondurable inputs.

2. Why does the issue of fairness arise when the prices of inputs are responsible for distributing income in an economy?

Basic Problems

1. In Table 16.3 below, information on a perfectly competitive firm in a perfectly competitive input market is given. The price of the final product is $10 and the price of labor (wage) is $20 per hour.
   a. Compute marginal product and average product in Table 16.3 and graph average product and marginal product in Graph 16.5(a) provided.
   b. Compute the value of marginal product and graph this in Graph 16.5(b) provided.
   c. At what level of labor use does the Law of Diminishing Returns begin?
   d. Using the information given in this problem and the information you have calculated, determine the profit maximizing amount of labor that this firm should hire.

Table 16.3

Labor (hours)	Total Output	Marginal Product	Average Product	Price of Final Good	Value of Marginal Product
1	5				
2	15				
3	27				
4	36				
5	44				
6	51				
7	57				
8	62				
9	66				
10	69				
11	71				
12	71				

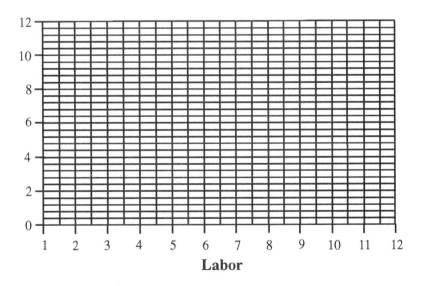

Graph 16.5(a)   Graph Average Product and Marginal Product.

Value of Marginal Product

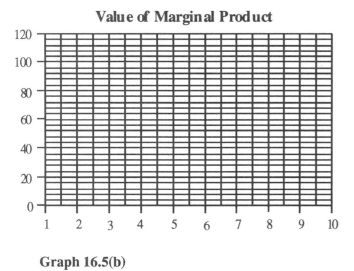

Graph 16.5(b)

2. How would your answers to Question 1 (d) change if the price of labor rose to $50?

3. How would your answers to Question 1 (d) change if the price of final output fell to $5.

Advanced Problems

1. Trace through verbally the sequence of changes that would take place in both input and output markets if the demand for a final good fell drastically.

2. Given Graph 16.6 showing long run production possibilities, what is the least cost method of producing 100 units of output in the long run if the price of capital is $10 per unit and the price of labor is $10 per unit. Why does the firm produce at only one point along the isoquant Q = 100?

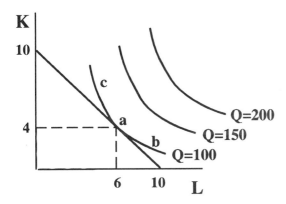

Graph 16.6

Chapter 17

Labor Markets

Learning Goals

1. Illustrate graphically and explain the conditions which would cause a government mandated minimum wage to increase unemployment.

2. Explain the conditions under which a firm will invest in improvements to the worker's human capital and pay for the worker's training.

3. Explain the theory behind a backward bending labor supply curve.

4. Distinguish between real and nominal wages.

5. Explain the conditions which cause some jobs to pay higher wages than others.

6. Describe the reasons why a firm would pay an efficiency wage.

7. Analyze some of the reasons for unemployment.

Key Term Matching Quiz

Terms

_____   1.   Labor Force

_____   2.   Backward Bending Labor Supply Curve

_____   3.   Real Wage

_____   4.   Compensating Differential

_____   5.   Human Capital

_____   6.   Labor Turnover

_____   7.   Unemployed Person

_____   8.   Underemployed Person

_____   9.   Labor Union

_____   10.   Implicit Labor Contract

_____   11.   Efficiency Wage

_____   12.   Job Tournament

_____   13.   Industrial Union

_____   14.   Craft Union

_____   15.   Closed Shop

_____   16.   Open Shop

_____   17.   Right to Work Law

_____   18.   Piece Rate

_____   19.   Signaling

_____   20.   Specific Human Capital

Definitions

a.   Covers workers in same occupation.

b.   Human capital useful in one industry.

c.   Does not have a job that makes use of his training, but wants one.

d.   Can work without being in union.

e.   Continuing flows of people into and out of the labor force.

f.   Wage paid above equilibrium to encourage productivity.

g.   State law that requires open shops.

h.   Skills, knowledge and abilities of people.

i.   Covers workers in the same industry.

j.   A labor supply curve that has a negatively sloped section.

k.   Informal agreement.

l.   Gives worker the incentive to work quickly, quality may not be important.

m.   Does not have a job, but wants one.

n.   Requires workers to be union member.

o.   Offsets differences in nonpay features.

p.   The chance of winning a good job motivates workers to perform well at their current jobs.

q.   Education tells the employer about the employees ability and motivation.

r.   Organizations of workers to improve working conditions and pay.

s.   Works in the market or is looking for work.

t.   Wage rate adjusted for inflation.

True/False Questions

_____ 1. Economists estimate that the average value of work in the home (caring for a family) is $30,000 per year.

_____ 2. A person who works in the home for no explicit pay is considered working in the market.

_____ 3. The income effect of a permanent increase in wages is less than the income effect of a temporary increase.

_____ 4. Nominal wages rather than real wages guide the decisions of workers.

_____ 5. The average wage of women has fallen since 1973 while the average wage of men has risen.

_____ 6. A worker's wages usually rise with age.

_____ 7. Older workers have higher marginal benefits from investing in human capital than younger workers.

_____ 8. Piece rate pay is more common in industries in which it is easy to judge quantity.

_____ 9. If a firm finds a way to get more information about people before they hired them, labor turnover will increase.

_____ 10. As a person remains unemployed longer, the likelihood that he will find a job declines as does the wage at an eventual job.

Multiple Choice Questions

1. A person works in the market if:
   a. someone pays the person to work.
   b. a person works in the home caring for their own children.
   c. a person is self employed working out of their own home.
   d. Answers a and c.

2. A person is more likely to participate in the labor force if:
   a. the benefit is high, the family has no other source of income.
   b. the opportunity cost is high.
   c. the value of time in the home is high because the person has small children.
   d. All of the above.

3. Labor supply decreases when:
   a. the work environment improves.
   b. stress or risk of injury fall.
   c. the nonpay features of a job become less attractive.
   d. family income from other sources falls.

4. The market supply of labor depends on:
   a. wages that could be earned in other occupations.
   b. the number of people with the required skills.
   c. their preferences for different kinds of work.
   d. All of the above.

5. The long-run elasticity of demand for labor for the entire U.S. economy is between -0.15 and -0.50; therefore, a 5 percent wage increase would reduce the quantity of labor demanded by between:
   a. 1.5 and 5 percent.
   b. 0.75 and 2.5 percent.
   c. 3 and 10 percent.
   d. None of the above.

6. A firm hires more employees and each employee works less hours if:
   a. hiring and training costs are high.
   b. more employees working fewer hours make the firm more productive.
   c. laws and regulations make it expensive to have many employees.
   d. employees want to work long hours.

7. When a firm provides a worker with the opportunity to acquire specific human capital:
   a. the firm will be likely to promote from within.
   b. the firm will charge the worker for this training by lowering his salary while he is being trained.
   c. the knowledge and skills gained by the worker will be useful regardless of where they work in the future.
   d. that firm is less likely to pay an efficiency wage to keep them from quitting.

8. Piece rate pay for workers:
   a. is common in industries in which quality is unimportant.
   b. may also provide an incentive to sacrifice quality for larger quantities.
   c. provides the incentive to work quickly for your income.
   d. All of the above.

9. Profit sharing plans for workers:
    a. reduce the risk of being laid off.
    b. cause their pay to fall when profits are low and business is slow.
    c. makes the worker's pay predictable.
    d. Both answers a and b.

10. The U.S. Bureau of Labor Statistics Current Population Survey will count people as unemployed if they:
    a. are not working and have not looked for work in the last month.
    b. work part-time.
    c. are a discouraged worker who has stopped looking for jobs.
    d. None of the above.

11. The supply of labor will increase due to all of the following except:
    a. an increase in population.
    b. the retirement of the Baby Boom population.
    c. an increase in technology that raises the marginal product of labor.
    d. Answers b and c.

12. Workers can be called underpaid if:
    a. the firm has a surplus of people applying for the job.
    b. their wages exceed the equilibrium wages for a job.
    c. firms face a shortage of workers for a job.
    d. Both answers a and b.

13. Unions, acting as monopoly sellers of labor:
    a. are legal cartels of workers that restrict their numbers.
    b. can raise the wages of their members.
    c. cause a deadweight social loss by restricting the number of workers.
    d. All of the above.

14. A firm will decide to pay efficiency wages to their employees:
    a. if they have given their employees firm specific training and are trying to keep them from quitting.
    b. if they want to keep the wage below its equilibrium level.
    c. to pay for increased supervision costs to prevent workers from shirking.
    d. Both answers b and c.

Chapter Review (Fill in the Blank)

1. Labor markets differ from market for goods because people earn _____ of their incomes from selling _____. The other _____ of income comes from owning _____. In addition, labor markets differ from other markets because labor services are _____ _____ to the worker. _____ care where they _____.

2. People decide _____ to be in the labor force, what _____ to choose, which _____ _____ to take, whether to operate their _____ _____ and _____ _____ hours to work. Labor supply curves may slope _____ if the _____ effect of a wage increase outweighs the _____ effect. If labor supply curves bend backward, the _____ effect of a wage increase outweighs the _____ effect . The demand for labor reflects the _____ of its _____ _____.

3. Labor market equilibrium consists of an equilibrium _____ _____ and an equilibrium number of _____ _____ for each type of labor. The _____ wage is measured in _____ power, that is the _____ (money wage adjusted for _____).

4. Wages differ across occupations partly because _____ aspects of occupations or jobs differ. _____ _____ are differences in wages that offset these differences in nonpay features of jobs. Wages also differ because some occupations require _____ levels of _____ capital. People invest in human capital through _____ _____ training and experience. The two main costs of investing in human capital through education are _____ expenditures for school and the _____ _____ of time in school. Wages usually rise with _____ and _____.

5. Workers are willing to accept _____ wages in jobs that provide them with _____ human capital. But, a firm must pay most of the costs of _____ that gives workers _____ capital that has little value outside of the _____.

6. Firms pay workers based on the _____ they work (time rate), the quantity they produce (_____ rate), or the firms _____ (_____ sharing). Each type of pay creates different _____. Firms also have _____ costs of employment such as _____, _____ _____, and _____ based on employment.

7. _____ _____ occur when the person who gets a job receives a much higher wage than rivals. Firms use _____ to _____ workers. _____ may help to explain high _____ _____.

8. Labor turnover occurs constantly as people _____ or _____ the labor force. The median length of time that a U.S. worker spends in one job is _____ years. The amount of _____ _____ in equilibrium depends on labor _____, the amount of information that workers have about their _____ and the extent of underlying _____ in the economy. Constant _____ _____ is one reason for _____. Unemployment also occurs if wages are kept _____ equilibrium levels. A person is _____ if he _____ a job but does not have one. A person is _____ if he wants a job that makes use of his _____ and _____ but does not have one.

9. Unions can _____ the wages of their members by acting as _____ sellers or labor that _____ the number of workers in an industry. Members gain even more if their union bargains to reduce the _____ _____ _____ and divide it between the _____ and the _____.

10. Firms may pay wages above equilibrium (_____ _____) to _____ workers with _____ training, provide workers with _____ to work effectively and not to _____, or to raise worker _____.

Priority List of Concepts

Labor Supply Decisions

Whether to Work: A person works in the market if someone pays the person to work or if that person is self employed. A person is in the labor force if he works in the market or is looking for a job in the market.

What Occupation to Choose: depends on a person's job preferences and opportunities. Opportunities depend on abilities, training and experience.

Which Job Offer to Take: Cost/benefit decision.

How many hours to work each year.

Labor Supply Curves: show the quantity of labor supplied as a function of the wage received. Labor supply curves may slope upward as the substitution effect of a wage rise makes them want to work more or bend backward as the income effect of a wage rise makes them want to work less.

Substitution Effect of a Wage Increase: People work more as their wage rate rises because they sacrifice more for each hour not spent working. The cost of leisure time = the wage rate.

Income effect of a wage increase makes people want to work less because the wage rate increase raises the worker's income and leisure is a normal good, so the worker chooses more leisure and less work.

Changes in Labor Supply: Labor supply increases (curve shifts right) when the nonpay features of a job improve or when family income from other sources decreases.

Market Supply of Labor: Supply to a particular occupation or industry.

May slope upward because an increase in wages in that occupation may lead more people to choose that kind of work.

Labor Market Equilibrium: determines total labor hours. The number of employees hired to work those hours depends on the costs and benefits of more employees vs. more hours per employee.

Nominal Wage: wage rate measured in money.

Real wage: wage rate adjusted for inflation.

Compensating Differentials in Wages: offset the differences in the nonpay features of different jobs. If workers realize that a job is risky, they will not take that job without a wage differential, wage premium for the risk they take.

Types of Pay	Pro	Con
Piece Rates	Gives worker an incentive to work quickly and not to shirk.	Worker faces the risk that circumstances beyond his control can decrease his productivity and pay (i.e., bad weather or machinery breaks).
		Can only be used in industries where quality is unimportant or easy to judge, otherwise the firm has to enforce a minimum quality standard.
Time Rates	Predictable income.	Gives workers less incentive than piece rate pay to work hard.
	Common in industries in which you can judge quantity.	
Profit Sharing	Pay increases when the demand for the product increases.	Pay decreases when the demand for the product decreases.
	Gives workers the incentive to maximize profits.	Pay is variable and unpredictable
	Gives firm less incentive to lay off workers in bad times.	

Human Capital: can be created by education and experience.
  Wages differ across occupations because some occupations require higher levels of skill and training.

The value of human capital is the discounted present value of the wages that the person can receive with it.
The Present Value of a person's human capital = [Wage (Yr. 1)/ $(1 + i)$] plus [Wage (Yr. 2) / $(1 + i)^2$] plus Wage (Yr. n) / $(1 + i)^n$

General Human Capital: knowledge and skills that are useful at many jobs. Workers pay many of the costs of this training, many times by taking low salaries while they train, because this training will help them earn more in the future regardless of where they work.

Specific Human Capital: knowledge and skills useful only in one industry, one occupation or one firm. The firm must pay most of the costs of training and the firm will have a strong incentive to retain that worker and to promote from within the firm.

Job Tournaments: the person who gets a job earns a much higher wage for only slightly higher productivity. Chance of winning a job tournament motivates workers to perform well at their current jobs.

Labor Turnover: flows of people into and out of the labor force:
  Depends on labor mobility, the amount of information that workers have on other job opportunities, the information firms have about workers and the state of the economy.

The Bureau of Labor Statistics considers a person to be:

Unemployed if he does not have a job, but is looking for one.

Employed if he has a job no matter whether that job is part-time or does not make use of his training or skills.

Unemployment: occurs if the wage is above the equilibrium wage and time or market imperfections prevent the wage from adjusting quickly down to equilibrium level.

Increase in labor supply can occur due to an increase in population, or changes in tastes for the final product.

Increase in labor demand can occur due to an increase in technology.

Overpaid workers: wages exceed the equilibrium wage and there is an excess supply of labor.

Underpaid Workers: shortage of workers.

Labor unions: organization of workers designed to improve the working conditions and pay of their members. Monopoly sellers of labor. Restrict employment and raise the wage to maximize profits.

Efficiency wages: wages paid above the equilibrium level to:
1. retain workers that have been given firm specific training,
2. give employees incentives not to shirk to help keep their jobs and to reduce supervision costs,
3. to increase productivity.

However, efficiency wages, being above equilibrium, can cause unemployment.

Short Answer Questions

1. Describe the factors that have caused labor turnover in our economy to increase in the last few decades.

2. The measure of the unemployment rate is imperfect at best. Describe some of the imperfections and the effect that these imperfections have on the magnitude of the unemployment rate.

3. Why does unemployment occur?

Basic Problem

1. What is the value of a 25 year old man's human capital if he expects to earn $25,000 + $1000 per year worked over the next 10 years and the interest rate is 10%?

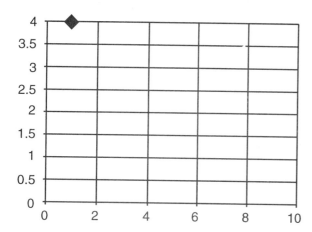

Chapter 18

Rich and Poor: Income Distribution, Poverty and Discrimination

Learning Goals

1. Develop a factual knowledge about the distribution of income in the U.S. and a conceptual knowledge of the terms and statistical measures used to describe and analyze income distribution.

2. Illustrate graphically the distribution of income within a country.

3. Interpret the distribution of income using the Gini coefficient.

4. Explain the government's definition of poverty and who falls below that line.

5. Explain the economic consequences of discrimination.

6. Describe the pros and cons of various theoretical arguments that if implemented, would claim to be able to improve income distribution.

Key Term Matching Quiz

Terms		Definitions

Terms

_____   1. Income

_____   2. Wealth

_____   3. Median Income

_____   4. Mean Income

_____   5. Money Income

_____   6. Family

_____   7. Household

_____   8. Lorenz Curve

_____   9. Gini coefficient

_____   10. Affirmative Action

_____   11. Egalitarianism

_____   12. Utilitarianism

_____   13. Negative Income Tax

_____   14. Human Wealth

_____   15. Non-human Wealth

_____   16. Veil of Ignorance

_____   17. Natural Right Argument

Definitions

a. Justice is maximizing the total amount of happiness.

b. Society would guarantee a set of fundamental rights.

c. Before-tax income including transfer payments, excluding noncash transfers and noncash benefits paid by employers.

d. Hire and promote people from under-represented groups.

e. Accumulated savings.

f. Income level at which half of the people have more income and half have less.

g. A graph of an income distribution.

h. People with very low incomes would receive money from the government.

i. Value of money and goods one receives during some time period.

j. People living with others to whom they are related or married.

k.. Fairness requires equal results.

l. People meet before they are born, in "the original position."

m. Total value of a person's accumulated savings plus the discounted PV of that person's expected future labor income.

n. Equal to zero, incomes are equal.

o. Discounted PV of expected future labor income.

p. Total Income divided by the number of people.

q. Families and individuals living alone.

True/False Questions

_____ 1. The government definition of money income overstates poverty because it does not include nonmoney income such as food stamps.

_____ 2. The distribution of money income (pretax income excluding noncash transfers) has shown less increase in inequality in recent decades than has the distribution of after-tax income, including non-cash transfers.

_____ 3. Poverty in the U.S. falls more heavily on females and children.

_____ 4. The Gini coefficient for U.S. family income is 0.4 and for individuals living alone is 0.45. Thus, families have less equality in income distribution than individuals living alone.

_____ 5. Income is distributed more equally than wealth.

_____ 6. Countries that redistribute more income from rich to poor, tend to have more equal distributions of income.

_____ 7. Economic growth tends to increase both poverty and inequality.

_____ 8. Studies of discrimination often overstate its effect on wages because they do not include the extent that lower education and experience levels from past discrimination.

_____ 9. The distribution of income that results from a perfectly competitive market system is equitable.

_____ 10. A lessening in discrimination against hiring women would raise women's wages and lower men's wages.

Multiple Choice Questions

1. Median income is:
    a. total income divided by the number of people.
    b. equal to the mean income when the income distribution is skewed.
    c. the income level at which half of the people have more income and half have less.
    d. Both answers b and c.

Refer to Graphs 18.1, (a) to (d) for questions 2 to 4.

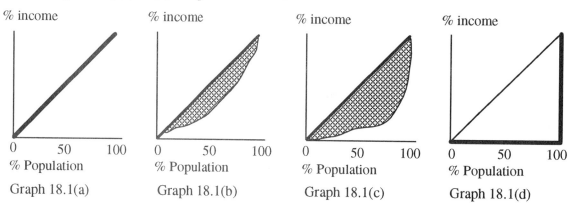

Graph 18.1(a)   Graph 18.1(b)   Graph 18.1(c)   Graph 18.1(d)

2. If everyone in the population had the same income, the Lorenz curve would be represented by Graph 18.1:
    a. (a).
    b. (b).
    c. (c).
    d. (d).

3. If all the money and wealth in the economy went to one person and everyone else received nothing the Lorenz curve would be represented by Graph 18.1:
    a. (a).
    b. (b).
    c. (c).
    d. (d).

4. The income distribution represented by Graph 18.1(c)
    a. shows greater inequality than Graph 18.1(d).
    b. shows greater inequality than Graph 18.1(b).
    c. shows less inequality than Graph 18.1 (b).
    d. shows less inequality than Graph 18.1(a).

5. The Gini coefficient for Graph 18.1(d) would be:
    a. less than the Gini coefficient for Graph 18.1(a).
    b. equal to zero.
    c. greater than zero but less than one.
    d. equal to one.

6. Over the last two decades, average wages have:
    a. fallen due to a shift of workers to service industries.
    b. fallen due to technology advances that have reduced the demand for low-skilled workers.
    c. risen due to increased international trade.
    d. Answers a and b.

7. Relative poverty is a measure of:
    a. the ratio of a person's income to average per capita income in a country.
    b. the ratio of the income received by the highest fifth of the population to the income received by the lowest fifth.
    c. the ratio of the income received by the lowest fifth of the population to the income received by the highest fifth.
    d. the ratio of one country's income per capital to income per capital in the U.S.

8. Studies of relative poverty have shown that:
    a. income tends to be less equal within richer countries.
    b. when countries become richer, absolute poverty increases.
    c. income tends to be more equal within richer countries.
    d. Answers a and b.

9. Inequality in the U.S. has risen in recent decades due to all of the following except:
    a. changes in technology.
    b. increased economic mobility of the labor force.
    c. discrimination.
    d. increase in international trade.

10. Egalitarianism is described by all of the following except:
    a. justice consists of maximizing the total amount of happiness.
    b. some people get more income than others to compensate them for other differences.
    c. "From each according to his abilities, to each according to his needs."
    d. Fairness requires equal results.

Chapter Review (Fill in the Blanks)

1. Median household income in the United States has _____ since the middle of the 20th century.

2. Poverty in the United States falls more heavily on _____ and _____. Families tend to have _____ incomes than individuals living alone. The official _____ _____ for a family of four is intended to equal three times estimated basic minimum _____ costs, based on a survey of food consumption. Based on after tax income, _____ of the population lived _____ the poverty line in 1993. _____ of all children under the age of six lived in households with incomes _____ the federal poverty line.

3. Wealth is distributed _____ equally than income. In the United States, the richest 2 percent of the population own about _____ of all household assets (_____ wealth). The richest 25 percent own about _____ of all household assets. The Gini coefficient for the distribution of wealth in the United States is about _____.

4. The difference between the average wealth of blacks and whites in the United States is much _____ than the difference between their _____. Measuring nonhuman wealth by financial assets minus _____, plus the value of real estate and motor vehicles, the median nonhuman wealth of white households is about _____, but for black and Hispanic households, it is only about _____. Married couples have _____ _____ nonhuman wealth than individuals living alone.

5. The United Nations estimates the _____ below which a person cannot afford a _____ _____ _____ and nonfood requirements to be _____ per year in 1995 U.S. dollars. Using this definition, 1 billion people, _____ of the world's population, live in _____.

6. Overall, world poverty is _____. World food production per person has _____. Consumption of food, however, has risen more _____ in poorer countries than in advanced countries.

7. Governments of many _____ countries pursue _____ programs. Many people believe that the recipients of welfare programs receive welfare only _____ when bad luck strikes their life. Critics of the welfare system argue that it discourages people from seeking _____ _____ and fosters a culture of welfare _____, sometimes creating perverse _____ to _____ break-up families or _____ employment.

8. The U.S. antipoverty programs: AFDC, SSI, Food Stamps and Medicaid are _____ _____ programs; only people with _____ incomes can collect benefits. The largest transfer program in the United States is the _____ _____ _____. U.S. government spending on Social Security in 1994 was about _____ billion. Social Security and Medicare are _____ means-tested, that is, people receive benefits _____ of their incomes or wealth. Some have proposed _____ the welfare system with a _____ _____ _____. Most studies indicate that the current welfare system allows people to keep _____ of any income they earn because they _____ welfare payments. A negative income tax might _____ the incentive to work.

9. Women and minorities earn less than white men because they face _____ in labor markets, they have less _____ _____ on average, and they take _____ jobs on average.

10. The _____ _____ Act of 1963 and the Act of 1964 outlawed many forms of _____. In 1965, the U.S. federal government began requiring firms with large government contracts to take _____ _____ to employ more _____ and _____ or to risk losing their government contracts.

Priority List of Concepts

Income: value of money and goods that a person receives during some time period.

Wealth: the total value of a person's accumulated savings plus the discounted present value of that person's expected future labor income.

Median income: the income level at which half of the people have more income and half have less.

Mean income: total income divided by the number of people.

Money income: as reported in government statistics refers to income before taxes including transfer payments, excludes noncash transfers from the government, noncash benefits paid by employers.

This measure overstates poverty because it does not include nonmoney income: such as food stamps.

Income Distribution: often described by the percentage of income received by the top fifth of the population (the 20% of the population with the highest incomes) or the bottom fifth of the population (the 20% of households with the lowest incomes).

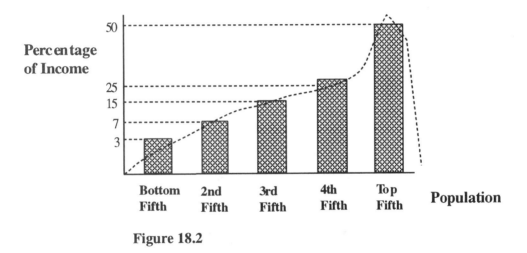

Figure 18.2

Figure 18.2, above, illustrates a distribution of income skewed toward the wealthy. Twenty percent of the population controls 50% of the income. The poorest twenty percent of the population controls or earns only 3% of the income generated in the country.

In a distribution of income with greater equality, the filled boxes would be more equal in size and each box would approach 20% of income representing the fact that each segment of the population was able to earn their fair share of income.

Lorenz Curve: a graphical representation of the income distribution in an economy. It shows the percentage of the economy's total income that is received by people below a given level in the income distribution.

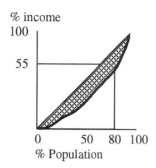

% income

Graph 18.3

The heavy black curve in Graph 18.3 is a Lorenz Curve which measures the inequality in the distribution of income.

A straight, 45 degree line would indicate equality of income.

The more curvature in the Lorenz curve, the more inequality in income distribution.

If the Lorenz curve forms a right angle, backwards L, the income in that economy is extremely unequally distributed, one person   controls all the income.

Gini Coefficient: a numerical measure of the inequality of an income distribution. It is equal to twice the area of the shaded region in the Lorenz curve graph. Income is equally distributed if the Gini coefficient equals 0, and extremely unequally distributed if the Gini coefficient equals 1.

If everyone had the same income, that is, income is equally distributed, the size of the shaded area would be zero and the Gini coefficient would be zero.

If income went to just one person, and the rest of the population received no income, the size of the shaded area would equal 1.

Graph 18.3 indicates that 80% of the people earned 55% of the income. Thus the top 20 % of the people receive 45% of the income.

Distribution of Income: What is Just? Questions of fairness or justice arise when people make judgments about the distribution of income or the effects of government programs on the distribution of income.

Egalitarianism: Fairness requires equal results.

Pro
Achieves a more equal distribution of income.

Con
Reduces incentives to work

Utilitarianism: Justice consists of maximizing the total amount of human happiness.

Pro
Redistribute income from rich to the poor because the poor value money more than the rich (i.e., have a higher marginal utility of money).

Con
Requires impossible interpersonal comparisons of utility (i.e., no one can compare one person's happiness with that of another).

Treats the distribution of happiness as unimportant.

Ignores people's fundamental rights (i.e., could force an old person to donate her kidney to a young person because the gain in happiness to the young person exceeds the loss in happiness to the old donor!).

Has "morally monstrous" implications.

Justice: an implicit contract, before you play a game or participate in the economy, you agree on rules. If people could meet before they were born, "in the original position," "behind the veil of ignorance," they would choose the legal rules and government policies that would affect their lives. These rules would be fair and give meaning to the concept of justice. One view of justice says: only rules can be fair, not outcomes.

Pro	**Con**
Guarantee a set of human rights	What are these human rights? Whether a natural rights proponent views redistribution of income as just or unjust depends on what specific natural rights he believes in!

Government Antipoverty Programs: programs designed to reduce poverty. Policy analysts disagree about their effects and possible desirable changes in these policies. The disagreements over these programs arise due to peoples interpretations of the principles of justice and fairness and the evidence on the effectiveness of programs already in place.

Inequality and Wealth: is affected by education, experience, ability, effort, luck, inheritance, discrimination, risk taking, and past savings.

Discrimination: in the labor markets affect wages, creating an equilibrium price for discrimination. The price is measured by the lower profits earned by a firm which discriminates in hiring. For example, by discriminating, the firm increases the demand for white males, and decreases the demand for minority labor. The wage of minority labor falls, and the wage of white males rises. The discriminating employer employs high wage labor and decreases his profits because he is not producing at least cost.

Affirmative Action: requires employers to try to hire and promote people from under-represented groups.

Pro	**Con**
Positive externality: promotes diversity and increases tolerance.	Creates reverse discrimination against white males and weakens incentives because people in the favored group have less incentive to acquire skills if the affirmative action policy can guarantee a job, while people in the disfavored group have less incentive to acquire skills if they believe affirmative action reduces the value of those skills.

Short Answer Questions

1. Median household income rose only 1.8% between 1970 and 1993 whereas total U.S. output of goods and services increased from $18,127 per person in 1970 to $25,716 per person in 1993. How could household income grow by such a smaller percentage than goods and services per person?

2. "A person who discriminates pays a price, as a result, prejudiced people do not always discriminate." Discuss the economic reasoning behind this statement.

Basic Problem

1. In country A, the highest fifth of the population earns 80% of the income whereas the lowest fifth earns 5 % of the income. In country B, the highest fifth of the population earns 60% of the income whereas the lowest fifth earns 6% of the income. Compute the relative poverty level of each country. Which country has the greatest poverty according to this measure?

PART VII

Advanced Topics in Microeconomics

Chapter 19

Economics of Information

Learning Goals

1. Analyze the economic effects of imperfect information.

2. Explain the method for determining the expected value of a future event.

3. Explain the incidence of moral hazard and adverse selection in industries and companies dealing with imperfect information.

4. Describe ways in which the agent can be motivated to work in the interest of the principal.

5. Distinguish between a person who is risk averse and a person who is risk neutral.

Key Term Matching Quiz

Terms

_____ 1. Expected Value

_____ 2. Search Cost

_____ 3. Distribution of Prices

_____ 4. Diversification

_____ 5. Risk Averse

_____ 6. Risk Neutral

_____ 7. Principal

_____ 8. Agent

_____ 9. Moral Hazard

_____ 10. Optimal Contract

_____ 11. Monitoring

_____ 12. Adverse Selection

Definitions

a. Some sellers charge higher prices than others.

b. A situation in which a principal cannot observe the actions of an agent who lacks an incentive to act in the best interests of the principal.

c. An agent is the person hired to do something for the principal. An employee.

d. An average of numbers weighted by the probabilities that they will occur.

e. Indifference towards risk.

f. Obtaining information about a person's actions (by watching).

g. Spreading risks across many different unrelated investments.

h. An agreement that maximizes the principal's profit while providing an incentive for the agent to participate in the agreement.

i. Prefers a less risky income, holding fixed its expected value.

j. A person who hires someone else to do something.

k. Hidden information. Two people might trade with each other and one person has relevant information about some aspect of the product's quality that the other person lacks.

l. Time and money costs of obtaining information about prices and products.

True/False Questions

_____   1.   Firms face downward sloping demand curves when buyers have limited information about prices.

_____   2.   When most consumers are well informed, stores charge low prices.

_____   3.   When buyers have perfect information about quality, high quality and low quality products sell for the same price.

_____   4.   When buyers have limited information, all stores charge low prices equal to marginal cost as in perfect competition.

_____   5.   When most consumers are well-informed, the perfect competition model applies.

_____   6.   Evidence from financial markets shows that most people are risk neutral.

_____   7.   Moral Hazard occurs when people know what an agent is doing, but not why.

_____   8.   Adverse Selection occurs one person does not know what another person is doing, a principal cannot see whether an agent is acting in the principal's best interest.

_____   9.   Executive compensation should be related to changes in the value of the firm to prevent moral hazard.

_____   10.   Profits rise when CEO compensation is tied to firm performance.

Multiple Choice Questions

1. The optimal amount of search occurs when:
   a. total search costs are minimized.
   b. the buyer finds the product at its lowest cost.
   c. the expected marginal benefit of searching equals its expected cost.
   d. All of the above.

2. The toss of a coin has the probability of 50% heads and 50% tails. What is the expected value of a bet that will pay $100 for heads and $0 for tails?
   a. zero.
   b. $50.
   c. $100.
   d. $150.

3. When firms have limited information about price:
   a. if one firm raises its price above the equilibrium price, it loses all of its customers.
   b. if one firm raises its price above the equilibrium price, it may only lose some of its customers, because many buyers may not realize that it is cheaper elsewhere.
   c. a buyer pays no search costs to obtain information about prices.
   d. All of the above.

4. A risk averse person would:
   a. take risks if the expected profits are high enough to make risk taking worthwhile.
   b. be willing to pay to take chances.
   c. not buy insurance or diversify
   d. None of the above.

5. Firms have tried all these innovative ways of monitoring their agents except:
   a. cash registers.
   b. auditing by accountants.
   c. give spouse a prize for making sure their mate shows up at work.
   d. All of the above.

6. To reduce the possibility of moral hazard, insurance companies:
   a. place deductibles in their policies.
   b. sell incomplete insurance.
   c. provide no incentives for the policy holder to prevent a loss.
   d. Both answers a and b.

7. A product guarantee:
   a. reduces an owners incentive to take proper care of a product.
   b. increases an owners incentive to take proper care of a product.
   c. increases the possibility of moral hazard if the principal can tell whether a problem results from a defect or poor care by the owner.
   d. decreases the possibility of moral hazard when a principal cannot tell why a problem occurs.

8. Service contracts:
   a.   are subject to moral hazard.
   b.   are not subject to moral hazard.
   c.   encourage moral hazard when they pay only for parts, not labor.
   d.   Both answers a and c.

9. Bondholders and stockholders:
   a.   differ in their view of risky investments for the firm.
   b.   are both risk averse as regards the investments of the firm.
   c.   are the firm's creditors and owners, respectively.
   d.   Both answers a and c.

10. The price of insurance:
   a.   reflects the perfect information that the insurance company has on the population applying for insurance.
   b.   to a low-risk person is lower than it would be if insurance companies had more information.
   c.   to a low-risk person is higher than it would be if insurance companies had more information.
   d.   Both answers a and c.

Chapter Review (Fill in the Blanks)

1. Information is not always _____, and this accuracy can be difficult or _____ to verify. The existence of _____ information has _____ consequences.

2. People often _____ at numbers they don't know. Under certain circumstances, a _____ _____ is the _____ _____. A(n) _____ _____ is an average of numbers weighted by the chance that they will occur.

3. When consumers have _____ information about _____ and they incur costs of _____ for the lowest _____, sellers face _____ demand curves. The optimal amount of _____ occurs when the expected marginal _____ of search equals the marginal _____.

4. When some customers have better _____ than others, a _____ of prices can exist in equilibrium. Some sellers charge _____ prices than others and better informed consumers buy from _____- price sellers. A firm can _____ between well-informed and poorly informed buyers by operating several stores that charge _____ prices or by selling essentially the _____ product under _____ brand names at _____ prices. _____ informed consumers are more likely to buy at the _____ price stores or to buy the _____ priced brands. As consumers get _____ information, the distribution of prices _____ and the average prices they pay _____. Firms with limited information about demand can learn about the demand curves they face by _____ and _____.

5. _____ (spreading risks across many different unrelated investments) can reduce _____.

6. The problem of _____ _____ arises when a principal has _____ information about the actions of a(n) _____. That agent may not have an incentive to act in the _____ interests of the principal. To give the agent a(n) _____ to take actions more consistent with the principal's _____, the principal wants to pay the agent for _____ results, even those due to good _____. As the agent's pay becomes more sensitive to outcomes that can be affected by luck, the agent's income becomes _____. Agents who are risk _____ dislike this risk, so the principal must pay a _____ expected income to attract agents.

7. An _____ contract between a principal and an agent _____ between the benefit to the agent of a _____ salary (low risk) and the incentive to act in the principal's interest that results from _____ pay for better outcomes. An optimal contract sets the marginal _____ of better incentives equal to their marginal _____. Principals can obtain some _____ about an agent's actions by _____ the agent, though obtaining _____ information is often too _____. _____ _____ problems arise in insurance, product guarantees, executive compensation, interest rates on personal loans and conflicts between bondholders and stockholders.

8. _____ _____ occurs when two people trade with each other and one has _____ _____ information about _____ _____ quality that the other person _____. A classic example involves _____ _____. Buyers do not _____ whether a person selling a car does so because it is faulty or for other reasons.

9. When buyers lack _____ about quality, high quality and low quality products sell for the _____ price. In addition, sellers offer mainly _____ quality products because they cannot charge _____ prices for higher quality products. Low quality products tend to drive _____ quality products out of the market under _____ _____.

10. Firms can _____ the problem of _____ _____ by offering _____. The problem of adverse selection is _____ severe when buyers and sellers deal _____ with each other or when people can _____ information about _____.

Priority List of Concepts

Economics of Information: economic consequences of imperfect information in a market.

Expected Values: People often guess at numbers they don't know. Under certain conditions, a rational guess is the expected value. Expected value equals the average of the sum of every possible number weighted by its probability (chance) of occurring.

For example, you plan to set up a lemonade stand on Monday. The lemonade stand will earn $10 on a sunny day, $4 on a cloudy day, and $0 on a rainy day. The chance of rain is 30%. The chance of a sunny day is 50% and a cloudy day is 20%. See Table 19.1

List your possible profits in column (1), list the chances of those profits occurring in column (2), multiply column (1) by column (2) and place these value in column (3). Sum the values in column (3) to get the expected value of the lemonade stand.

Table 19.1

(1) Lemonade Profit		(2) Probability	(3) (Profit multiplied by probability)
Sunny	$10	0.5	$5.00
Cloudy	$ 4	0.3	1.20
Rainy	$ 1	0.2	0.20
		Expected Value	$6.40

According to Table 19.1, the expected value of your lemonade profits is $6.40.

Limited Information About Prices: Firms face downward sloping demand curves. When a store raises its price, many buyers may not realize that the product is cheaper elsewhere, so the firm may lose only some of its customers.

A buyer may search for the best price. This search has costs, the time and money costs of obtaining information about prices and products.

The optimal amount of search occurs when the expected marginal benefit of searching equals its expected marginal cost.

A distribution of prices can exist between stores.

Better Information about Prices: reduces prices. The better information improves the rational guesses of consumers.

Examples of Search Theory:
Search requires time and money.
Firm, for example, has limited information about the prices that buyers are willing to pay. A firm may charge a high price at first, the reduce the price over time, and put the good on sale if it doesn't sell well.
    Firm benefits: charges more to buyers who are willing to pay more.
    Firm Costs: some consumers postpone purchase until the store reduces the price on its merchandise, and the firm sells goods more lowly so it has higher inventory costs.

Diversification: People can reduce the risk of their investments by diversifying, spreading risks across many different unrelated investments.

Beth has $100 to invest. She can invest in one or two stocks, each costing $50 a share. The profit possibilities depend on whether or not the Romer company corrects a flaw in its new technology. If it corrects, Romer profits and Solow loses. If Romer leaves the flaw uncorrected, Solow profits and Romer loses.

Table 19.2

Investment	Romer Corrects the Flaw	Flaw is Uncorrected	Expected Profit
Buy 2 shares of Romer at $50 each.	Stock value rises to $80 each.	Stock value falls to $30 each.	$(0.5) * (60) + (0.5) * (-40) = \$10$.
Buy 2 shares of Solow at $50 each.	Stock value falls to $30 each.	Stock value rises to $80 each.	$(0.5) *(-40) + (0.5)* (60) = \$10$.
Diversify. Buy 1 share of Romer and 1 share of Solow, each costing $50 each.	Romer value rises to $80 and Solow value falls to $30.	Solow value rises to $80 and Romer value falls to $30.	$(0.5) *(10) + (0.5) * (10) = \$10$.

In Table 19.2 the expected profit is the same for all three investment decisions, but the risk varies. Diversification reduces the risk. Beth is certain to make $10. The other two investment decisions, invest all in Romer or invest all in Solow, have the possibility of causing Beth to lose $40.

Risk Averse: A person who prefers a less risky income, holding fixed its expected value. In Table 19.2, a risk averse person would buy one share of each stock to be certain of the $10 profit and to avoid the risk of losing $40.

Risk Neutral: A person who is risk neutral does not are about risk. Would not care which investment decision was taken in Table 19.2

(Risk Lover): Likes risk. Would pay to take a gamble. Would not buy insurance or diversify investments.

Moral Hazard: an agent lacks the incentive to act in the best interests of the principal and the principal can't observe the actions of the agent.

Optimal Contracts: maximize the principal's profit while providing an incentive for the agent to participate in the agreement. Sets the marginal benefit of the additional sensitivity of the agent's pay to the results (what incentive does it provide for the agent to try harder?) equal to the marginal cost of the additional sensitivity (the additional effect of luck on the agent's pay).

Example: A principal hires an agent to sell a product. The amount the agent sells depends on both the agents luck and effort. The principal knows only the firm's profit. The chance of the profit is based on the agents actions.

Table 19.3.

Agent's Actions	Profit	No Profit
Try Hard	2/3 chance	1/3 chance
Try a Little	1/2 chance	1/2 chance
Shirk (Don't Try)	1/3 chance	2/3 chance

The profit to be made is $300,000 or zero. If the agent tries hard, Table 19.3 shows there is a 2/3 chance of earning $300,000 or a 1/3 chance of earning zero. The expected profit is $200,000. If the agent shirks, the expected profit is $100,000 and the chance of a $300,000 profit is only 1/3.

How do you get the agent to work hard? A high base salary would give the agent the incentive to shirk. However if the agent receives $45,000 if the firm earns $300,000 and receives nothing if the firm earns zero profits, the agent has an incentive to try hard, because effort can raise the expected salary. The agent may not like the risk of a zero salary and may not take the job. The firm has to raise the expected salary to compensate the worker for the risk of a zero salary.

Monitoring: Obtaining information about a person's actions (by watching). Perfect monitoring is too costly. Monitor until the expected marginal cost of monitoring equals the expected marginal benefit.

Adverse Selection: When two people trade with each other, one person has relevant information about the product's quality that the other person lacks.

Example: In the used car market, buyers can't tell if a car is being sold because it is faulty or because it is a good car. Good cars get underpriced by the market and faulty cars are overpriced. Good cars are under-represented in the used car market and faulty cars are over-represented. The term adverse selection refers to this result. As a result, buyers overpay for faulty cars and underpay for good used cars. Low quality cars offered for sale drive the higher quality cars out of the used car market.

Limits on Adverse Selection: Firms that sell high quality goods can employ guarantees to ensure the quality of their products. Repeat Buying and the ability to buy information, such as product reviews, also limit adverse selection. Sometimes, the firm can separate the two types of people, high risk and low risk and charge them different prices (i.e., in insurance, charge a low rate for basic insurance and a high rate for comprehensive insurance). The heavy users will want comprehensive whereas the low risk types will choose the basic coverage.

Basic Problems

1. What is the expected value of the following project? The payoffs are $100,000, $50,000 or zero with a 1/3 chance of each payoff happening.

2. Determine the optimal search for the following buyer. The buyer is shopping for a clock radio. Two stores in his area charge $50 for the ratio, one store charges $35 and the other store charges $60. The buyer is willing to pay up to $60 for the product and knows the prices which the stores charge but does not know which store has the lowest price, $35.

    The buyer has gone to one store and found that the price of the radio at that store is $50. Using the concept of determining an optimal search, should the buyer go to another store?

Advanced Problems

1. Using the probabilities given in Table 19.4 for agent's actions, analyze the following employment situation. Will this employment compensation scheme be likely to cause moral hazard, (shirking), or will it cause the agent to work in the principal's best interest? The agent is hired on the agreement that he will earn $25,000 if the firm makes no profit and $35,000 if the firm makes a profit of $300,000.

Table 19.4

Agent's Actions	Profit	No Profit
Try Hard	2/3 chance	1/3 chance
Try a Little	1/2 chance	1/2 chance
Shirk (Don't Try)	1/3 chance	2/3 chance

    a.   Determine the expected salaries of the three types of agents.
    b.   How much risk does the agent accept in taking this job.
    c.   Is there any incentive for the agent to work hard?
    d.   Is there any incentive for the agent to shirk?
    e.   What is the expected profit of the firm in each of the three cases?
    f.   Is this an optimal contract?

Chapter 20

Environmental Economics and Public Goods

Learning Goals

1. Explain the economic consequences of externalities.

2. Discuss the reasons for overuse of a common resource.

3. Distinguish between social costs and private costs.

4. Explain the economic consequences of property rights.

5. Describe the rationale behind the government's decision to provide a public good.

Key Term Matching Quiz

Terms		Definitions

Terms

_____ 1. Private Cost

_____ 2. Social Cost

_____ 3. Private Benefit

_____ 4. Social Benefit

_____ 5. Externality

_____ 6. Negative Externality

_____ 7. Positive Externality

_____ 8. Internalizing an Externality

_____ 9. Transactions Cost

_____ 10. Property Right

_____ 11. Private Ownership

_____ 12. Common Resource

_____ 13. Tragedy of the Commons

_____ 14. Nonrival Good

_____ 15. Nonexcludable Good

_____ 16. Public Good

Definitions

a. Quantity available for others does not fall when someone consumes it.

b. Changing private costs or benefits so that they equal social costs or benefits.

c. The cost to everyone in the society, including people who do not produce or consume it.

d. Something that belongs to no one or to society as a whole.

e. Occurs when the social cost of a good exceeds its private cost.

f. Nonrival and nonexcludable good.

g. Costs of trading.

h. Benefit to the people who buy and consume it.

i. Overuse of a common resource relative to its economically efficient use.

j. Occurs when the social benefit exceeds the private benefit.

k. The cost paid by the firm that produces and sells it.

l. One person has a property right to use or sell a resource.

m. Occurs when the private cost or benefit of a good differs from its social cost or benefit.

n. Prohibitively costly to provide the good only to those who pay for it.

o. The total benefit to everyone in the society.

p. Legal right to decide the use of a scarce resource or to sell the resource to someone else.

True/False Questions

_____ 1. It is economically efficient to totally eliminate pollution.

_____ 2. When people are made responsible for all the costs of their own actions, an externality is internalized.

_____ 3. Output of a good is economically efficient if the Marginal Social Benefit is greater than the Marginal Social Cost.

_____ 4. Economic efficiency requires that total pollution from all sources be reduced with the lowest cost method implying that it is economically efficient to reduce pollution caused by some activities without reducing pollution caused by other activities.

_____ 5. Reverse side payments from a polluter to people harmed by the pollution lead to economic efficiency if the required side payments equal the marginal cost of the pollution to the other people.

_____ 6. Consumption of a nonrival good by one person leaves less for others to consume,

_____ 7. When the marginal private benefit is less than the marginal social benefit, (MPC < MSB), a negative externality exists.

_____ 8. When the marginal social cost is greater than the marginal private cost, (MSC > MPC), a negative externality exists.

_____ 9. A negative externality causes production at equilibrium to be less that the economically efficient production level.

_____ 10. If transaction costs are low and property rights are assigned, the Coase theorem predicts that negotiations between the two parties will produce the economically efficient solution.

Multiple Choice Questions

1. The economically efficient level of pollution:
   a. is not zero.
   b. is zero.
   c. occurs where the marginal benefit of reducing it is equal to the marginal cost of reducing it.
   d. Answers a and c.

Refer to Graph 20.1 for questions 2 to 5.

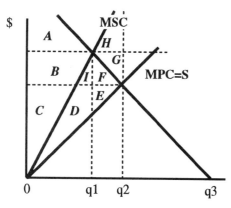

Graph 20.1

2. The economically efficient quantity is:
   a. q1.
   b. q2.
   c. q3.
   d. zero.

3. The deadweight loss of the negative externality is:
   a. area $H + G$.
   b. area $F + I$.
   c. area $F + E$.
   d. the $H + G + F + E$.

4. The economically efficient quantity is:
   a. greater than equilibrium quantity.
   b. equal to equilibrium quantity.
   c. less than equilibrium quantity.
   d. represents zero pollution.

5. The marginal cost to others of q2 units of the good:
   a. is greater than zero and indicates that this is a negative externality.
   b. is represented by the vertical distance between the MPC and the MSC at q2.
   c. is equal to zero, there is no externality.
   d. Answers a and b.

6. Internalizing an externality:
    a. eliminates the deadweight loss.
    b. is economically efficient.
    c. can be done with side payments.
    d. All of the above.

7. A side payment:
    a. lowers the firm's marginal cost of production.
    b. decreases the opportunity costs of the firm.
    c. is a payment or bribe for a specified action.
    d. Answers a and c.

8. The direction of a side payment:
    a. is determined by law and property rights.
    b. refers to who pays whom.
    c. affects the allocation of resources.
    d. Answers a and b.

9. The Coase Theorem:
    a. removes the effects of law and property rights on the distribution of income.
    b. applies to situations with high transactions costs.
    c. requires low transactions costs for the economically efficient result to occur.
    d. None of the above.

10. Once produced, this product is available to all:
    a. private good.
    b. public good.
    c. nonrival good.
    d. All of the above.

11. Second hand smoke is a cost visited upon others by smokers and this creates:
    a. a positive externality.
    b. a negative externality.
    c. a property right.
    d. a side payment.

Chapter Review (Fill in the Blanks)

1. A negative externality occurs when the _____ _____ of an action _____ its _____ costs. A negative externality raises the equilibrium quantity above the _____ _____ quantity. The _____ _____ quantity of pollution is not equal to _____. The _____ _____ level of pollution occurs when the _____ marginal benefit of reducing it equals the _____ marginal cost of reducing it.

2. Negative externalities occur when people do not pay all of the costs of their own actions so that other people bear some of the _____. _____ an externality makes people _____ for all of the costs of their _____ actions so that _____ and _____ costs are equal. When a(n) _____ is internalized, the equilibrium is _____ _____.

3. If transactions costs are _____, _____ payments can _____ externalities and make an equilibrium _____ _____ regardless of whether the law gives firms the _____ to pollute. The law determines only who make _____ payments to whom.

4. If transactions costs are _____, _____ payments do not occur. In this case, laws and _____ rights affect the equilibrium _____ and the equilibrium may not be _____ _____. The government may be able to create a more _____ situation with _____ or _____ or by issuing _____ _____ to pollute.

5. A property right is a _____ right to decide the use of a _____ resource or to sell a _____ to someone else. Private ownership of a resource gives one person or a small group of people a _____ right to _____ or _____ that resource. A _____ resource is something that belongs to no one or to _____ as a whole.

6. Owners of private property have _____ to protect its _____. But common resources are _____ because no one has an _____ and _____ right to prevent their _____. Private ownership of a resource can eliminate this _____ of the _____ by giving the owner a(n) _____ to care for the _____ and _____ its _____. The main drawbacks to this solution are the _____ of establishing and enforcing _____ rights and the problems of _____ _____ that high transactions costs may create.

7. A positive externality occurs when the _____ benefits of an action exceed its _____ benefits. With a positive externality, the equilibrium quantity is _____ than the _____ _____ quantity. _____ occurs because people who buy and sell a good _____ its benefits to other people. _____ transactions costs allow side payments to _____ positive externalities. When transactions costs are _____, the government may be able to _____ equilibrium output to the _____ _____ level through _____ or _____.

8. The quantity of a nonrival good available for other people does not _____ when someone consumes it. It is prohibitively _____ to provide a _____ good only to people who _____ for it and _____ or _____ other people from obtaining it. A _____ good is a nonrival and a _____ good.

9. Public goods present problems because firms have little _____ to produce them. Most buyers are _____ to pay for _____ goods because they can get them free; they prefer to be _____ riders and let other people _____. When everyone tries to _____ ride, _____ _____ pays for the good and _____ firm produces it. The free rider problem _____ the equilibrium quantity of a public good _____ the _____ _____ quantity. The free-rider problem provides a fundamental rationale for government financing of _____ goods.

Priority List of Concepts

Externality: Occurs when the private cost or benefit of a good differs from its social cost or benefit. Pollution occurs when people do not bear all of the costs of their actions.

> **Private Cost:** Cost paid by the firm that produces and sells the product. (Delivery truck using leaded gasoline.)
>
> **Social Cost:** Total private cost plus the total cost to other people from producing various quantities of a good. (Lead pollutes the air of all society.)
>
> **Private Benefit:** Benefit to the people who buy and consume the product. (Planting a garden.)
>
> **Social Cost:** Total benefit to everyone in the society. (Garden affords beauty and clean air to society.)

Negative (Harmful) Externality: Social Cost exceeds Private Cost of a good (i.e., Pollution). (As a firm produces, its smokestack pollutes the air.)

Positive (Beneficial) Externality: Social Benefit exceeds Private Benefit (i.e., Bee Keeper next to an apple orchard). (Bees pollinate the trees.)

Equilibrium and Economic Efficiency

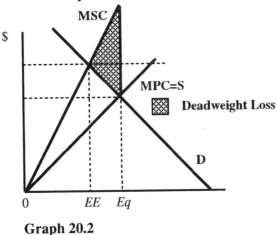

Graph 20.2

Equilibrium occurs at Eq where Demand and Supply intersect.

> This equilibrium is not economically efficient because at Eq, the MSC is greater than the MPC as seen by the vertical solid black line above quantity Eq between the MPC and the MSC.

A negative externality is shown by the fact that MSC is greater than the MPC. This vertical distance represents the Marginal Cost to others from producing or consuming one more unit.

> The negative externality causes the economy to find an inefficient equilibrium quantity at Eq that exceeds the economically efficient quantity, EE. The economically efficient quantity (EE) occurs where MSC = MSB.

The deadweight loss of the negative externality is represented by area of the shaded triangle in Graph 20.2.

Internalizing Externalities: making people responsible for all of the costs of their own actions.

Side Payments: a method of internalizing externalities when transaction costs are low. People who suffer harm from pollution can offer to pay the polluter to stop. This offer of a side payment creates an opportunity cost for the factory because it sacrifices the side payment if it keeps polluting.

A side payment of the right size would equalize the private costs with the social costs, internalizing the externality. The highest price that a person would be willing to pay to reduce pollution is the value of the harm that the pollution causes that person.

Economic efficiency can result from side payments in either direction. If pollution is legal, people can pay the polluter to reduce pollution to the economically efficient level. If pollution is illegal, firms can pay people to accept the pollution

Graph 20.3 shows that economic efficiency can result from Side Payments that raise the MPC sufficiently to equal the MSC.

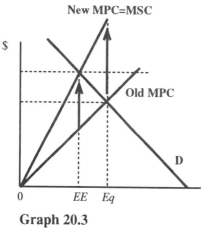

Graph 20.3

The law determines the direction of side payments, so it affects the distribution of income (who pays whom) but not the allocation of resources (actual production and modification or replacement of equipment).

Transactions Costs: Costs of trading.

High transactions costs impede the ability of side payments to internalize all externalities.

Coase Theorem: If transactions costs are sufficiently low, the equilibrium is economically efficient regardless of whether firms have the right to pollute, though the law affects who makes side payments to whom.

Taxes and Regulations: Government policies to internalize an externality in the presence of high transaction costs.

With high transactions costs, laws and property rights affect the equilibrium quantity, and the equilibrium may not be economically efficient.

Sellable Rights to Pollute	Taxes	Regulations
Sold by the government to the highest bidder.	Raise the private costs of a polluter. If the tax for each additional amount of pollution equals the marginal cost to other people of that pollution, then the tax equalizes the private and social costs and internalizes the externality.	Require the industry to produce at the economically efficient quantity.
Promotes the lowest cost method of reducing pollution to the specified level.	Provide better incentives than regulation. Generate revenue for the government.	Effective if the government can impose that quantity on firms in an efficient manner.

Property Rights: legal right to decide the use of a scarce resource. With high transactions costs, the assignment of property rights can determine whether the outcome is efficient.

Common Resource: something that belongs to no one or society as a whole. It is overused, because everyone has the right to use common resources.

'Tragedy of the Commons': Each person wants to use the resource free of charge, (free ride).
The resource use (Eq) is greater than the economically efficient amount. (EE) in Graph 20.5.
Eq minus EE gives the amount of overuse.
Overuse eventually causes depletion of the resource.
The negative externality is shown by the divergence between marginal private benefit and marginal social benefit.

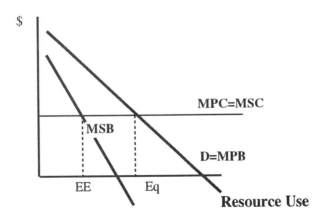

Graph 20.5

Private Ownership of a resource can internalize the externality and eliminate the 'Tragedy of the Commons' Private ownership would shift the MPB curve in Graph 20.5 down until it equaled the MSB, creating an economically efficient equilibrium at EE.

Drawbacks to the private property rights solution to externalities:
first, high costs of defining or enforcing property rights,
second, high costs of charging people to use the property,
and third, high costs of government regulation.

Solution to the use of a common resource may be no use (i.e., the of the Georges Bank fishing grounds in 1995).

Positive Externalities: creates underproduction at Eq rather than EE in Graph 20.5. With high transactions costs, when the marginal social benefit (MSB) exceeds the marginal private benefit (MPB), equilibrium quantity (Eq) will represent a point of underproduction compared to the economically efficient output (EE). Graph 20.5 below.
Underproduction occurs because people who buy and sell the good ignore its benefits to other people.

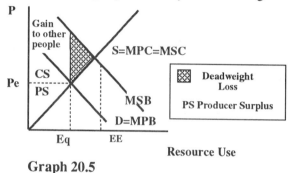

Graph 20.5

Solutions to promote economically efficient output in the face of positive externalities:
With high transactions costs, the government could subsidize production to raise equilibrium output to the economically efficient level, EE. (Government often subsidizes vaccinations)
With low transactions costs, side payments can be made to internalize the externality. (Apple growers pay beekeepers to operate their beehives near the apple trees.).

Positive Externalities: the case of Public Goods.

Public Goods: are nonrival and nonexcludable.
Nonrival: the use of the good by one person does not preclude its use by another person. The goods are not used up or depleted when people consume them (knowledge).
Nonexcludable: it is prohibitively costly to provide the good exclusively to people who pay for it.

Problems of Public Goods:
Firms have little incentive to produce them.
Few buyers willing to pay for public goods because they can get them free. This free rider problem holds the equilibrium quantity of a public good below the economically efficient quantity

Private Methods to Produce Public Goods: attempt partial excludability. (Software firms provide technical support only to registered users.)

Government Production of Public Goods: due to the free rider problem which discourages private production or production of the economically efficient quantity.

Government solves the free rider problem by coercion: taxes people to pay for the public good.

Underproduction occurs because people who buy and sell the good ignore its benefits to other people.

Government Production of Public Goods

Con	Pro
Lacks information about people's willingness to pay.	Enters production due to market failure (the private market fails to produce the economically efficient amount).
Can't calculate the economically efficient level of production.	Gets closer to the economically efficient level of the public good than private industry.
May tax people more than their willingness to pay.	Provides excludability through patents and copyrights.
May reflect the desires of special interest groups rather than considerations of economic efficiency.	

Short Answer Questions

1. What determines the direction of side payments?

2. How do sellable pollution rights promote the least costs method of pollution reduction?

3. Overfishing in the George's Bank area of the Atlantic Ocean off the New England coast became so damaging that the fishing area was closed in 1995. Could this Tragedy of the Commons have been prevented by the use of private property rights?

Basic Problems

1. A logging company and a resort hotel are located on a beautiful lake. The hotel has a beautiful view of the logging company's forest. The logging company is planning to clear cut the forest. The logging company has the property rights to the forest.
    a. According to the Coase theorem, can the hotel alter the use of resources and act to preserve its view of the trees?
    b. Given the result, what has happened to the distribution of income?
    c. If the hotel succeeds in preserving the view, will this be an economically efficient result?
    d. Would the result have been any different if the forest had been owned by the hotel?

Chapter 21

Government Regulations and Taxes

Learning Goals

1. Explain how a government can choose a combination of taxes to raise revenue with the lowest possible deadweight social loss from economic inefficiency.

2. Apply cost-benefit analysis to the effects of government regulations.

3. Describe the pricing options when regulating a natural monopoly.

Key Term Matching Quiz

Terms

_____   1. Government Regulation

_____   2. Deregulation

_____   3. Cost-Benefit Analysis

_____   4. Public Interest View of Regulation

_____   5. Special Interest View of Regulation

_____   6. Capture View of Regulation

_____   7. Concentrated Interest

_____   8. Diffuse Interest

_____   9. Nationalized Firm

_____   10. Privatization

_____   11. Optimal Taxation

_____   12. Average Tax Rate

_____   13. Marginal Tax Rate

Definitions

a. Minimizes the total deadweight social loss from taxes that raise a certain amount of revenue for the government.

b. Benefit to a small group of people or firms.

c. A previously nationalized firm becomes private property.

d. Limits or restricts the actions of people or firms.

e. Increase in taxes paid if income rises by $1.

f. Government regulations serve special-interest groups.

g. Removal of government regulations.

h. Politicians do what most voters want in order to be reelected.

i. Benefit that is spread across many people.

j. A firm that the government owns.

k. The process of finding and comparing the costs and benefits of a regulation, tax, or other policy.

l. Tax obligation divided by income.

m. Regulatory agencies, originally established to serve the public interest, end up serving the special interests of the industries they were intended to regulate.

True/False Questions

_____   1.   If the benefits of a regulation exceed its costs, then the regulation is a potential Pareto improvement.

_____   2.   A diffuse interest is a benefit to a small group of people or firms.

_____   3.   Rate of return regulation gives the firm an incentive to maximize profits.

_____   4.   Deregulation of the airline industry caused average fares to rise and decreased the cities served by more than one airline.

_____   5.   The Capture Theory of Regulation argues that the political power of concentrated interests exceeds that of equal-sized diffuse interests.

_____   6.   If government regulation can require that a natural monopoly charge the competitive price, the natural monopoly will cover its costs and make no economic profit.

_____   7.   Privatization occurs when government acquires a firm.

_____   8.   The main argument against private supply of a good is that government supply can ensure uniform quality standards.

_____   9.   The size of the deadweight loss from taxes increases as supply or demand becomes less elastic.

_____   10.   By placing high tax rates on goods with low elasticities of supply and demand and low tax rates on goods and services with high elasticities of supply and demand, the government is practicing optimal taxation.

Multiple Choice Questions

1. The view that regulatory agencies end up serving the special interests of the industries they were intended to regulate is:
   a. the public interest view of regulation.
   b. the special interest view of regulation.
   c. the capture view of regulation.
   d. a diffuse interest.

2. The view that politicians establish and operate regulations to serve the majority of voters is:
   a. the public interest view of regulation.
   b. the special interest view of regulation.
   c. the capture view of regulation.
   d. a diffuse interest.

3. Occupational licensure:
   a. prevents people from choosing lower quality goods or services at lower prices.
   b. restricts competition.
   c. raises prices to consumers.
   d. All of the above.

Use Graph 21.1 of a Natural Monopoly to answer questions 4 to 7.

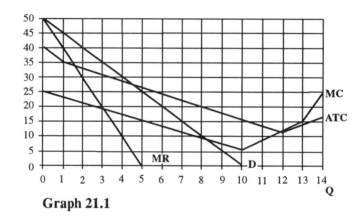

Graph 21.1

4. If the government requires that a natural monopoly charge the competitive price:
   a. the firm will break even.
   b. price will be set equal to marginal cost where the demand curve crosses marginal cost.
   c. the firm will make a profit.
   d. None of the above.

5. If the government requires that a natural monopoly engage in average cost pricing:
   a. the firm will break even and charge a price of $27.50.
   b. price will be set equal to marginal cost where the demand curve crosses marginal cost.
   c. the firm will break even and charge a price of $9.00.
   d. None of the above.

6. If the firm profit maximizes, monopoly price will be _____ and monopoly quantity will be _____ and the firm will make a _____:
   a. $26, 4.5, zero profit.
   b. $9, 8.1, loss of $10 per unit.
   c. $34, 3.1, profit of $3 per unit.
   d. $34, 3.1, loss of $3 per unit.

7. If the firm charges the competitive price, it will charge _____ and produce _____ quantity with a loss of _____ per unit:
   a. $26, 4.5, zero.
   b. $9, 8.1, loss of $10 per unit.
   c. $34, 3.1, loss zero per unit.
   d. $34, 3.1, loss of $3 per unit.

8. The government can minimize the economic inefficiency from taxes by:
   a. levying a head.
   b. only taxing goods with inelastic demands or supplies.
   c. only taxing goods with elastic demands or supplies.
   d. only taxing land.

9. The statement, "People in equal conditions should pay equal taxes," refers to:
   a. vertical equity.
   b. horizontal equity.
   c. the effects of a land tax.
   d. the effects of a head tax.

10. The statement, "People in unequal conditions should be treated differently," refers to:
    a. vertical equity.
    b. horizontal equity.
    c. the effects of a land tax.
    d. the effects of a head tax.

11. A flat tax:
    a. makes people with high incomes pay more than people with low incomes.
    b. requires the same percentage tax for all.
    c. makes people with higher incomes pay higher tax percentages on their incomes.
    d. Both a and b the price of inputs.

Chapter Review (Fill in the Blanks)

1. Government regulations _____ the actions of people and firms. Government regulations _____ the environment, _____ economic efficiency, _____ fairness, _____ people from their own bad decisions, _____ products, or _____ _____ for using common resources. Some regulations are intended mainly to _____ certain special-interest groups at the _____ of other people.

2. Economists use _____ analysis to compare the benefits and costs of regulations, taxes and other government policies. The _____ of a regulation results from an _____ in economic inefficiency (lost _____ and _____ surplus and costs to other people from _____ (such as pollution). Economists measure costs and benefits of _____ (such as safety) by the _____ of _____ that people are willing to _____ for that intangible in other situations. When a regulation or a tax has _____ costs or benefits, economists compare the _____ _____ _____ of the costs and benefits. When the costs are _____, economists compare the discounted present values of the _____ values of the costs and benefits. One criticism of cost-benefit analysis is that the _____ and _____ from a regulation or tax may _____, and cost-benefit analysis shows only whether it would be a _____ Pareto improvement, but not whether it would be a(n) _____ _____ improvement. A second criticism is that the _____ of discounted present values causes cost-benefit analysis to place _____ weight on the effects on future generations that some critics deem _____.

3. Critics of government regulations contend that the _____ effects of regulations frequently differ from their _____ effects. The three main economic views of regulation are the _____ view, the _____ view, and the _____ view. The _____ and _____ views are based on the argument that the political power of _____ interests exceeds that of equal-sized _____ interests, so regulations tend to benefit groups with _____ interests such as firms in the regulated industries. The possibility that government will help producers through regulation gives them a(n) _____ to spend resources to obtain _____ regulations: this _____ _____ is economically inefficient.

4. Nationalized firms (those _____ by the government) have different _____ than privately owned firms. Nationalized firms have _____ incentives to _____ _____, partly because nationalized firms face _____ potential takeovers. Many nationalized firms are _____ _____ that would have _____ _____ to maximize value if they faced _____ and did not receive government subsidies. One argument against allowing private firms to compete with nationalized firms, the _____ arguments, states that private firms would take away only _____ customers. The counter argument is that _____ occurs only when nationalized firms _____ some customers at the expense of others: competition would _____ this. Private firms could supply many products and services that _____ supply; an alternative method of supply is for the government to _____ for a good with _____ _____ and to hire the _____ private supplier to produce it.

5. _____, like regulation, have _____ _____: They _____ government programs, _____ income, and achieve _____ _____ _____. Because most taxes create _____ _____, different combinations of taxes that give the government the same amount of revenue can create _____ amounts of economic _____. _____ _____ sets tax rates that _____ the total deadweight social loss from taxes while raising a certain amount of _____ _____ for the government. Optimal tax rates are _____ on goods with more _____ supplies and demands and _____ on goods with more _____ supplies and demands. If the government can identify goods with _____ _____ _____ _____ _____, it is optimal to tax only those goods. Other considerations such as _____, may suggest that the government should _____ choose tax rates _____ to minimize economic inefficiency.

Priority List of Concepts

Evaluating Regulations: Cost-Benefit Analysis. Economist measure the costs and benefits of a regulation or tax by the changes in consumer surplus and producer surplus and the effect on people of externalities.

Intangible Costs and Benefits: Economists measure the intangible benefits of a lower chance of accidental death (i.e., by measuring the amounts of money that people are willing to pay for a lower chance of accidental death). How much will they pay for increased safety devices on their cars, etc.?

Uncertain Costs and Benefits: Economists measure the expected values of costs and benefits.

Future Costs and Benefits: Economists discount these to present value. Criticism of this method comes from those who feel this method gives too little weight to future costs and benefits.

Public Interest View of Regulation: Politicians do what most voters want in order to be reelected. They serve the majority of voters.

Special Interest View of Regulation: Special interest groups have enough political power to convince the government to create regulations for their benefit.

Capture View of Regulation: Regulatory agencies end up serving the special interests of the industries they were intended to regulate.

Regulations:

    Occupational Licensure: Reduces competition by creating a barrier to entry and raising prices. It guarantees a minimum level of quality but prevents people from choosing lower-quality goods or services at lower prices.

    Regulating a Natural Monopoly Graph 21.2: The economically efficient level of output, Qc, occurs where price is equal to marginal cost, where the Demand curve crosses the marginal cost curve. The firm would not sell Qc units at the price of Pc because this Qc entails a loss.

Natural Monopoly

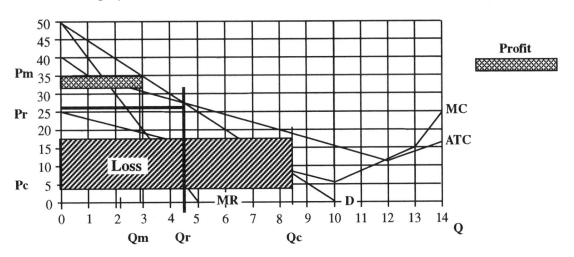

Graph 21.2

Government regulation could require average cost pricing, Pac occurs where the demand curve crosses the average cost curve. The quantity produced is Qr. At this price the firm covers his costs and breaks even. Although Qr is not the economically efficient quantity, it is closer than the quantity produced by an unregulated monopoly that simply profit maximizes. (Pm, Qm).

Government regulation could also require the natural monopoly to charge a two-tier price which covers its costs and produces at the economically efficient quantity, Qc. The two tier price consists of a monthly fee that covers the firms fixed costs and a use charge. Together these fees allow the firm to cover costs.

Real life regulation of natural monopolies is a political process where the interests of the producer are more concentrated than the interests of the consumer.

Rate of return regulation gives the firm an incentive to raise its costs in ways to give nonmoney forms of benefits to its employees and executives.

Nationalized Firm: Extreme case of government regulation, government owns a firm.

Privatization: a government sells a nationalized firm and creates property rights to that firm.

Taxes: most create economic inefficiencies.

Optimal Taxation: Minimize the deadweight social loss. By placing high tax rates on goods with high elasticities of demand and supply the government can minimize the economic inefficiency of collecting any amount of total tax revenue.

Horizontal Equity in Taxes: People with the same characteristics should be treated equally.

Vertical Equity in Taxes: People in unequal conditions should be treated differently. Thus, taxes should be based on the ability to pay.

Average Tax: Tax obligation divided by income.

Marginal tax: increase in taxes if your income rises by $1.

Flat rate tax: Everyone pays the same percentage. Main argument against this is fairness. Critics believe higher income people should pay a higher tax rate on increments to their income.

Graduated Tax: Higher incomes pay higher income tax percentages.

Short Answer Questions

1. State governments are heavily involved in occupational licensure. What is the economic argument for occupational licensure? Does it cause the market to approach an equilibrium quantity that is economically efficient?

2. What are the drawbacks to regulating a natural monopoly using rate of return pricing?

3. Is the corporate income tax an optimal tax?

Basic Problem

1. Identify the deadweight loss of a $1 tax in each of the following graphs by darkening in the area of loss. In which graph below does the tax cause the greatest inefficiency?

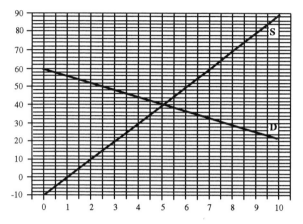

Graph 21.3(a)

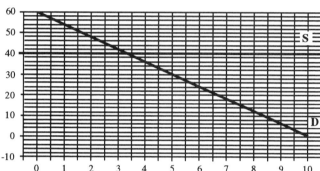

Graph 21.3(b)

Advanced Problem

1. Graph 21.4 represents the supply and demand for cigarettes. Levy an optimal tax on cigarettes and identify the net benefit of the tax.

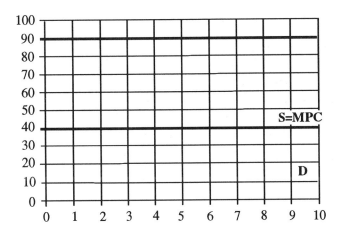

Graph 21.4

Chapter 22

Economics of Public Choice and Law

Learning Goals

1. Describe how political markets differ from markets for most products.

2. Evaluate the economic efficiency of laws and contracts.

Key Term Matching Quiz

Terms

_____   1. Political Equilibrium

_____   2. Median Voter

_____   3. Median Voter Theorem

_____   4. Arrow Impossibility Theorem

_____   5. Tort

_____   6. Liability Rule

_____   7. Expectations Damages

_____   8. Reliance Damages

_____   9. Logrolling

Definitions

a. Any social decision rule must violate at least one of the axioms of rational choice.

b. The person who breaks the contract should pay enough money to make the other people as wealthy as they could have expected to be if the contract had been honored.

c. Under certain conditions, the equilibrium government policy chosen in political markets is the policy favored by the median voter.

d. A situation, characterized by peoples' votes and campaign contributions, the positions and strategies of candidates for office, and the decisions and actions of government officials, that shows no tendency for change.

e. Vote-Trading.

f. Voter whose views on a policy issue are in the middle of the spectrum; half of the other voters are on one side of this voters views, and half are on the other side.

g. The person who breaks the contract should pay enough money to make the other people as wealthy as they would have been if the contract had never been signed.

h. A legal statement of who is responsible under what conditions for injuries in a tort.

i. Acts that injure other people either intentionally or by accident.

True/False Questions

_____ 1. If someone suggests that the government should eliminate wasteful government spending, public choice analysis would assume that the government will carefully carry out the suggested policy.

_____ 2. The median voter theorem is that the politician tries to obtain votes by changing voter's views.

_____ 3. All political situations have equilibria.

_____ 4. One person's vote is unlikely to affect the outcome of a political race.

_____ 5. The economically efficient level of damage payments is the level that creates incentives for people to honor contracts when doing so is economically efficient and to break contracts when that is economically inefficient.

_____ 6. Expectations damages requires the person who breaks the contract should pay enough money to make the other people as wealthy as they would have been if the contract had never been signed.

_____ 7. It would be economically efficient to eliminate crime completely.

_____ 8. It is economically efficient for the criminal justice system to use fines rather than prison sentences as long as the fine has the same deterrent effect as the prison sentence.

Multiple Choice Questions

1. The median voter theorem:
    a. applies when voters' choices are limited because someone has previously established an agenda for voters.
    b. applies when voters prefer high spending or low spending.
    c. applies to situations with more than one candidate or more than one issue.
    d. explains the tendency for politicians to take middle-of-the road positions.

2   Because one person's vote is unlikely to affect the outcome of an election:
    a. this may increase the political power of groups with diffuse rather than concentrated interests.
    b. people have less incentive to stay informed on government policies.
    c. politicians have more incentive to favor policies with long run benefits rather than short run benefits.
    d. politicians have less incentive to inform voters about short run benefits.

3. A tort is:
    a. Acts that injure other people either intentionally or by accident.
    b. A legal statement of who is responsible under what conditions for injuries.
    c. Vote-Trading.
    d. All of the above.

4. Expectations Damages are:
    a. Acts that injure other people either intentionally or by accident.
    b. The person who breaks the contract should pay enough money to make the other people as wealthy as they could have expected to be if the contract had been honored.
    c. The person who breaks the contract should pay enough money to make the other people as wealthy as they would have been if the contract had never been signed.
    d. None of the above.

5. Using economic analysis, you can reduce crime efficiently by:
    a. raising the expected cost of crime to the criminals.
    b. lowering the chance of catching the criminals.
    c. eliminating all crime completely.
    d. All of the above.

6. The expected cost of crime to the criminal is:
    a. the fine he pays if caught.
    b. the income he loses while in prison.
    c. the chance of being caught multiplied by the punishment if caught.
    d. All of the above.

Chapter Review (Fill in the Blanks)

1. Political markets _____ from markets for most products. Production is determined by a _____ vote and _____ customers get a single type of product or service. A politician _____ in political markets must appeal to a _____ enough set of voters to survive _____ from opponents.

2. When the views of elected officials _____ with those of the majority of the people who elected them, their desires to _____ the policies that seem _____ to them can _____ with their desires to be _____.

3. Governments are not _____ decision makers; they consist of many people with _____ interests that sometimes _____ and who often _____ important information for the formulation of policies. The _____ method of evaluating government policies takes into account the _____ and _____ that create a _____ equilibrium.

4. The Median Voter Theorem states that, under certain conditions, the equilibrium _____ _____ chosen in _____ markets is the policy favored by the _____ _____. Although the median voter model explains the tendency of politicians to establish positions in the _____ center, the model has several limitations. For example, it does not apply to certain situations in which voters' choices are limited by _____ _____ voting agendas.

5. _____ affect all behavior, including _____. _____ the benefits of crime increases the crime rate, and _____ the cost of crime _____ it. It would not be _____ _____ for society to eliminate crime _____. The _____ _____ amount of crime is the amount at which the _____ _____ _____ of reducing crime equals the _____ _____.

6. Economically efficient punishments _____ across crimes. The marginal expected _____ for a more _____ crime must be _____ enough to achieve the _____ _____ amount of _____ at each level of severity

Short Answer Questions

1. Describe the characteristics of an economically efficient law.

2. Evaluate the economic efficiency of the theft of a sentimental piece of jewelry?

Chapter 23

International Trade

Learning Goals

1. Define comparative advantage, and explain how international trade is based on comparative advantage.

2. Describe the welfare gains from international trade.

3. Be able to list several sources of comparative advantage.

4. Define and measure the balance of trade and the current account.

5. List and evaluate the common arguments for protectionism.

Key Term Matching Quiz

Terms

____ 1. Exports

____ 2. Imports

____ 3. Merchandise trade balance

____ 4. Comparative advantage

____ 5. Production possibilities frontier

____ 6. Gains from trade

____ 7. Dynamic gains from trade

____ 8. Current account

____ 9. Protectionism

____ 10. Tariff

____ 11. Quota

____ 12. World Trade Organization

Definitions

a. Shows the combinations of products that can be produced with available resources and technology.

b. Sales of goods and services to people in other countries.

c. Benefits of increased economic growth and development due to international trade.

d. An organization and a series of related treaties that reduce trade restrictions.

e. Measures the amount that a country lends to or borrows from other countries.

f. Purchases of goods and services from people in other countries.

g. Government policies that restrict imports.

h. Net benefits to people as consumers and producers from trading.

i. Balance on goods only.

j. Restricts the number of imports of goods of a certain type.

k. A country can produce a product at a lower opportunity cost than other countries.

l. A tax on imports.

True/False Questions

____ 1. International trade increases economic efficiency.

____ 2. International trade increases competition.

____ 3. The U.S. has recently enjoyed a substantial trade surplus.

____ 4. The U.S. imports more from Japan than from any other nation.

____ 5. The merchandise trade balance is smaller than the balance of trade on goods and services in that it omits trade in services.

____ 6. International trade can be viewed as a technology to transform coffee beans into tractors.

____ 7. The basis for international trade is absolute advantage.

____ 8. Comparative advantage permits total world output to increase.

____ 9. If a nation does not trade, then its production possibilities curve is the same as its consumption possibilities curve.

____ 10. Total world imports of an item must be equal to total world exports of an item.

____ 11. The losses from trade generally offset the gains from trade, so that a nation is usually wise to restrict trade.

____ 12. If a nation imports very little of an item, its gain from trade is correspondingly little.

____ 13. Trade increases total production, but does not allow persons to increase consumption.

____ 14. The slope of a production possibilities curve measures the absolute price of two products.

____ 15. If Japan gains from international trade, then Japan's trading partners have clearly had a loss.

____ 16. Small countries have no reason to trade with large countries, because small countries have no comparative advantage.

____ 17. If all nations had equal resources endowments, technology, and tastes, there would be little or no international trade.

____ 18. Every country has a comparative advantage in something.

____ 19. A country which can outproduce every other nation can still gain from international trade.

____ 20. A country with a current account surplus is lending to other nations.

____ 21. If a country's trade deficit decreases, its GDP will tend to rise.

____ 22. A country has a current account deficit if it saves less than it invests.

___ 23. A country can save more than it invests by borrowing from other countries.

___ 24. Few economists think that budget deficits can lead to trade deficits.

___ 25. A tariff is a quantity restriction on imports.

___ 26. Because a tariff raises tax revenue for government, total societal welfare is the same with or without a tariff.

___ 27. The main difference between a tariff and a quota is that a government collects no money with a quota.

___ 28. The welfare costs of protectionism is only a few hundred million dollars per year.

___ 29. The GATT has been replaced by the WTO.

___ 30. Increased free trade raises living standards in countries which practice it.

___ 31. Because U.S. firms have no comparative advantage, they need protection at home in order to survive.

___ 32. Selling a product at very low prices to foreigners is known as dumping.

Multiple Choice Questions

1. International trade promotes
   a. economic efficiency.
   b. economic competition.
   c. specialization.
   d. world economic output.
   e. All of the above.

2. If imports exceed exports, a nation has a
   a. budget deficit.
   b. trade deficit.
   c. trade surplus.
   d. budget surplus.

3. The largest single trading partner for the U.S. is
   a. Japan.
   b. Britain.
   c. Canada.
   d. Mexico.
   e. South Korea.

4. The merchandise trade balance includes trade in goods and
   a. nothing else.
   b. services.
   c. financial flows.
   d. tourism.
   e. inter-government aid.

5. Japan's largest export market is
   a. Canada.
   b. Britain.
   c. China.
   d. Taiwan.
   e. U.S.

6. Suppose the U.S. has limited the import of French wine. If trade restrictions are completely removed, the U.S. price of French wine will _____, and the world price will _____.
   a. rise, fall
   b. rise, rise
   c. fall, fall
   d. fall, rise

7. In the summer of 1995, the US and Japan settled a trade dispute regarding automobiles and parts. If Japan buys more parts from US suppliers, the price of parts in the US will _____, and in Japan the price will _____.
   a. rise, fall
   b. rise, rise
   c. fall, fall
   d. fall, rise

8. Suppose that in a particular trade situation, Canada has a large gain. Its major trading partner, the U.S., probably
   a. had a loss the size of Canada's gain.
   b. had a loss smaller than Canada's gain.
   c. had a gain as well.
   d. had a smaller gain than did Canada.
   e. had no change in economic well-being.

9. Countries tend to trade because
   a. trading provides opportunities to earn profits.
   b. the rate of interest is not the same in all countries.
   c. resources are not equally distributed among all nations.
   d. some nations like to build one thing, while others build another.

10. The actual gains from trade are likely to be larger than commonly thought because of
    a. dynamic gains from trade.
    b. gains from industries with economies of scale.
    c. political gains from trade.
    d. All of the above.

11. A country will have a current account deficit if it
    a. spends more than it borrows.
    b. earns more than it spends.
    c. saves less than it invests.
    d. imports less than it exports.
    e. All of the above.

12. Tariffs decrease economic welfare because
    a. tax revenue is less than the deadweight loss.
    b. prices increase and total trade decreases.
    c. quantity increases less than commonly thought.
    d. the gain to winners exceeds the loss to losers.
    e. All of the above.

Chapter Review (Fill in the Blanks)

1. If a nation exports more than it imports, it has a trade _____; if it imports more than it exports, it has a trade _____.

2. The largest trade partner for the U.S. is _____.

3. International trade as a percentage of GDP is _____ for the U.S. than for other industrialized nations.

4. If a nation has comparative advantage in some item, it can produce the item for _____ than other nations.

5. The U.S. has a comparative advantage in two classes of goods: _____ and _____.

6. A restriction on imports tends to _____ the price of the item in that country, and _____ the world price of that item.

7. If trade begins to open up between two nations, there are winners and losers. In the importing country, the winners are _____, and the losers are _____.

8. In the exporting country, the winners are _____, and the losers are _____.

9. Production possibilities frontiers differ across countries because of differences in _____ and _____.

10. The actual gains from trade are likely to exceed what is commonly thought because of _____, _____, and _____.

11. If a nation runs a trade deficit, it is _____ another country.

12. A tariff is a _____, and a quota is a _____.

13. If a tariff is imposed on a particular good, the price will _____, and the quantity will _____.

14. The most important difference between a tariff and a quota is that with a _____ the government collect revenue, and with the other it doesn't.

15. Current costs of protectionism in the U.S. is about _____ per year.

16. The organization founded in 1947 to promote trade was the _____, and it has been replaced by the _____.

17. The two groups of nations in Europe which have reduced trade restrictions between themselves are _____ and _____.

18. _____ is the practice of selling at very low prices to foreigners.

Priority List of Concepts

Comparative Advantage: if a country can produce a good at a lower opportunity cost than other countries, it has a comparative advantage in that good. Comparative advantage permits gains from specialization and trade, which increases total world output and raises standards of living.

Gains From Trade: consumers gain from lower prices, exporters gain from increased sales abroad. Losers from increased trade include sellers who face stiffer import competition, and consumers abroad who see higher prices of products that they make and also buy.

Current Account: a country that saves less than it invests has a current account deficit, and borrows from other nations.

Protectionism: a common response to trade competition is protection of domestic firms or industries. Protection *does* protect some jobs, but also costs jobs in other industries. The World Trade Organization and other treaties seek to reduce protection, and extend free trade.

Arguments For Protection: seven common arguments in favor of protection were examined. All are fallacious, or subject to serious qualification. Most or all arguments for protection are forms of rent-seeking.

Short Answer Questions

1. Is international trade more important to the U.S. than to Canada and Japan? Explain.

2. Explain why comparative advantage and specialization permits total world output to increase.

3. In what product(s) has the U.S. a comparative advantage? What does this mean in concrete terms?

4. Since trade creates winners and losers, is trade "worth it"? Explain.

5. Is lobbying to restrict trade an example of rent-seeking? Explain.

6. Countries gain from trade because of differences of some sort. What sort of differences affect the gains from trade?

7. Explain why a nation which has lower production costs in all goods still has a comparative advantage in only some goods.

8. Explain why a country with a current account deficit is by definition borrowing from other countries.

9. Do large budget deficits cause trade deficits? What is the evidence on this question?

10. Although many persons think that a trade deficit is bad, economists often argue that such is not the case. What are the reasons that a trade deficit isn't really so bad for the country?

11. What are the main types of trade restrictions?

12. Trade restrictions cause welfare losses for countries; why do countries impose them?

13. Is national defense a valid reason to restrict free trade?

Basic Problems

1. For the U.S., has international trade increased in importance in the past twenty years or decreased? Draw an appropriate graph to help answer this question.

2. Explain why consumption possibilities and production possibilities are different when nations trade. Draw an appropriate diagram to illustrate your answer.

3. Show (with production and consumption possibilities curves) how trade allows persons in each country to consumer more of every product.

4. Explain why trade restrictions which protect jobs also cost jobs.

Advanced Problems

1. Explain why trade is based on comparative advantage.

2. Who gains and who loses when international trade takes place? Draw an appropriate diagram to illustrate your answer.

3. Suppose you are a Congresswoman. What sorts of constituents will ask you to restrict trade? What sorts will ask you to lower trade barriers? Which groups will you tend to follow? Explain.

4. What are the major arguments that have been offered in favor of trade restrictions? How valid are they?

5. Suppose that the government of Gwandanaland decides to subsidize the export of widgets and gadgets. The delivered price to U.S. ports will be zero—the goods are free. What is an appropriate policy on the part of the U.S. in response to this unfair competition?

6. If the U.S. removed all trade restrictions, would welfare increase or decrease? Explain. What problems, if any, do you anticipate? How would you solve them?

7. Ontario is capable of producing 100 kilograms of corn or 80 kilograms of soybeans with one unit of labor. South Dakota is capable of producing 120 kilograms of corn or 120 kilograms of soybeans with one unit of labor. Assume that this is typical of the labor force as a whole. Discuss this situation it terms of comparative advantage and gains from trade. Should South Dakota buy grain from Ontario?

PART VIII

ANSWERS

Answers to Chapter 1

Key Word Matching Quiz

1. c	6. j	11. m
2. g	7. a	12. n
3. h	8. k	13. b
4. e	9. l	14. f
5. i	10. d	

True/False Questions

1. F. Factual question, the average person is five times as rich.

2. T.

3. F. Factual question, Government buys 18% of the U.S. economy's output.

4. T.

5. F. Theory, a free good is found abundantly on our planet and its use involves no opportunity cost or sacrifice.

6. F. A market occurs wherever a trade takes place in a specific grocery store, over the phone, on a street corner, via E Mail.

7. T.

8. F. The market process works best when there are clearly defined property rights.

9. T.

10. T.

Multiple Choice Questions

1. a	5. b
2. d	6. d
3. b	7. b
4. c	8. d

Chapter Review (Fill in the Blanks)

1. 5.7: 40; 7,000.
2. 13.
3. 5, 12.
4. 7.5, 28,000.
5. 1 1/2, 2, 1.8, double.
6. 50, 5.
7. 1/4, 15,000.
8. 28,000; 5,000; 4,000; 19,000.
9. 1/2 10.59.5 cents; 38.5 cents; 2.3 cents.

Basic Problems

1. Benefits include the savings in tuition and board, a year's salary and getting job experience and promotions a year before your peers. Opportunity costs include the loss of summer job earnings, the cost of summer school tuition, the loss of the social benefits of senior year with your class and the loss of all those school vacations. Estimate the dollar value to you of these costs and benefits and compute your incentive. Would the effort at graduating early be worth it to you?

2. Some of the benefits a college junior would gain from accepting a professional sports team draft include the salary and perhaps a contract with provisions that may be different and better this year rather than next, and the certainty of your health this year rather than risking injury in your senior year. The opportunity costs which the college junior would incur include the possibility that he might not finish his college degree, the loss of social benefits of senior year in college and the loss of more college conditioning. Estimate the value of these costs and benefits and compute your incentive to accept a Pro Draft.

Advanced Problems

1. If you are a free market advocate, you might divide the resources equally and let everyone engage in free market competition to use their resources for their own profit trusting that the "invisible hand" would guide the economy to a benevolent result.

    If you were a skeptic about free markets, you might control all the resources yourself and direct everyone else in their use and consumption of these resources. You would be a benevolent dictator/central planner .

Answers to Chapter 2

Key Term Matching Quiz

1. e	6. d	11. j
2. i	7. l	12. b
3. m	8. a	13. f
4. c	9. g	
5. h	10. k	

True/False

1.   F.   A Normative statement is a value judgment.

2.   T.

3.   F.   A Positive statement is either true or false.

4.   F.   Logical thinking plus evidence would be sufficient to reach conclusions about economics.

5.   F.   Evidence can support or disprove an economic model but it can never conclusively prove a model.

6.   T.

7.   T.

8.   F.   Unconditional predictions answer the question, What will happen?

9.   T.

10.   F.   A positive slope refers to a shape that runs upward and to the right.

11.   T.

12.   F.   "If...then..." statements are the predictions of a model.

13.   T.

14.   F.   Conditional predictions answer questions of the form, "What will happen if?"

15.   T.

16.   F.   Rational behavior implies that a person does not make the same mistake twice.

Multiple Choice Questions

1.	c	6.	b
2.	b	7.	c
3.	a	8.	d
4.	c	9.	d
5.	a	10.	a

Chapter Review (Fill in the Blanks)

1. statistical analysis, uncertainty.
2. assumptions, assumptions, conclusions. conclusions.
3. understanding, prediction, interpretation.
4. the best they can.
5. other conditions.
6. move.
7. same.
8. opposite.
9. a period of time.
10. Conditional.

Basic Problems "Using Graphs"

1. Graph (B) & (C), their shapes run **upward** and to the right.

2. Graph (A) & (D), their shapes run downward and to the right.

3. Graph (A). To compute slope, pick a point on the graph as a starting point, move one unit to the right and then see how many units you must move vertically to get back to the graph. Did you move up (+) or down (-). You moved down (-), thus for Graph (A), slope is negative (-) 1.

4. Graph (C).

5. 2, Each point on the curve indicates two numbers, a quantity and a price. Along the graph at the point where price is equal to 4, quantity is equal to 2.

6. 4.

7. 50, Make the triangle into a rectangle, compute the area of a rectangle, (base * height) and divide by 2.

Advanced Problems

1. The slope of the line is negative two fifths, -2/5.

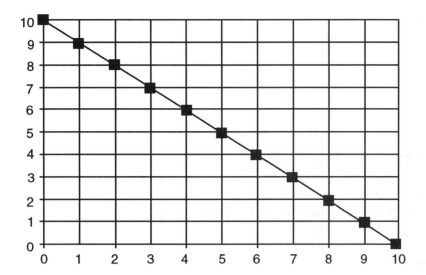

Answers to Chapter 3

Key Word Matching Quiz

1. b	6. j	11. k
2. i	7. e	12. d
3. f	8. l	13. n
4. m	9. h	14. g
5. c	10. a	

True/False Questions

1. T.

2. T.

3. F.   In a zero sum game, if someone wins, someone else loses.

4. T.

5. F.   Producing inside the production possibilities frontier is inefficient.

6. F.   If the production possibilities frontier shifts inward, the economy has experienced a decline in its ability to produce through some destruction or depletion of technology or resources.

7. T.

True/False Questions (continued)

8. T.

9. T.

10. F.   Economics deals with statements about facts and efficiency. Economics says nothing about fairness.

Multiple Choice Questions

1. e   6. b
2. d   7. b
3. b   8. c
4. d   9. b
5. a   10. d

Chapter Review (Fill in the Blanks)

1. positive statements.
2. fairness, equal, fairness, rules.
3. inefficient, efficient, gain, lose, gain.
4. Production possibilities frontier, inputs, technology.
5. Economic growth.
6. 1.8.
7. comparative advantage, lower.
8. efficient, losing.
9. good, bad, distribution, income.

Short Answer Questions

1. People have incentives to trade when the trade can create a gain to one or both parties without either party losing anything. The parties to the trade can share the gains from changing an inefficient situation into an efficient one.

2. A tax creates an inefficient situation if its existence prevents a trade and in addition the government will collect no revenue from the tax .

Basic Problems

1.

Productivity of Jan & Tom per hour

	Lawns Mowed	Cars Washed
Jan	5	5
Tom	4	2

Relative Productivity at Mowing Lawns

	(lawns/hour)/(cars/hour)	
Jan	(5/5)	1
Tom	(4/2)	2***

Relative Productivity at Washing Cars

	(cars/hour)/(lawns/hour)	
Jan	(5/5)	1***
Tom	(2/4)	0.50

***The person with the higher relative productivity at a job has the Comparative Advantage.

2.

Costs of Production	Minutes	
	Jan	**Tom**
Mow Lawn	12.5	15
Wash Car	12.5	30

Relative Costs

Mow Lawn	12.5M/12.5W=1	15M/30W=0.5***
Wash Car	12.5W/12.5M=1***	30W/15M=2

***Jan has the lowest relative cost of washing cars and Tom has the lowest relative cost of mowing lawns. **Lowest relative cost determines** the one who has the comparative advantage. Jan should wash cars and Tom should mow lawns. Note that in the case of Jan and Tom, Jan is absolutely more productive in both activities than Tom, but because they have different relative abilities you can still determine a comparative advantage by comparing relative costs.

3. **Production Possibilities Frontier for Jan**

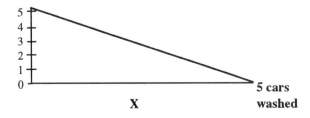

4.   Production Possibilities Frontier for Tom

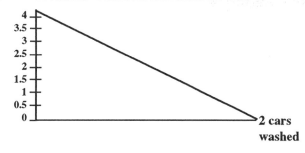

2 cars
washed

Advanced Problems

1.   Time required to mow one lawn or wash one car.

	Jan	Tom
Mow Lawn	12.5 minutes	15 minutes
Wash Car	12.5 minutes	30 minutes

Results of the trade of 1 lawn mowed by Tom for 1 car washed by Jan

Jan still gets her chores done in 25 minutes. She washes two cars. If she had washed a car and mowed a lawn it would still have taken her just 25 minutes. She gets no increased leisure time from the trade but she is no worse off because of it either.

Tom gets his chores done in 30 minutes instead of 45. With the trade he mows two lawns in 30 minutes. Without the trade he would have had to mow his lawn and wash his own car which would have taken him 45 minutes. Tom gained 15 minutes of leisure time.

This trade is efficient because there was a gain of leisure time. The gains from the trade were not equally shared. Tom gained but Jan was no worse off so she would consent to the trade. The trade is efficient because there was a gain with no one losing.

Answers to Chapter 4

Key Term Matching Quiz

1. j	6. b	11. e
2. a	7. f	12. l
3. d	8. i	13. h
4. m	9. c	
5. g	10. k	

True/False

1. F. A demand schedule lists hypothetical prices of the good. It does not say what price buyers actually pay.

2. T.

3. F. The price on a demand or supply curve is a relative price.

4. T.

5. F. Prices will fall towards equilibrium price.

6. F. Its relative price rises.

7. T. This change is shown by a movement along the demand curve.

8. F. The nominal price of a good is its money price.

9. T.

10. T.

Multiple Choice

1. d	5. b	9. b
2. a	6. b	10. b
3. a	7. b	11. b
4. a	8. b	12. a

Chapter Review (Fill in the Blanks)

1   price.
2   conditions, shifts.
3   vertical, horizontal.
4   time.
5   conditions, price, tastes, useful, income, complements, substitutes, time, change.
6   other conditions, falls, demand.
7   downward, negative.
8   rises, conditions, Law.
9   positive, raises.
10   price, movement along.
11   conditions other than the price of the good in question.
12   price of inputs, technology, price of other goods, adjustment time, number of potential sellers.
13   equilibrium, equilibrium, change, condition, equilibrium.
14   below, rise.
15   above, fall.

Short Answer Questions

1. The graph 4.4A below shows that a decrease in supply shifts the supply curve left from S1 to S2. Equilibrium moves from position E1 to E2. As a result, equilibrium price increases to P2 and equilibrium quantity decreases to Q2. On this graph P2 represents a price of 10 and Q2 represents a quantity of 5.

Decrease in Supply

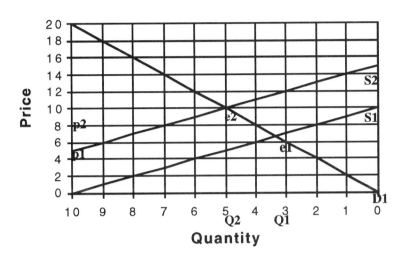

Graph 4.4A

2. The graph 4.5A below shows that an increase in both demand and supply shifts the supply curve right from S1 to S2 and shifts the demand curve right from D1 to D2. Equilibrium moves from position E1 to E2. As a result, equilibrium price decreases to P2 and equilibrium quantity increases to Q2. On this graph P2 represents a price of 6.5 and Q2 represents a quantity of 7.5.

Increase in Supply and Demand

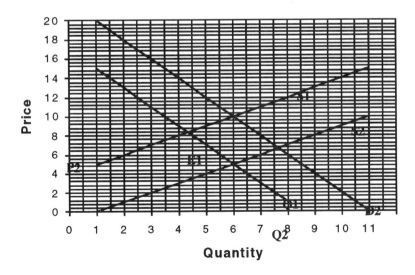

Graph 4.5A

Basic Problems

1. Graph 4.6 shows the demand for pizza.

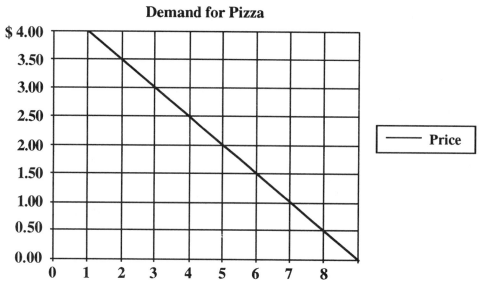

Demand for Pizza

Graph 4.6

2. Graph 4.7 shows the Demand and Supply for Pizza.

Quantity Demanded	Quantity Supplied	Price
1	9	4.0
2	8	3.5
3	7	3.0
4	6	2.5
5	5	2.0
6	4	1.5
7	3	1.0
8	2	0.5
9	1	0.0

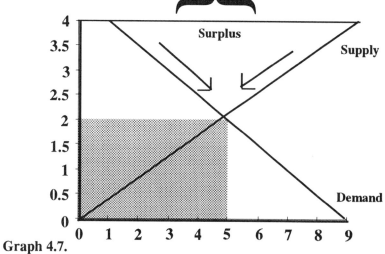

Graph 4.7.

3. Equilibrium price is $2.00 and equilibrium quantity is 5.

4. The shaded rectangle represents Total Spending at equilibrium (price multiplied by quantity or $5 multiplied by 5 equals $25 Total Spending).

5. A surplus exists at a price of $4.

6. That surplus equals quantity supplied at $4 less quantity demanded at $4 or 9 Qs less 1 Qd = a surplus of 8.

7. Due to this surplus situation at a price of $4, price will fall to move the economy towards equilibrium.

Advanced Problems

1. A tariff is similar to a tax on cars and would decrease supply. A tariff represents a rise in price and would cause a movement along a demand curve. Equilibrium price would rise and equilibrium quantity would decrease.

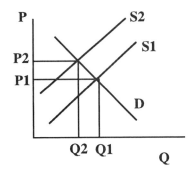

2a. As the Baby Boom population ages, there will be decrease in the population in the labor force causing a decrease in supply, a rise in the equilibrium price of labor and a decrease in the equilibrium quantity of labor. [Same graph as in question 1 above.]

2b. There will be a decrease in demand for these foods causing a decrease in price and a decrease in quantity.

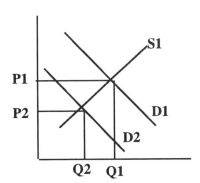

2c.   There will be an increase in demand for these goods causing an increase in price and an increase in equilibrium quantity.

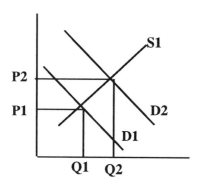

2d.   Less students enrolling in college, a decrease in demand for college. Same answer and graph as 2b.

3a.   The demand for construction increased. Same answer and graph as 2c.

3b.   The demand for furniture increased. Same answer and graph as 2c.

3c.   The supply of hotel room decreased due to destruction and the demand for hotel room decreased due to lack of anything to see except destruction. Equilibrium price increased and equilibrium quantity decreased

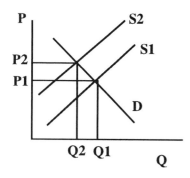

Answers to Chapter 5

Key Term Matching Quiz

1. b	6. e	11. g
2. f	7. c	12. l
3. m	8. k	13. h
4. j	9. i	14. n
5. a	10. d	

True/False Questions

1. F. Elasticity of demand is different from slope.

2. T.

3. T.

4. F. If demand is inelastic, Disney would lose money by lowering the prices on its videos. Disney should keep its price high because its customers will buy the classic children's videos without much reaction to the price.

5. T.

6. F. Demand for a good is more elastic the more substitutes that are available for a product. Then, people can switch to another product if the price rises.

7. T.

8. T.

9. T.

10. F. A long run demand curve is more elastic than a short run demand curve because people have had more time to adjust to the price change.

Multiple Choice

1. b, Box C represents the increase in spending. Box A represents the loss in spending. Box C is larger in answer b.
2. b
3. b
4. c
5. d

6. d, $\left(\dfrac{\%\text{ change in Qd}}{\%\text{ change in P}}\right) = \left(\dfrac{-\left(\dfrac{1}{15}\right)}{+\left(\dfrac{2}{10}\right)}\right) = -\left(\dfrac{1}{15} \times \dfrac{10}{2}\right) = -\left(\dfrac{1}{3}\right) = -0.3$

7. c
8. a, In the inelastic range of demand curve, when price rises, spending rises
9. a
10 a

Chapter Review (Fill in the Blanks)

1. elasticity.
2. quantity demanded.
3. same.
4. differs.
5. perfectly inelastic.
6. perfectly elastic.
7. rises.
8. less.
9. same.
10. less.

Short Answer Questions

1. Elasticity is measured as a percentage. Elasticity measures the percentage change in quantity demanded along the horizontal axis when the variable on the vertical axis (Price) changes by one percent. Slope measures the change along the vertical axis when the variable on the horizontal axis changes by one unit.

2. Total spending is positively related to changes in price along the inelastic portion of a demand curve. If price increases, spending increases and if price decreases, spending decreases.

    Total spending is negatively related to changes in price along the elastic portion of a demand curve. If price increases, spending decreases and if price decreases, spending increases.

    Total spending does not change along the unit elastic portion of a demand curve. If price increases, total spending remains the same and if price decreases, total spending remains the same.

3. Increases in any of these factors will increase elasticity.

4. The competition from a cheap substitute would increase the elasticity of demand for gasoline.

Basic Problems

1. Formula: Percentage Change in Quantity Demanded

   = (Percentage Change in Price $\times$ Elasticity of Demand)

   $= \left(-50\% \text{ X } (-.25)\right) = +12.5\%.$

2. Formula: Percentage Change in Quantity Demanded

   = (Percentage Change in Income $\times$ Income Elasticity)

   $= \left(-50 \times (+1)\right) = +10\%$ change in Quantity Demanded d

3. Formula: Elasticity of Demand $= \left(\dfrac{\text{Percentage Change in Quantity Demanded of X}}{\text{Percentage Change in Price}}\right)$

   $= \left(\dfrac{-50\%}{+5\%}\right) = -10$ Elasticity of Demand. This is a very elastic demand.

4. Cross Price Elasticity of Demand $= \left(\dfrac{\text{Percentage Change in Quantity Demanded of X}}{\text{Percentage Change in Price of Y}}\right)$

   $= \left(\dfrac{-50\%}{+20\%}\right) = -2.5.$ The Cross Price Elasticity of Demand is negative, thus these products are complements.

Advanced Problems

1. Formula: In equilibrium, if demand changes, the percentage change in the equilibrium price of cellular phones =

   $\left(\dfrac{\text{Percentage Change in Equilibrium Quantity}}{\text{Elasticity of Supply}}\right) = \left(\dfrac{+50\%}{+3}\right) = +16.7\%.$ Price rises by 16.7%.

2. Along the inelastic portion of a demand curve, changes in price are positively related to total spending or sales. Thus, if price rises, total spending will rise.

3. Formula: In equilibrium, if supply changes:

   Percentage Change in Price $= \left(\dfrac{\text{Percentage Change in Equilibrium Quantity}}{\text{Elasticity of Demand}}\right)$

   $= \left(\dfrac{50\%}{-1}\right) = -50\%$ change in Price, Price falls by 50%.

Answers to Chapter 6

Key Term Matching Quiz

1.	e	7.	j
2.	h	8.	b
3.	a	9.	k
4.	i	10.	f
5.	c	11.	g
6.	d		

True/False Questions

1. T.

2. F.   An increase in Government Demand for a good raises private purchases.

3. T.

4. F.   People with high values of time will pay higher prices to save time.

5. T.

6. F.   The cost of raising children on the farm was cheaper because food was plentiful and the children also contributed to the work of the farm.

7. T.

Multiple Choice Questions

1.	d	7.	b
2.	c	8.	a
3.	a	9.	b
4.	c	10.	a
5.	d	11.	d
6.	a	12.	c

Chapter Review (Fill in the Blank)

1.   increase, decreases.
2.   raises, decreases.
3.   borrowing, government budget deficit, year, more.
4.   government borrowing.
5.   supply, demand, interest rate.
6.   raises, interest rate, private sector, crowds out.
7.   demand, demand.
8.   an increase in government spending, a decrease in taxes.
9.   high, support, lower, more.
10. reducing, less productive, productive, deficiency.
11. time, money, opportunity.
12. time, parties, movies.
13. upward ,rises, falls, time, money.
14. money, non-money, non-money, raises, reduces.
15. money, expected punishment, caught, punished, increases, rise, decrease, increase, decrease.
16. free, safety, injury, safety.
17. higher, higher, self-interest, raise, profit, incentive.

Short Answer Questions

1.   The rise in wealth and wages has increased the price of time and decreased our demand for sleep.

2.   Demand for healthy food increases, demand curve shifts right increasing equilibrium quantity and price.

3.   Supply of health food increases. Equilibrium quantity increases. Equilibrium price falls.

4.   Expected punishment price decreases. The Demand for fireworks increases and equilibrium price and quantity increase.

Basic Problems

1.   For a graphical answer to this ,see priority concepts, increase in government demand for goods. The increase in government demand for healthcare will increase the price of healthcare and decrease the private demand for healthcare. Equilibrium quantity of healthcare produced will rise but not by as much as the increase in the government demand for health care because the quantity demanded of private health care has decreased due to the rise in price.

2.   For a graphical answer to this, see pp. 134-135 in the text, figure 6.1. If Medicare spending was drastically reduced, government spending on healthcare would decrease, the price of healthcare would decrease, the private demand for healthcare would increase and the total quantity produced at equilibrium would decrease but not by as much as the original decrease in Medicare spending because private quantity demanded would have risen due to the lower price.

Basic Problems (continued)

3. In Graph 6.3 below, the supply of natural gas increases, S1 shifts right to S2. Equilibrium price remains the same at P. Equilibrium quantity increases to Q2m for the total market. The government increases its quantity demanded to Og2 while the quantity consumed privately remains the same at Qp.

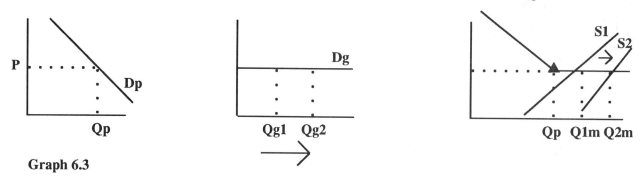

Graph 6.3

4. The total price of the concert is $35.

Advanced Problems

1. The increase in the time price of dinners in the city is $6 (1/2 hour * $12).

    The demand curve D1 shifts downward vertically by $6, the increased time price. The new equilibrium price is $21. It has fallen less than the increase in the time price. The quantity consumed per year will drop from 10 to 6. Thus, although the money price of a restaurant dinner in the city dropped to $21, the total price is $21 + 6 = $27. Formerly the total price had been $25 + a minimal travel time into the city, perhaps $1 worth in time.

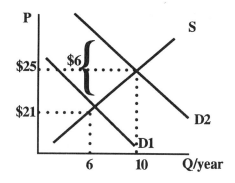

Graph 6.4

2. Legalization decreased the expected punishment price, and thus increased demand for numbers betting. With no change in supply, an increase in demand will increase price and increase equilibrium quantity.

3. Increase the supply of labor and decrease the formal wage. It should also discourage honest ushers from working since they would make less pay.

4. The increased demand for safety would shift the demand for Co2 detectors to the right, increasing both price and equilibrium quantity.

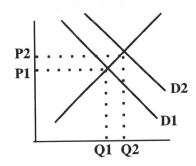

5. The expected punishment price would fall which would increase the demand for illegal goods and increase the opportunity cost of living an honest life.

Answers to Chapter 7

Key Term Matching Quiz

1. f	6. g	11. m	16. h
2. a	7. c	12. l	
3. n	8. e	13. o	
4. i	9. j	14. p	
5. b	10. d	15. k	

True/False Questions

1. F. Winners from international trade gain more than losers, thus trade is economically efficient.

2. F. With international trade, world supply and demand curves determine equilibrium price world equilibrium price and the equilibrium price in each country which trades.

3. T.

4. T.

5. F. Arbitrage tends to eliminate price differentials.

6. T.

7. T.

8. F. With costless speculation, a good's expected future price cannot exceed its current price.

9. T.

10. F. The gains from speculating are larger than the losses if speculators have reasonably accurate expectations about the future.

Multiple Choice Questions

1. d	6. b	11. b
2. a	7. c	12. b
3. c	8. b	
4. a	9. d	
5. d	10. d	

Chapter Review (Fill in the Blanks)

1. one-tenth, growing, one-twentieth, international, interregional, speculation.
2. each country's, world, produces, consumes.
3. exports, imports.
4. world equilibrium.
5. lower, higher, higher, lower.
6. economically efficient.
7. low, high, reduce.
8. time, later, uncertain, risk, lower, profit, exceed, zero.
9. goods, lend, borrow, interest rate, raises, raises.
10. future, spot, future.

Answers to Chapter 8

Key Term Matching Quiz

1. h	6. a	11. j
2. k	7. e	12. l
3. g	8. i	
4. b	9. c	
5. d	10. f	

True/False Questions

1. F.   Rationing by waiting lets the buyer pay more than the money price, he also pays a time price.

2. F.   The government is trying to keep prices high by setting price floors, minimum legal prices above equilibrium price.

3. T.

4. T.

5. F.   Beyond a certain point on the Laffer curve, an increase in tax rates will decrease tax payments.

6. T.

7. F.   The extra money goes to foreign sellers who export goods to the U.S.

8. T.

9. F.   Sugar costs more in the U.S. than in the rest of the world.

10. T.

Multiple Choice Questions

1. c	6. a	11. a
2. b	7. c	
3. c	8. d	
4. a	9. d	
5. b	10. c	

Chapter Review (Fill in the Blanks)

1. low, above, supply, demand, maximum legal prices, long lines, shortages, production.
2. demanded, supplied, nonprice, queuing, coupons, bribery.
3. minimum wage, price floor, minimum legal price, price floor, surplus, output, supplied, demanded, sell, sell, minimum.
4. surplus, unemployment, demanded, lowers, teenagers, adults.
5. minimum, support, support, export, import quotas, doubled, producers.
6. gap, per unit tax, raises, lowers, lowers.
7. price, price.
8. raises, lowers, tariff. raises, reduces, lowers, raises. reduces, quota, government, revenue, none, raises, money, tariff.

Short Answer Questions

1. It reduces the number of organs available for transplant by decreasing the quantity supplied. Eventually it will lead to the invention of subtle indirect ways to pay for transplants so that there is a greater quantity supplied.

2. When a price floor is set above equilibrium price, a surplus is created and because the price is not permitted to fluctuate, the surplus will not disappear. Thus minimum wage can create a surplus of labor on the market, unemployment.

Basic Problems

1. A $3 legal price will cause a shortage. At $3 only 3 Q will be available for sale while 9 Q will be demanded. There will be a shortage of 6Q. With rationing by coupons, 3 coupons will be sold at a price $3. Although the equilibrium price is $6, the true cost to buyers is $9, ($3 for the coupon and $6 for the equilibrium price. Giving away the coupons rather than selling them would make no difference as to who finally buys the merchandise. See Graph 8.15 below.

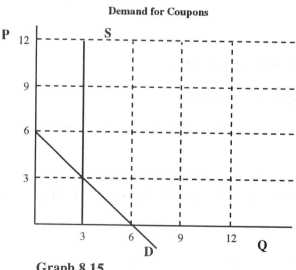

Graph 8.15

2. The supply curve is relatively inelastic (steeper than the demand curve) so the producer will pay relatively more of the tax. See Graph 8.16 below. The Producer or seller pays $1.80 of the $2 tax or 90% of the tax.

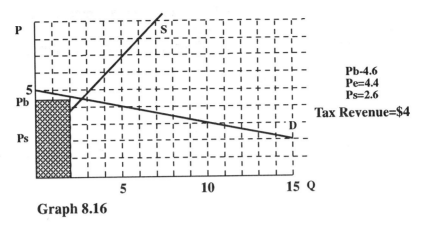

Pb-4.6
Pe=4.4
Ps=2.6
Tax Revenue=$4

Graph 8.16

Advanced Problems

1. The producer would pay none of the tax if the Demand for the product was perfectly inelastic and the supply was relatively elastic.

Answers to Chapter 9

Key Terms Matching Quiz

1. m	6. j	11. f
2. a	7. c	12. l
3. d	8. n	13. i
4. b	9. k	14. e
5. g	10. h	

True/False Questions

1. T.

2. F. Willingness to pay does depend on income.

3. F. There is probably no way to measure this.

4. F. Equilibrium price does not measure the importance of the good to people.

5. T.

6. F. Marginal benefit is the extra benefit you get from doing something once more.

7. F. The budget line will rotate inward along the horizontal axis where good X is measured.

8. F. Indifference curves do not cross one another or intersect.

True/False Questions (continued)

9. F.   Rational choice suggests doing the action only so long as Marginal Benefit is equal to or greater than Marginal Cost.

10. T.

Multiple Choice Questions

1.	d	6.	c
2.	d	7.	c
3.	b	8.	d
4.	d	9.	b
5.	c	10.	c

Chapter Review (Fill in the Blanks)

1. Consumer Surplus, demand curve, equilibrium price.
2. budget line.
3. relative, horizontal, vertical.
4. income, slope.
5. price, rotate, slope.
6. benefit, cost, net benefit.
7. rationally.
8. opportunity, sunk, recovered, rational.
9. tastes.
10. highest.

Short Answer Questions

1. Although a very important good, necessary for life, water may be very inexpensive in terms of its equilibrium price as compared to oil. Equilibrium price is not a measure of water's importance to people. Consumer surplus, a measure of people's willingness to pay for the good, would be much higher for water than for oil. Consumer surplus would affirm the relative importance of water over oil.

Basic Problems

Answers to questions 1 to 3 refer to Graph 9.10 and the table below.

1. Budget Line B

Budget Line B	Budget Line C	Budget Line D
$100	$200	$200
Py = $25	Py = $25	Py = $25
Px = $10	Px = $10	Px = $20

2. Budget Line C shows a shift outward and to the right indicating that the consumers opportunities for spending have increased.

3. When the price of X increases, the budget line rotates in along the X axis to budget line D.

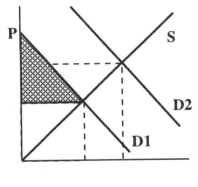

Graph 9.9a

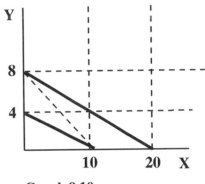

Graph 9.10

4. Graph 9.9a
    Consumer surplus decreases.

5. Consumer surplus = [1/2 ({4.00-2.50} * 4)] = [1/2 {1.50*4}] = $3.00

6. Engage in the activity 5 times to maximize net benefit at 55.

Number of Times	Total Benefit	Marginal Benefit	Total Cost	Marginal Cost	Net Benefit
1	20	20	1	1	19
2	38	18	3	2	35
3	54	16	6	3	48
4	68	14	13	7	55
5	78	10	23	10	55
6	85	7	37	14	48
7	91	6	56	19	35
8	96	5	81	25	15
9	100	4	113	32	-13
10	103	3	153	40	-50
11	105	2	203	50	-98
12	106	1	268	65	-162

Advanced Problems

1. Solve for equilibrium price by setting $Q^s = Q^d$

$$10 - 2P = P + 2$$
$$8 = 3P$$
$$8/3 = P$$
$$P = 2.67 = \text{Equilibrium Price}$$

Substitute the value for P into the equation for $Q^s = P + 2$

$$Q^s = 2.67 + 2$$
$$Q^s = 4.67 \text{ Equilibrium Quantity}$$

Graph 9.11 shows consumer surplus as a filled triangle.
    To compute Total Consumer Surplus:
    calculate 1/2 of the area of the rectangle equal to
    ({[Height of Demand Curve for the unit (Willingness to Pay)] minus [Equilibrium Price]} multiplied times Equilibrium Quantity) equals [Total Consumer Surplus].
    (1/2{[5.00 - 2.67] *4.67})= 5.44 Total Consumer Surplus, the area of the filled triangle in Graph 9.11.

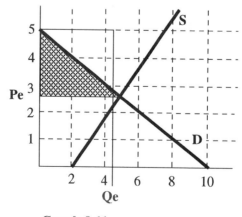

Graph 9.11

Answers to Chapter 10

Key Term Matching Quiz

1.	m	6.	c	11.	n	16.	f
2.	e	7.	a	12.	d		
3.	1	8.	k	13.	g		
4.	b	9.	h	14.	p		
5.	i	10.	o	15.	j		

True/False Questions

1. T.

2. F. A method of production is technically efficient if the firm could not produce the same amount using less of any one input without using more of the other inputs.

3. T.

4. F. There are usually many technically efficient ways to produce, usually only one of them is economically efficient, it minimizes the costs of production.

5. F. The value of the firm will decrease.

6. T.

7. T.

8. F. Average cost and average variable cost differ in the short run due to the existence of fixed costs, but are equal in the long run because there are no fixed inputs in the long run, thus no fixed costs.

9. F. In the long run, producer surplus is equal to profit. In the short run producer surplus is equal to profit plus fixed cost.

10. F. When marginal cost is greater than average cost, average cost is rising as output increases.

Multiple Choice Questions

1.	c	6.	d	11.	b
2.	a	7.	d	12.	b
3.	b	8.	c	13.	c
4.	d	9.	d	14.	b
5.	a	10.	b	15.	a

Chapter Review (Fill in the Blanks)

1. firm, contracts, obligations, rights.
2. one, personal, personally, all sole proprietorship, 3/4, 6 percent.
3. two, ownership, written, all, all, debts, 10 percent 4 percent.
4. corporation, artificial, owners, stockholders, 20 percent, 90 percent.
5. how, how much.
6. quantity, technically, least cost.
7. Marginal Cost, Marginal Revenue, rising, constant, Total Revenue, Total Variable Cost, Total Revenue, Total Variable Cost, Average Revenue (Price), Average Variable Cost, Average Revenue (Price), Average Variable Cost.
8. rising, falling.
9. discounted present value.
10. perfectly elastic (horizontal).

Short Answer Questions

1. If firms make irrational choices repeatedly, competitors will come along to drive that firm out of business. Takeovers are a continuing example of the ability of the free market to keep the firm focused on maximizing its value (profits).

Basic Problems

1. At a quantity of 3. Shade in the elliptical area in the graph to show profit. That area reaches its greatest height at a quantity of:

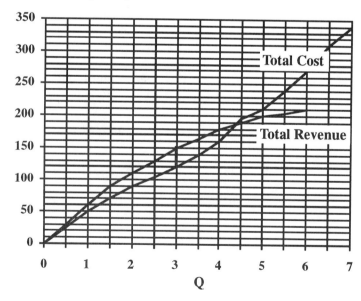

2. Marginal cost equals marginal revenue where marginal cost is rising at approximately 3.5 units. Quantity produced and profit can't be determined without information on the Price of the product, average variable cost and average total cost.

Q	TR	AR	MR	TC	TFC	TVC	AC	AVC	AFC	MC	Profit
		TR/Q	*		TC-TVC	TC-TFC	TC/Q	TVC/Q	TFC/Q	**	TC-TR
0	0			13	13	0	####				
1	20	20	20	26	13	13	26	13	13	13	-6
2	38	19	18	38	13	25	19	6.5	6.5	12	0
3	54	18	16	49	13	36	16.33	4.33333	4.33333	11	5
4	68	17	14	58	13	45	14.5	3.25	3.25	9	10
5	80	16	12	65	13	52	13	2.6	2.6	7	15
6	90	15	10	74	13	61	12.33	2.16667	2.16667	9	16
7	98	14	8	84	13	71	12	1,85714	1.85714	10	14
8	104	13	6	95	13	82	11.88	1.625	1.625	11	9
9	108	12	4	107	13	94	11.89	1.44444	1.44444	12	1
10	110	11	2	120	13	107	12	1.3	1.3	13	-10

3. Data and Graph showing Marginal Cost and Marginal Redvenue from the above table. Profit maximizing quantity is 6 units. Total Revenue less Total Cost at 6 units equals a profit of $16.

Q	MR	MC
0		
1	20	13
2	18	12
3	16	11
4	14	9
5	12	7
6	10	9
7	8	10
8	6	11
9	4	12
10	2	13

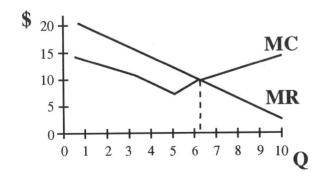

Advanced Problem

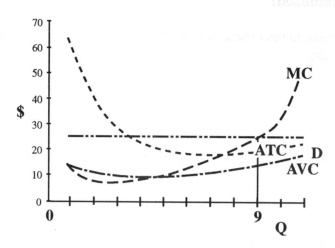

Profit maximizing output is 9, where MC = MR and MC is rising. Price (average revenue is greater than AVC. Producer surplus is the area above marginal cost and below the demand curve. Since this is short run, it is equal to Profit plus Fixed Cost. At 9 units of output, producer surplus equals Total Revenue less Total Variable Cost. At 9 units of output, producer surplus equals Total Revenue less Total Variable Cost, equals $193 less $122, equals $71.

Answers to Chapter 11

Key Terms Matching Quiz

1. c   6. d
2. f   7. e
3. b
4. g
5. a

True/False Questions

1. T.

2. F.   Producer surplus is larger when supply is more inelastic.

3. F.   In a potential Pareto improvement there can be losers, but in a Pareto improvement no one loses and at least one person gains.

4. T.

5. T.

6. F.   The loss from an economic inefficiency is measured in part by the deadweight loss.

True/False Questions (continued)

7. F. It is a potential Pareto improvement because some may lose while others gain, but the gainers can compensate the losers.

8. T.

9. T.

10. F. Subsidies cause economic inefficiency and a deadweight social loss. The government loses because it provides the subsidy.

Multiple Choice Questions

1. b
2. d
3. d
4. b
5. b
6. d

To answer questions 7 to 11 you must be able to measure consumer surplus (the area under the demand curve but above the equilibrium price from zero to the quantity sold.) and producer surplus (the area above the supply curve but under equilibrium price from zero to the quantity sold).

Original Equilibrium

Imposition of Maximum Legal Price

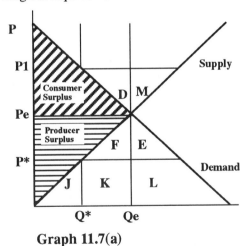

Graph 11.7(a)

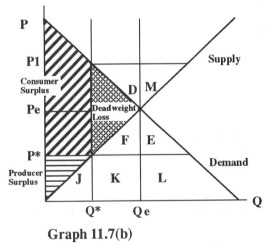

Graph 11.7(b)

7. c
8. a
9. b
10. a
11. b

Chapter Review (Fill in the Blanks)

1. consumer, producer surplus. total benefit, total variable.
2. gains, loses. potential Pareto, winners.
3. economically efficient.
4. deadweight social loss.
5. potential Pareto, helps, hurts, higher, gain more, lose. hurts, helps, gains, losses, compensate, economically efficient. economically efficient.
6. inefficiency. less, consumer, producer surplus, perfectly inelastic, deadweight social loss.
7. inefficient. exceeds, buyers, sellers, deadweight social loss.

Short Answer Questions

1. It is unlikely anyone would argue against a Pareto improvement in the economy because no one would lose and at least one person would gain. However, there is usually much controversy surrounding a potential Pareto improvement because there are both winners and losers as a result of the change. Even if the winners gain more than the losers lose, it's hard to accept if you are on the losing side.

2. The ban on smoking in most buildings would be termed by smokers, a potential Pareto improvement. Smokers lost their freedom and the rest of the world improved their health.

3. A potential Pareto improvement, such as improved technology, can cause unemployment and lost income to those who lose their jobs to a machine. This causes a redistribution of income from the laborer to the owner of the machine. The gains to the producer from producing more goods at a cheaper cost, and to the consumer from being able to buy the goods at a lower price outweigh the loss in jobs and the need to retrain.

Basic Problems

1. In Graph 11.8 below, the deadweight loss of producing less than equilibrium quantity is the shaded area. It's value is equal to 1/2 (base * height) of the triangle or 1/2 (10 * 5) equals 25.

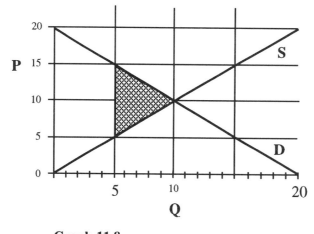

Graph 11.8

2. Trade causes consumers in the high price country to gain and consumers in the low price country lose. Trade causes producers in the high price country to lose and producers in the low price country to gain. This happens because the world price at which goods are traded is lower than the high price country and higher than it had been in the low price country. With trade, there is a benefit to both countries which becomes a deadweight loss to both countries if trade were restricted.

3. The deadweight loss of a $1 tax is the shaded area below.

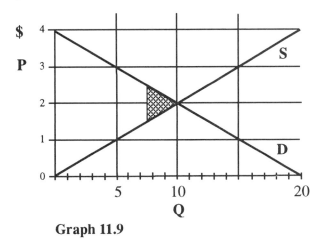

Graph 11.9

Advanced Problems

1. Assuming the countries had been trading before this trade embargo was enacted, the U.S. consumer gains, the U.S. producer loses. The foreign consumer loses and the foreign producer gains. There is a deadweight loss which is evidence that total gains fell and that this condition has caused economic inefficiency. The distribution of income has changed to favor the consumer in the U.S. and the producer in the foreign country.

    With trade, (refer to Graph 11.10) total gains from trade in the U.S. are (A + B + C + D) and total gains from trade in Japan are (E + F + G+ H).

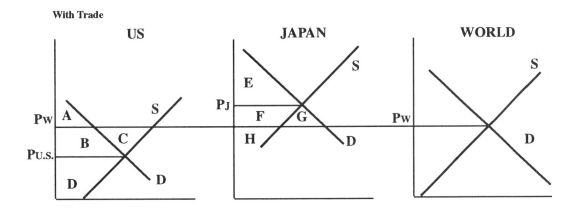

Graph 11.10

After the trade restriction (refer to Graph 11.11):

1. the U.S. consumer gains B but loses C. The U.S. producer loses B, the deadweight loss that neither producer nor consumer captures is C.
2. Japanese consumers lose F and G and the Japanese producer gains F. G is the deadweight loss that neither Japanese producer or consumer captures.
3. Income redistribution may be analyzed by looking at producer vs. consumer in the U.S., the producer is the loser. In Japan, the consumer is the loser.

With Trade

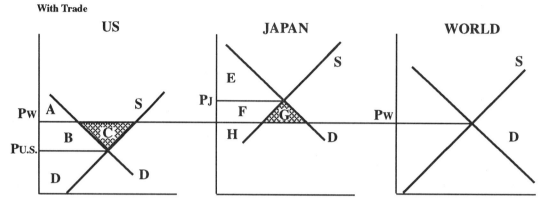

Graph 11.11

2. $Q_D = 10 - P_B$
    $Q_{S=} 2P_S$
    $10 - P_B = 2 P_S$
    $P = 3.33$
    $Q_S = 2P_S$
    $Q_S = 2 (3.33) = 6.7$
    Equilibrium price = 3.33, Equilibrium quantity = 6.7

A tax of $1 is imposed. Now the $P_B = (P_s + 1)$
    $Q_D = 10 - (P_s + 1)$
    $Q_S = 2P_S$
    $10 - (P_s + 1) = 2 P_S$
    $9 = 3 P_S$
    $P_s = 3$
    $P_B = (P_s + 1) = 4$
    $Q = 2P_S = 6$

After the tax, equilibrium price has risen to $4 and equilibrium quantity has fallen to 6.

The deadweight loss of the tax is equal to 1/2 (Q) (Tax), equals {1/2 [(0.7)($1)]} = .35.

Answers to Chapter 12

Key Term Matching Quiz

1.	p	6.	d	11.	e	16.	t
2.	i	7.	n	12.	b	17.	o
3.	s	8.	g	13.	l	18.	c
4.	a	9.	q	14.	h	19.	m
5.	k	10.	j	15.	r	20.	f

True/False Questions

1. T.

2. F. Historical costs fail to measure true costs because they do not measure price changes over time or the implicit rental rate of capital.

3. T.

4. F. Depreciation of an intangible asset is an implicit cost.

5. F. Entrepreneurs risk the chance of suffering losses as well as the possibility of profits.

6. F. In the short run, a firm's profit is equal to total revenue minus total cost not total variable cost. Total cost includes total variable cost and total fixed cost.

7. F. Depreciation is the fall in the value of the capital good due to its age and accumulated usage.

8. F. Total economic costs include both explicit and implicit costs.

9. F. Implicit costs do not require direct payments.

10. T.

Multiple Choice Questions

1.	a	6.	d
2.	c	7.	d
3.	c	8.	d
4.	d	9.	b
5.	d	10.	d

Chapter Review (Fill in the Blanks)

1. desires, lowest, profits, competition, losses, out of business.
2. Competition, cooperate, want, lowest.
3. price taking.
4. opportunity.
5. true economic costs, historical, opportunity, implicit, economic.
6. zero
7. externalities, want, willingness to pay, all, all.
8. tradeoff, production, marginal cost.
9. want, can.
10. can, want, potentially Pareto-improving, two.

Short Answer Questions

1. If each firm produces only a small fraction of total industry output and if buyers do not care which firm's product they buy (the products are perfect substitutes), each firm is approximately a price taker.

2. Accounting measures of costs omit explicit costs and use historical rather than opportunity costs.

3. The firm pays its workers their opportunity costs. They can't do any better doing something else.

4. Each firm's average cost may depend on industry output. Some firms may operate more efficiently than others.

5. If there are no externalities, in equilibrium with perfect competition, the economy makes the tradeoffs that consumers want to make, as revealed by their willingness to pay for various goods. In equilibrium with perfect competition, the relative price of each good equals the tradeoff that consumers are willing to make to buy the good. The relative price of each good also equals the tradeoff in production, that is the marginal cost of producing the good, measured in terms of other goods. The tradeoff that consumers want to make equals the tradeoff that the economy can make to produce the goods.

Basic Problems

1. World output rises to 100,000,002. It increases by 0.000002 percent.
    Elasticity of demand = $\% \Delta Q / \% \Delta P$, $= -1/2$.
    $-1/2 = +0.000002\% / ? \% \Delta P$.
    Thus $\% P = +0.000002\% / -0.5$
    $\% \Delta P = -.000004\% \Delta P$. An increase in Farmer Brown's output of corn has an infinitesimally small effect on the equilibrium price in the market. Farmer Brown, for all intents and purposes, is a price taker. His output changes do not affect market price.

Advanced Problems

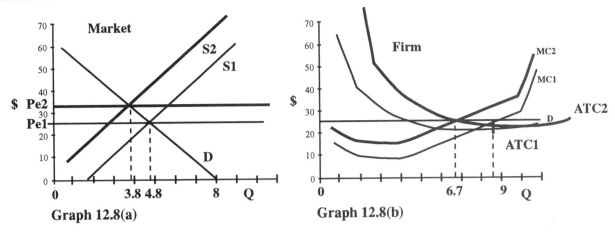

Graph 12.8(a)

Graph 12.8(b)

The rise in marginal cost (Graph 12.8(b)) means a decrease in Supply (Graph 12.8 (a)) which raises equilibrium price and lowers equilibrium quantity. Firms in the industry see their short run profits fall to zero economic profits. The fall in supply reduces the number of firms in the industry. Because economic profits are zero there is no incentive for firms to either exit or enter the industry from this point.

Answers to Chapter 13

Key Term Matching Quiz

1. c	6. d	11. e
2. h	7. j	12. i
3. k	8. l	
4. f	9. a	
5. b	10. g	

True/False Questions

1. F. An industry with perfect competition produces the economically efficient quantity and charges a price equal to marginal cost.

2. T.

3. F. A natural monopoly has increasing returns to scale over sufficiently large quantities produced. It has a large portion of its LRATC that is downsloping, decreasing cost industry.

4. T.

5. F. Monopolies do not fully pass on all cost increases to their consumers. See Figure 13.15 in the text.

6. F. License requirements are legal requirements of the government which serve as barriers to entry.

7. T.

True/False Questions (continued)

8. T.

9. F.   It is not price discrimination if you charge different prices when the goods costs of production differ.

10. F.   Free agency gave players the power to offer their services to other teams and reduced the monopsony power of baseball club owners.

Multiple Choice Questions

1.	a	6.	b
2.	a	7.	d
3.	c	8.	b
4.	b	9.	d
5.	d	10.	d

Chapter Review (Fill in the Blank)

1. sole, downward, regardless, no, demand, profit, marginal cost, marginal revenue, mark-up.
2. inefficiency, less, not, restricts, economically efficient quantity, above.
3. entry, resist, barriers to entry, out, lower, patents, license.
4. Anti-trust, "unreasonable conduct", tie-in, merger, price discrimination.
5. different, different, same, raise.
6. economic inefficiencies, inferior, obsolete.
7. monopsony, upward, independently, marginal cost, marginal revenue, lowest, economic efficiency.

Short Answer Questions

1. Price takers sell all their product because they do not have to reduce the price to sell more. Sellers, who face downward sloping demand curves can sell more, however, only by reducing the price. If reducing the price, reduces their profits, they don't sell more, but they choose to sell less.

2. Monopoly compared to Perfect Competition has a lower consumer surplus, a greater producer surplus and causes a deadweight loss

3. The highest price it would pay is the discounted present value of all its future monopoly profits. If a town gets several cable companies bidding for the right to become its monopoly, they are likely to bid until the winner pays the discounted present value. This reduces the winner's economic profit to zero and the town government collects a fee equal to the discounted present value of the monopoly profit that the firm would have earned.

Basic Problems

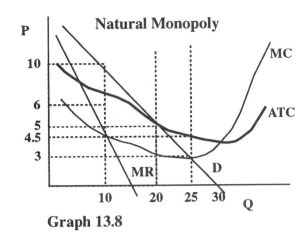

Graph 13.8

1. Given the Graph 13.8 on an industry which will foster the development of a natural monopoly, identify and illustrate with the appropriate abbreviations on the graph provided and the numerical answer in the spaces provided below:

Monopoly Output Qm_10____
Monopoly Price Pm__10___
Profit _4 * 10 = 40_____

If the firm is regulated to sell the Economically Efficient Quantity?

Economically Efficient Quantity Qe_25_____
Perfectly Competitive Price Pc___3_____
Profit or Loss at Pc paid and Qe sold {1.5 * 25 }= 37.50_____

If the firm is regulated to sell at its Average Cost, Q_{ac} _20_____
Price = Ac, P_{ac} __5_____

Would there be profit or loss at P_{ac}? Economic profit is equal to zero. At P_{ac} would the firm be producing the economically efficient quantity. No.

How could the firm produce the economically efficient quantity and not suffer a loss?
    Charge a multipart price. Charge a per use fee equal to P_c = \$3 and a monthly fee to cover the loss.

Answers to Chapter 14

Key Term Matching Quiz

1. k   6. i   11. g
2. a   7. l   12. d
3. h   8. b
4. c   9. j
5. f   10. e

True/False Questions

1. T.

2. F.   Inflexible technologies can deter entry and help a cartel to prevent cheating.

3. F.   Concentration ratios are not related to costs of production or economic efficiency.

4. T.

5. F.   A duopoly under the Cournot model will charge a price below the monopoly price and above marginal cost.

6. F.   Under the Bertrand model, one firm expects the other firm not to change his price. Thus one Bertrand firm will undercut the other firm to increase his market share and profits all the while assuming the other firm will not decrease his price.

7. T.

8. T.

9. T.

10. T.

Multiple Choice Questions

1. a	6. b	11. b
2. c	7. a	12. a
3. c	8. c	
4. c	9. c	
5. d	10. d	

Chapter Review (Fill in the Blanks)

1. many, differentiated, independently. Free, zero, long run.
2. Downward sloping, below, profit, quantity, highest, demand curve.
3. excess.
4. Non-price, better.
5. profits, enter, demand, falls, left, zero, new, no, enter. Average Cost, zero.
6. acts independently, free entry.
7. downward sloping, differentiated product, not, exceeds, excess.
8. free entry, economic, zero.
9. not, strategically, decisions, reactions, effects.
10. profits, economic profits, barriers to entry.
11. Nash, best, profit, rival.
12. rivals, different.
13. prices, quantities.
14. monopoly, monopoly price, leftover, smaller.
15. Monopoly, Cournot, Perfect Competition, many, same, repeatedly, few, monopoly (cartel).

Short Answer Questions

1. To produce more and decrease average costs would require the firm to decrease price which would decrease profits.

2. If the price was greater than marginal cost under the Bertrand model of oligopoly, each firm would have an incentive to cut price and grab customers, market share, from other firms and raise its own profit. This incentive continues until price is driven down to marginal cost.

3. If firms believe that the others won't change their quantity, then they have an incentive to cheat on the cartel by raising their own output. Thus the cartel solution is not a Nash equilibrium in the Cournot model.

4. Under Cournot model conditions, setting price equal to marginal cost would not be a Nash equilibrium. Firms would have an incentive to raise price. They would assume the others would not change their quantity. Thus the last firm would look at leftover demand and charge the monopoly price and the restricted monopoly quantity.

Basic Problems

1. In Graph 14.6 below, Company A sells 4 units of Quantity initially at a price of $12. Then to compute Company B's production decision, use the Cournot model of oligopoly behavior and assume that Company A will not change its output level from 4 units of quantity. Company B computes leftover demand, (Db), which is the Market Demand curve (D) minus the 4 units Company A produces. Company B sells 2 units of quantity at a price of $8. It is producing where MC = MR and sells this quantity at the highest price it can along its demand curve, this would be a price of $8.

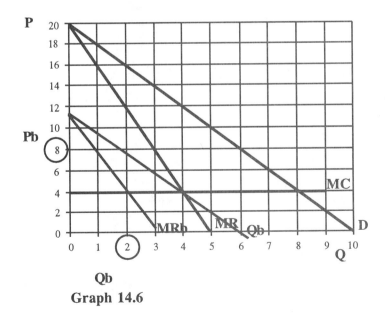

Graph 14.6

Now, continuing with the Cournot oligopoly model, Company A sees that Company B is selling 2 units, and estimates its leftover demand as Da in Graph 14.7, following.

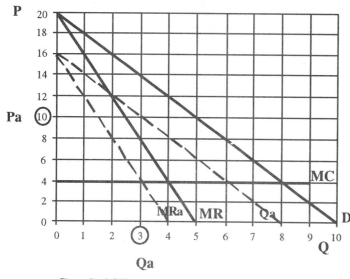

Graph 14.7

This reaction between companies A and B continues until they reach an equilibrium price of $9 and each sells approximately 2.7 units of quantity, that is, a total quantity of 5.4. See Graph 14.8. Profit per unit would equal Price minus AC. In this situation with no fixed costs, AC = MC. Profit per unit would be $9 minus $4, or $5 per unit. Total profit would equal $5 multiplied by total quantity, 5.4 or $27.00.

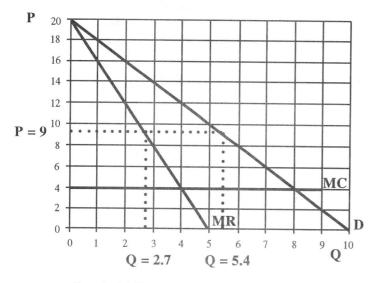

Graph 14.8

2.   Using the Bertrand model of oligopoly behavior in which each firm believes that the other firm will keep its price fixed, the Nash equilibrium price will equal MC. In Graph 14.9 below, price will equal $4 and total quantity sold will equal 8 units. The quantity will be divided arbitrarily between the firms in the industry. Each firm will maximize its own profit by charging a price equal to marginal cost.

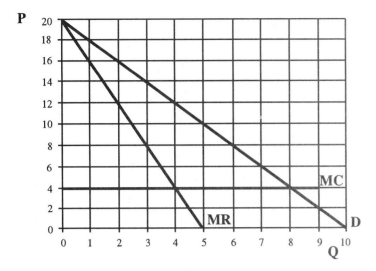

Graph 14.9

Advanced Problems

1. To get the greatest amount of customers for your new product you don't want to differentiate your product too much. See the Brownie example in the text.

2. The logic of Monopolistic Competition would predict that Atlanta would earn zero economic profits after it offered tax breaks, new stadiums and everything else that the Olympic Committee desired.

3. To ban advertising of perceived differences in products would ban half the TV ads that advertise a lifestyle if you consume the product rather than the characteristics of the product. This type of advertising should be viewed as consumer fantasy rather than consumer fraud. If the consumer didn't want to be entertained by this fantasy, they would insist that it be banned. Sometimes such fantasy is even beneficial. An example would be the soft drink commercials that make people think about the beautiful views or the beautiful people when they drink the beverage. Smoking commercials are banned because they cross the line from fantasy to fraud and deception. The fantasy that smoking commercials promote with the camel that appeals to children is not a harmless frivolity, but a life threatening charade that is a dangerous deception. The question to be asked to distinguish the difference between a harmless fantasy and a dangerous deception is, Will this advertising do harm?

Answers to Chapter 15

Key Term Matching Quiz

1. m	6. e	11. g
2. f	7. k	12. d
3. j	8. b	13. l
4. a	9. n	14. c
5. i	10. h	

True/False Questions

1. F. If both commit to keep quiet, both would have the incentive to keep quiet and both would gain. However, if only one makes the commitment to keep quiet, the other prisoner would still have an incentive to confess.

2. T.

3. T.

4. F. Repeated games tend to encourage cooperative behavior.

5. F. Best response, for example, in the case of a tariff, does not erase the deadweight loss which is evidence of inefficiency.

6. T.

7. T.

8. F. A subgame perfect Nash equilibrium has players with credible strategies, economic efficiency is not guaranteed.

9. F. The other player would still have the incentive to confess.

10. T.

Multiple Choice Questions

1. d	6. b	11. a
2. a	7. a	12. a
3. d	8. d	
4. d	9. c	
5. a	10. d	

Chapter Review (Fill in the Blanks)

1. strategic behavior, rules, strategies and payoffs.
2. Nash, best response.
3. prisoner's, deviating, lower, cooperative, prisoners' cheating, trade, advertising.
4. dominant, best.
5. coordination.
6. sequential, subgame perfect Nash equilibrium, credible.
7. commits, gain, limit.
8. repeated, repeated, punish, bad, experience.
9. tit for tat, cooperation, cooperate, do, uncooperative, cooperation.

Short Answer Questions

1. A firm would invest in excess capacity to make credible its threat to glut the market and depress the price if a new competitor were to enter the market.

Basic Problems

1. This is the decision tree for Harding based on information in Table 15.4.

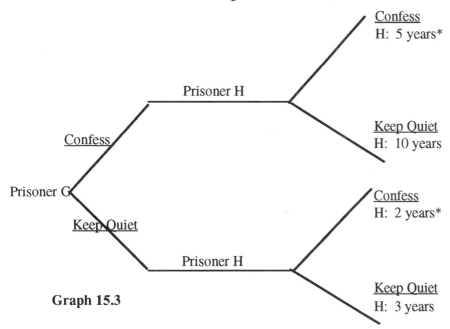

Graph 15.3

No matter what strategy Prisoner Gilooley decides, confess or keep quiet, H's (Harding's) best strategy is to confess. Harding has a dominant strategy, confess.

Decision Tree for Prisoner Gilooley from Table 15.4

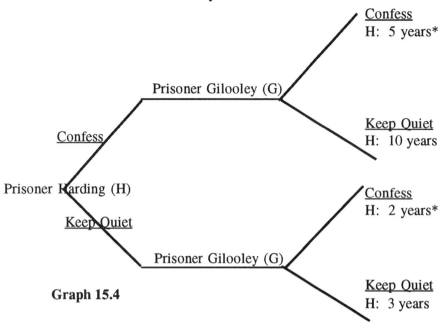

Graph 15.4

Gillooley also has a dominant strategy no matter what Harding does, that is to confess.

Advanced Problems

1(a).   Prior to the tariff, producer surplus and consumer surplus in the U.S. are shown in Graph 15.5 below.
Consumer surplus equals ((1/2 * (5*25)) = $62.5.
Producer surplus equals $62.5.
Equilibrium price is $5 and equilibrium quantity is 25.

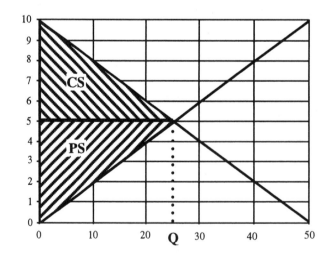

Graph 15.5

1(b).   After the $2 tariff is imposed:
         In the TV market:
                 the U.S. government collects a tariff revenue of $40 on U.S. imports of TVs,
                 the tariff increases the U.S. price of TVs to consumers from $5 to $6,
                 the U.S. consumer surplus from buying TV's falls to ((1/2*(4*20)) = $40,
                 the Japanese producer surplus from producing TVs falls to $40,
                 the Japanese producer loses 1/2 of the deadweight loss, 1/2 ((1/2 (2 * 5)) = $2.5,
                 the U.S. gains (1/2 G) - (1/2 DL) or $20 - $2.5 or $17.5,
                 the Japanese lose (1/2 G) + (1/2 DL) or $22.5.
                 the Deadweight Loss is equal to $2.5 and is graphical evidence of the inefficiency of the
                 tariff.

         In the Food market:
                 a similar tally of gains and losses could be made with the roles of Japan and the U.S.
                 reversed.

Graph 15.6(a) and (b) shows the markets after the tariff is imposed

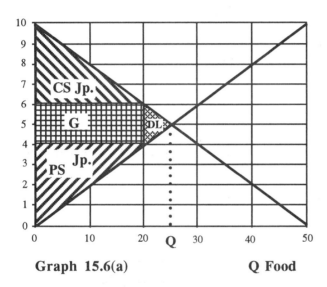

Graph 15.6(a)   **Q Food**

CS - Consumer Surplus
G - Government Revenue
PS - Producer Surplus
DL - Deadweight Loss

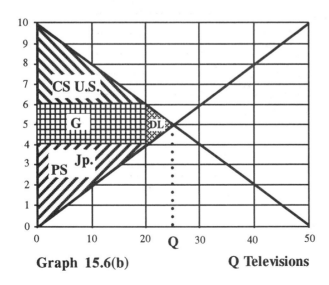

Graph 15.6(b)   **Q Televisions**

CS - Consumer Surplus
G - Government Revenue
PS - Producer Surplus
DL - Deadweight Loss

1(c).   To construct the payoff matrix, sum the producer and consumer surpluses minus the deadweight loss for each situation.

Table 15.5

		Japan	
Cartel		*Tariff*	*No Tariff*
U.S.	*Tariff*	U.S.: 80+40=120	U.S: 80+62.5=142.5
		JP: 40+80=120	JP: 40+62.5=102.5
	No Tariff	U.S.: 40+62.5=102.5	U.S.: 62.5+62.5=125
		JP: 80+62.5=142.5	JP: 62.5+62.5=125

1(d).   Decision Tree for Japan from Table 15.5

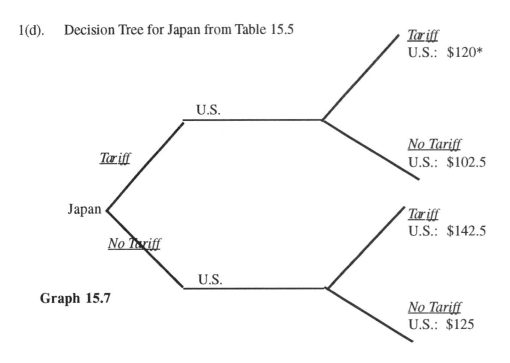

Graph 15.7

1(e).   No matter what strategy Japan decides, Tariff or No Tariff, U.S.'s best strategy is a tariff. U.S. has a dominant strategy, tariff.

1(d).   Decision Tree for JAPAN from Table 15.5

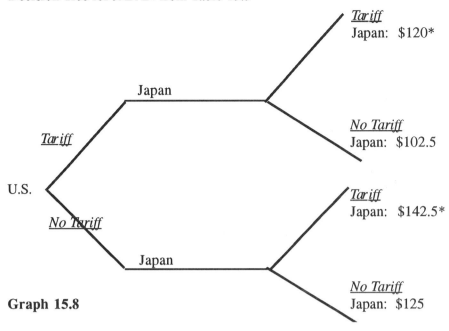

Graph 15.8

Tariff
Japan: $120*

No Tariff
Japan: $102.5

Tariff
Japan: $142.5*

No Tariff
Japan: $125

1(e)   Japan also has a dominant strategy to levy a tariff. This strategy is a Nash equilibrium but it is not economically efficient as evidenced by the deadweight loss in Graph 15.6.

Both countries would have been better off, judged by the sum of their producer and consumer surpluses, if they engaged in free trade. With free trade they would each have received a payoff of $125 rather than the Nash equilibrium of $120. The Nash equilibrium in this case in each countries best response given the actions of the other party, but it is not optimal or economically efficient

Answers to Chapter 16

Key Term Matching Quiz

1. i	6. g	11. p	16. f
2. a	7. j	12. h	
3. l	8. b	13. k	
4. d	9. m	14. c	
5. o	10. e	15. n	

True/False Questions

1. F.   This statement demonstrates an example of the fallacy of composition. It is true for one seller but not for the economy as a whole. The price of final goods and inputs are jointly determined by supply and demand in each market.

2. F.   The demand for inputs is more elastic in the long run because people have time to adjust to change.

3. T.

4. F.   Under perfect competition in input markets, the value of marginal product is equal to the marginal physical product of the input multiplied by the price of the final good.

5. F.   An increase in the demand for the final product increases the demand for the input used to produce that final product.

6. F.   To maximize the value of a firm, buy a durable input with a positive net present value.

7. T.

8. F.   Economic rent is the producer surplus.

10. F.   Isoquants production of a final good by inputs that are perfect substitutes, are diagonal straight lines which slope downward and to the right.

Multiple Choice

1. b	6. c	11. b
2. d	7. c	12. d
3. b	8. d	13. b
4. d	9. a	14. c
5. d	10. d	

Chapter Review (Fill in the Blanks)

1. low skilled labor, technical progress, technical progress, forty percent, fifteen percent.
2. inputs, final, inputs, productivity, price.
3. marginal product, total output, one more, fixed.
4. Law of Diminishing Returns, marginal product, fixed. Diminishing returns, rise, increasing.
5. value of marginal product, marginal product, price.
6. marginal product, final good. input, final good, demand, marginal product, demand, price, demand.
7. durable, repeatedly, saved. value of the firm, durable, positive.
8. economic rent, opportunity cost.
9. output. raises, production, raises.
10. allocate, highly valued use, incentives, exceed, distribute, fairness.
11. market, command, coordinate, transactions costs.

Short Answer Questions

1. The rule for rational decisions applied to inputs: a firm maximizes its value (the discounted present value of its profits) by choosing a quantity of each input that equates its marginal benefit and its marginal cost. A firm maximizes its profit by choosing a quantity of each nondurable input so that the value of its marginal product equals the price of the input. The logical rule also applies to durable inputs. The height of a firms demand curve for a durable input indicates the discounted present value of the future value of the marginal product of that input. To maximize profits, a firm buys any durable input with a positive net present value.

2. The question of fairness arises when the equity of income distribution by the prices of inputs is analyzed. Who owns the inputs? How is the ownership of inputs distributed in society? Is that distribution equitable? Does everyone in society own their own proper share of inputs? How is this distribution decided, subject to change, determined by wealth and advantage rather than by some equitable rule? The answers to these questions abound with controversy!

Basic Problems

Labor (hours)	Total Output	Marginal Product	Average Product	Price of Final Good	Value of Marginal Product
1	5	5	5	10	50
2	15	10	7.5	10	100
3	27	12	9	10	120
4	36	9	9	10	90
5	44	8	8.8	10	80
6	51	7	8.5	10	70
7	57	6	8.1	10	60
8	62	5	7.8	10	50
9	66	4	7.3	10	40
10	69	3	6.9	10	30
11	71	2	6.5	10	20
12	71	1	5.9	10	10

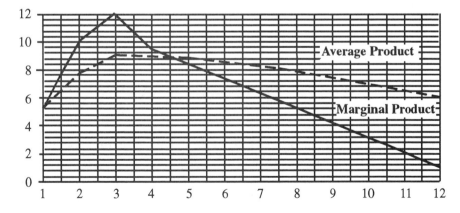

Graph 16.2(a)

1. d.   At a wage of $20, VMP = Price of labor when 11 units of labor are hired.

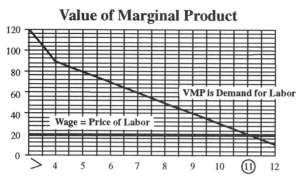

2. If the price of labor rose to $50, the amount of labor hired would fall to 8 units.

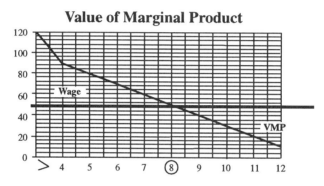

3. If the price of final output fell to $5, the VMP would fall as shown in the graph below, and the labor hired at a wage of $20 would fall to 9 units.

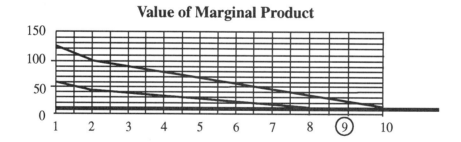

Advanced Problems

1. A decrease in the demand for a final good would:
    first, cause the price of the final good to decrease,
    second, cause the value of marginal product of the inputs used to produce it to decrease,
    third, the VMP is the demand curve for the inputs, so the demand for inputs would decrease,
    fourth, because the demand for inputs decreases, the employment of inputs decreases,
    fifth, in a perfectly competitive input market the prevailing wage is given by market forces.
        If there is less demand in general for this input, the price of the input would eventually fall.

Advanced Problems (continued)

2. Produce at point a in Graph 16.6 where the budget line is tangent to the isoquant representing 100 units of output. The least cost method of producing is to use 4 capital (K) and 6 labor (L). They cost $10 each so total cost is $100. Points b and c would both produce 100 units of Q but their production technique would cost more

Answers to Chapter 17

Key Term Matching Quiz

1. s	6. e	11. f	16. d
2. j	7. m	12. p	17. g
3. t	8. c	13. i	18. l
4. o	9. r	14. a	19. q
5. h	10. k	15. n	20. b

True/False Questions

1. T.

2. F. To be considered working in the market, the work must be done for explicit pay.

3. F. The income effect of a permanent increase in income is greater than the income effect of a temporary increase. You would not feel much richer if your income doubled for just one day, but you would feel wealth if your income were to double permanently.

4. F. Real wages guide the decisions of workers because real wages have been adjusted for inflation.

5. F. The average wage of women has risen, while the average wage of men has fallen since 1973.

6. T.

7. F. Younger workers have higher marginal benefits of investing in human capital because they have more years ahead of them.

8. F. Time rate pay is more common in industries in which it is easy to judge quantity.

9. F. Labor turnover will decrease because more information creates better matches and less turnover.

10. T.

Multiple Choice Questions

1. d	6. b	11. b
2. a	7. a	12. c
3. c	8. d	13. d
4. d	9. d	14. a
5. b	10. d	

Chapter Review (Fill in the Blanks)

1. three-fourths, labor, one-fourth, capital, physically connected, workers, work.
2. whether, occupation, job offer, own business, how many. upward, substitution, income. income, substitution, value, marginal product.
3. real wage, hours worked, real, purchasing, nominal, inflation.
4. nonpay, compensating differentials, higher, human, education, on-the-job, direct, opportunity cost, age, experience.
5. lower, general, training, specific, firm.
6. time, piece, profit, profit, incentives, nonwage, insurance, pension plans, taxes.
7. Job tournaments, tournaments, motivate, Tournaments, executive compensation.
8. enter, leave, 3.6, labor turnover, mobility, opportunities, change, labor turnover, unemployment, above, unemployed, underemployed, training and skills.
9. raise, monopoly, restrict, deadweight social loss, firms, union.
10. efficiency wages, retain, firm-specific, incentives, shirk, productivity.

Short Answer

1. Increasing labor mobility, information about other job opportunities and volatile economic conditions have increased labor turnover in recent years.

2. The unemployment rate is imperfect in that it does not count people as unemployed who have become discouraged by the job market and have altogether stopped looking for work. The discouraged worker is not even counted in the labor force. The unemployment rate counts people as employed if they are only working part-time. These two imperfections make the unemployment rate as measured, lower than it probably is. The third problem is that people will respond to a phone survey by saying that they looked for work, even though they did not. This last imperfection would make the unemployment rate smaller than the BLS measured one.

3. Given the supply and demand for labor in graph 17.1 below, if the wage is above equilibrium wage, equilibrium will occur and will be equal to L_3 minus L_1. Normally, the wage will tend to fall to equilibrium due to competitive market forces. However, the time it takes to fall to equilibrium creates a period of temporary unemployment. In addition, less than perfect competition in the labor market can cause unemployment. These conditions include government regulations, such as the minimum wage, union contracts that may have bargained a wage above equilibrium or firms setting efficiency wages, wages above equilibrium.

Labor Market

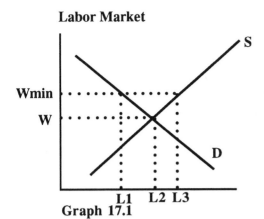

Graph 17.1

Basic Problems

1. PV of a person's human capital = Wage (Yr. 1)/ $(1 + i)$
    plus Wage (Yr. 2) / $(1 + i)^2$
    plus Wage (Yr. n) / $(1 + i)^n$

Wages	$(1 + i)n$	
25,000		25,000
26,000	1.1	23,636.36
27,000	1.21	22,314.05
28,000	1.331	21,036.81
29,000	1.4641	19,807.39
30,000	1.61051	18,627.64
31,000	1.771561	17,498.69
32,000	1.948717	16,421.06
33,000	2.143589	15,394.74
34,000	2.357948	14,419.32
35,000	2.593742	13,494.02
	PV wages	**207,650**

Answers to Chapter 18

Key Term Matching Quiz

1.	i	6.	j	11.	k	16.	l
2.	r	7.	q	12.	a	17.	b
3.	f	8.	g	13.	h	18.	m
4.	p	9.	n	14.	o		
5.	c	10.	d	15.	e		

True/False Questions

1. T.

2. F.   The distribution of money income has increased in inequality whereas the distribution of after-tax income including non-cash transfers is roughly the same as it was in 1970.

3. T.

4. F.   The Gini coefficient for individuals living alone is larger, thus individuals have greater inequality in their income distribution than families.

5. F.   Wealth is distributed less equally than income.

6. T.

7. F.   Economic growth tends to decrease economic inequality and poverty.

8. F.   These reasons cause studies to normally understate the effect of discrimination.

9. F.   The distribution of income that results from a perfectly competitive market system depends on the distribution of income which the system began with and there is no guarantee that perfect competition can take a skewed income distribution and make it equitable.

10. T.

Multiple Choice Questions

1.	c	6.	d
2.	a	7.	b
3.	d	8.	c
4.	b	9.	b
5.	d	10.	a

Chapter Review (Fill in the Blanks)

1. doubled.
2. women and children, higher, poverty line, food, fifteen percent, below, one-fourth, below.
3. less, one-fourth, non-human, three-fourths, 0.7.
4. larger, incomes, debt, $75,000, $5,000.
5. income, nutritionally adequate diet, $525, one fifth, absolute poverty.
6. declining, risen, slowly.
7. developed, antipoverty, temporarily, productive work, dependence, incentives, avoid.
8. means tested, low, Social Security System, $500, not, regardless, replacing, negative income tax, less, lose, raise.
9. discrimination, human capital, lower-paying.
10. Equal Pay, Civil Rights, discrimination, "affirmative action," women, minorities.

Short Answer Questions

1. The income figures do not include noncash income provided by the government or employers, and this income has risen over time. Second, median income differs from mean income. When the distribution of income becomes more unequal (as it has since 1970) the median income per person rises more slowly than the mean. Third, average household size has fallen over time. and many more households consist of a female, her children and no adult male. These latter households are often poor.

2. A person who discriminates pays a price. He refuses to hire (i.e., blacks and women) lowering their equilibrium wages. Each firm that discriminated by hiring white males instead of blacks and women would pay more for labor and would sacrifice profits by not hiring lower-wage women and blacks with equally good skills. A prejudiced person's decision to hire blacks and women might well be motivated by least cost production goals, rather than his underlying prejudice. Prejudice, by restricting the proper operation of the labor market, exacts a price not only from producers in the form of paying higher wages to white males than blacks and women, but also to buyers, in that these higher costs of prejudiced production are passed on to consumers in the form of higher product prices.

Basic Problems

1. Relative poverty level is determined by the ratio of the income received by the highest fifth of the population to the income received by the lowest fifth.

	Country A	Country B
Highest Fifth	80%	60%
Lowest Fifth	5%	6%
Relative Poverty Level	80/5=16	60/6=10

Poorest country is Country A as determined by the fact that it has the highest relative poverty level.

Answers to Chapter 19

Key Term Matching Quiz

1. d	6. e	11. f
2. l	7. j	12. k
3. a	8. c	
4. g	9. b	
5. i	10. h	

True/False Questions

1. T.

2. T.

3. F.   When buyers *lack* information about quality, high quality and low quality products sell for the same price.

4. F.   When buyers have limited information about prices, some stores charge high prices and some stores charge low prices, a distribution of prices prevails.

5. T.

6. F.   Evidence shows that most people are risk averse, risky investments must pay higher expected returns to induce people to buy them.

7. F.   Adverse Selection occurs when people know what an agent is doing, but not why.

8. F.   Moral Hazard occurs when one person does not know what another person is doing, a principal cannot see whether an agent is acting in the principal's best interest.

9. T.

10. T.

Multiple Choice Questions

1.	c	6.	d
2.	b	7.	a
3.	b	8.	a
4.	a	9.	d
5.	d	10.	c

Chapter Review (Fill in the Blanks)

1. accurate, costly, imperfect, economic.
2. guess, rational guess, expected value, expected value.
3. limited, prices, searching, price, downward-sloping, search, benefit, cost.
4. information, distribution, higher, lower price, price-discriminate, different, same, different, different, poorly, higher, higher, better, narrows, fall, trial, error.
5. diversification, risk.
6. moral hazard, imperfect, agent, best, incentive, interests, good, luck, riskier, averse, higher.
7. optimal, compromises, flat, higher, benefit, costs, information, monitoring, perfect, costly, moral hazard.
8. adverse selection, important, product, lacks, used cars, know.
9. information, same, low, higher, higher, adverse selection.
10. reduce, adverse selection, guarantees, less, repeatedly, buy, quality.

Basic Problems

1. Expected value equals $\{[(1/3) * \$100,000] + [(1/3) * \$50,000] + [1/3*0]\}$ equals $(\$33,333) + (16,666) + 0 = \$49,999$

2. The optimal amount of search occurs when the expected marginal benefit of searching (the expected benefit from trying one more store) equals its expected marginal cost.

The benefits from shopping at the three other stores would be:
      saving \$15 at the store with the radio for \$35,
      saving nothing at the store with the radio for \$50, and
      saving nothing at the store with the radio for \$60.

The shoppers benefit from searching one more store equals 1/3 (\$15) plus 1/3 (zero) + 1/3 (zero) = \$5.

If \$5 is greater than the extra cost of the time and effort to go to the next store, the shopper will shop one more store. If the benefit is less than the cost, it is rational to stop shopping and buy from the first store.

Advanced Problem

1. Using the probabilities given in Table 19.4 for agent's actions,

Table 19.4

Agent's Actions	Profit	No Profit
Try Hard	2/3 chance	1/3 chance
Try a Little	1/2 chance	1/2 chance
Shirk (Don't Try)	1/3 chance	2/3 chance

1(a). The expected salaries of the three types of agents are determined in Table 19.5 below.

(1)	(2)	(3)	(4)
Agent's Actions	Firm Profits	No Profit	Expected Salary Sum of columns (2) and (3)
Try Hard	2/3 * \$35,000 = \$23,100	1/3 * \$25,000 = \$8,250	\$31,350
Try a Little	1/2 * \$35,000 = \$17,500	1/2 * \$25,000 = \$12,500	\$30,000
Shirk (Don't Try)	1/3 * \$35,000 = \$11,500	2/3 * \$25,000 = \$16, 500	\$28,000

Advanced Problem (continued)

The agent who tries hard will make an expected salary of $31,350.
The agent who tries a little will make an expected salary of $30,000.
The agent who shirks will make an expected salary of $28,000.

1(b).   In accepting this job, the agent risks not making more than $25,000 in his job.

1(c).   For a basic shirker, there is no incentive for the agent to work hard. He can make an easy $25,000 doing nothing. The incentive to work hard to make $300,000 profit for the firm is that the firm will pay him a salary of $10,000 more, or in expected value terms, that the expected value of his salary would rise from $28,000 to $31, 350 or $3,350 for hard work.

1(d).   The agent has no risk from the effect of luck on his earnings. He earns $25,000 even if the firm makes no profit.

1(e).   The expected profit of the firm is shown in Table 19.6 below.

(1)	(2)	(3)	(4)
Agent's Actions	Firm Profits	No Profit	Expected Salary Sum of columns (2) and (3)
Try Hard	2/3 * $300,000 = $200,000	1/3 * $00 = $0	$200,000
Try a Little	1/2 * $300,000 = $150,000	1/2 * $0 = $0	$150,000
Shirk (Don't Try)	1/3 * $300,000 = $100,000	2/3 * $0 = $0	$100,000

Table 19.6 shows that a Firm:
> with an agent who shirks expects to make $100,000,
> with an agent who tries a little, expects to make $150,000, and
> with a hard worker, expects to make $300,000.

This employment compensation scheme would be likely to cause moral hazard (shirking) or cause the agent to work in the principal's best interest depending upon the agent's attitude toward the extra benefit of working hard. The shirker sees this extra benefit as $3,350 and the agent who tries a little sees the extra benefit as $1,350.

To say this was an optimal contract, you would have to have experimented with salaries for these agents and discovered by trial and error how much salary difference it takes to get the shirker to work hard.

An optimal contract is a compromise between:
> the benefit to the agent of a flat salary (low risk) [$25,000] which is [$28,000 expected value], and
> the incentive to act in the principal's interest that comes from a higher salary ($35,000) which is [$33,350 expected value]for a better outcome ($300,000 profit).

> The marginal benefit is the incentive for the agent to try harder ($3350 expected value). The marginal cost is the effect of luck on the agents pay which makes the agent bear more risk and raises the expected salary that the principal must pay to attract an agent to the job.
> (This agent does not bear any risk due to the effect of luck.)

An optimal contract sets the incentive to try harder equal to the effect of luck on an agents salary. At this point these ratios are not equal. There is no optimal contract here.

Answers to Chapter 20

Key Term Matching Quiz

1. k	6. e	11. l	16. f
2. c	7. j	12. d	
3. h	8. b	13. i	
4. o	9. g	14. a	
5. m	10. p	15. n	

True/False Questions

1. F. The economically efficient level of pollution is not zero. The economically efficient level of pollution occurs when the marginal benefit of reducing it equals the marginal cost of reducing it.

2. T.

3. F. Output of a good is economically efficient if the Marginal Social Benefit equals the Marginal Social Cost.

4. T.

5. T.

6. F. A non-rival good does not get used up. Consumption by one person does not decrease the amount of the nonrival good available for the next person.

7. F. When the MPB < MSB, there is a positive externality.

8. T.

9. F. A negative externality causes the market to produce more than the economically efficient output.

10. T.

Multiple Choice

1. d	6. d	11. b
2. a	7. c	
3. c	8. d	
4. c	9. c	
5. d	10. c	

Chapter Review (Fill in the Blanks)

1. social costs, exceed, private costs, economically efficient, economically efficient, zero, economically efficient, social, social.
2. costs, internalizing, responsible, own, private, social, externality, economically efficient.
3. low, side, internalize, economically efficient, right, side.
4. high, side, property, quantity, economically efficient, efficient, taxes, regulations, sellable rights.
5. legal, scarce, resource, property, use, sell, common, society.
6. incentives, value, overused, incentive, legal, overuse. Tragedy, Commons, incentive, resource, prevent, overuse, costs, property, economic inefficiency.
7. social, private, lower, economically efficient, underproduction, ignore, low, internalize, high, raise, economically efficient, subsidies, regulation.
8. fall, costly, nonexcludable good, pay, prevent, exclude, public, nonexcludable.
9. incentive, unwilling, nonexcludable, free, pay, free, no one, no, reduces, below, economically efficient, public.

Short Answer Questions

1. The law and property rights determine the direction of side payments, the distribution of income.

2. Firms with the highest costs of reducing pollution would have incentives to pay the highest prices for these sellable rights. Firms with lower costs of reducing pollution would have incentives to reduce pollution rather than buy the sellable rights.

3. The drawbacks to giving private property rights to an ocean fishing are would be myriad. The problems and costs of defining and enforcing the property rights would be enormous. The area involves international waters, so regulations would have to be international regulations. How to charge for the use of these rights would also be an expensive and even dangerous puzzle. The fishing grounds have already seem some gunboat diplomacy.

Basic Problems

1a. If the transactions costs are low and property rights are assigned, the economically efficient result will occur if the two parties negotiate. The hotel can preserve the view of the forest if it values that view more than the logging company values its logging profits and it the hotel is ready to pay for the value of the view.

b. The income is redistributed from the hotel to the logging company.
c. The Coase theorem would predict that the result would be economically efficient.
d. If the hotel owned the trees, there would be a negotiation and if the same values prevailed, (that the hotel values the view of the trees more than the logging company's profits) the view would remain but there would be no income redistribution and no clear cut logging.

Property rights determine the direction of side payments, so they affect the distribution of income but not the allocation of resources.

Answers to Chapter 21

Key Term Matching Quiz

1. d	6. m	11. a
2. g	7. b	12. l
3. k	8. i	13. e
4. h	9. j	
5. f	10. c	

True/False Questions

1. T.

2. F.   A diffuse interest is a benefit that is spread across many people.

3. F.   Rate of return regulation gives the firm an incentive to raise its costs in ways that will give its employees and executives nonmoney forms of benefits.

4. F.   Deregulation caused average fares to fall and increased the cities served by two or more airlines.

5. T.

6. F.   At the competitive price (price equals marginal cost), where the demand curve crosses the marginal cost curve, a natural monopoly will not necessarily cover its costs, it may suffer a loss.

7. F.   Privatization occurs when a previously nationalized firm becomes private property.

8. T.

9. F.   The size of the deadweight loss from taxes increases as supply or demand becomes more elastic.

10. T.

Multiple Choice Questions

1. c	6. c	11. d
2. a	7. b	
3. d	8. b	
4. b	9. b	
5. a	10. a	

Chapter Review (Fill in the Blanks)

1. restrict, protect, reduce, increase, protect, improve, set rules, benefit, expense.
2. cost-benefit, cost, increase, consumer, producer, externalities, intangibles, amount, money, pay, future, discounted present values, uncertain, expected, winners and losers, differ, potential, actual Pareto, use, lower, appropriate.
3. actual, intended, public-interest, special interest, capture view, special interest and capture views, concentrated, diffuse, concentrated, incentive, beneficial, rent seeking, inefficient.
4. owned, incentives, weaker, maximize value, no, legal monopolies, stronger incentives, competition, cream-skimming, profitable, cream-skimming, subsidize, prevent, governments, pay, tax revenues, lowest-cost.
5. Taxes, several purposes, fund, redistribute, achieve other social goals. economic inefficiencies, different, inefficiency. Optimal taxation, minimize, tax revenue, higher, inelastic, lower, elastic, perfectly inelastic supplies or demands, fairness, not, solely.

Short Answer Questions

1. The argument for occupational licensure claims that licenses provide people with information about quality that otherwise would be costly to ascertain. To the extent that occupational licensure adds to costs, reduced competition and higher prices, licensure is not economically efficient.

2. Rate of return pricing gives the natural monopoly no incentive to control costs.

3. The efficiency argument against the corporate income tax is that it taxes some corporate income twice. First, corporations pay taxes on their profits; second, people who receive those profits in the form of stock dividends or capital gains pay personal income taxes on it again. This raises the overall tax on savings and may reduce economic growth.

4. The author states that theft is economically efficient in certain situations. On an economic basis, how could theft be termed economically efficient?

Basic Problems

1. The deadweight loss is the shaded area in graphs below. The dollar value would be the area of the triangle, $5 in Graph 21.3(a) and $10 in Graph 21.3 (b). The $1 tax causes the greatest inefficiency, identified by the size of the deadweight loss, in Graph 21/3(b) where the supply curve is perfectly elastic. The inefficiency of a tax increases as supply or demand becomes more elastic.

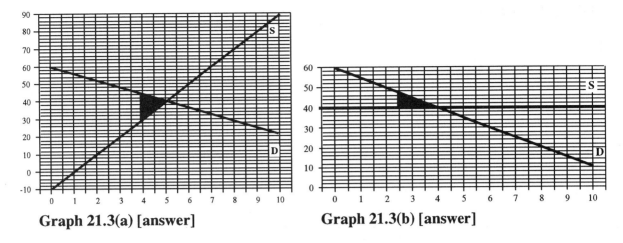

Graph 21.3(a) [answer]   **Graph 21.3(b) [answer]**

Advanced Problems

1. Levy an optimal tax that sets equilibrium quantity at the point where the MSC intersects the Demand Curve. The tax will equal $50 per unit.

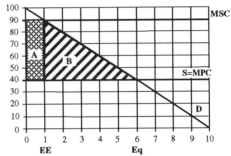

Graph 21.5 Effect of Tax on Consumer Surplus
Lose areas [A+B]

Benefits of the tax shown in Graph 21.6 below.

Due to the tax of $50 per unit of cigarettes, the consumer loses consumer surplus areas A + B,
    the government gains tax revenue equal to area A,
    the cost (deadweight loss) of the tax equals [(A + B) - A = B]
    the benefit of the tax is equal to area B + D.
    the net benefit of the tax equals cost less benefit, equals [(B + D) -B) = D]
    Net benefit is equal to area D, $125.

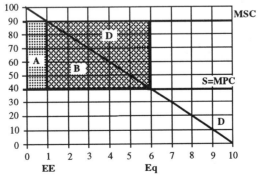

Graph 21.6 Government Revenue = Area A
Benefit of Tax = Area B + D
Net Benefit of Tax = Area D

Answers to Chapter 22

Key Term Matching Quiz

1.	d	6.	h
2.	f	7.	b
3.	c	8.	g
4.	a	9.	e
5.	i		

True/False Questions

1. F. Public choice analysis would ask what the government would actually do in a political equilibrium if it were to adopt the suggested policy.

2. F. The median voter theorem is that the politician will choose policies that are favored by the median voter. He will not try to change the median voter's mind.

3. F. Some political situations may have no equilibria at all.

4. T.

5. T.

6. F. Those are reliance damages.

7. F. According to marginal cost, marginal benefit analysis, it would not be economically efficient to eliminate crime completely. The economically efficient amount of crime is the amount at which the marginal benefit of reducing the crime equals the marginal cost.

Multiple Choice Questions

1. d
2. b
3. a
4. b
5. a
6. c

Chapter Review (Fill in the Blanks)

1. differ, majority, all, competing, broad, competition.
2. 2, conflict, follow, best, conflict, reelected,
3. single, various, conflict, lack, public-choice, incentives, constraints, political.
4. government policy, political, median voter, political, previously established.
5. incentives, crime, raising, raising, reduces, economically efficient, completely, economically efficient, marginal benefit, marginal cost.
6. differ, punishment, severe, large, economically efficient, crime.

Short Answer Questions

1. An economically efficient law creates incentives to solve problems in the cheapest, most economically efficient way and minimize transactions costs so that people can settle disputes cheaply. However, shouldn't courts be concerned with values other than economic efficiency? What about fairness and justice to name just a few!

2. The gain to the thief is the market value of the jewelry minus the productive time he lost. The loss to the victim is the market value plus the jewelry's sentimental value. The net loss to society is the time to catch the thief, the loss of the thief's productive time and the loss of the jewelry's sentimental value.

3. Economics judges decisions based on marginal cost marginal benefit equality. If the marginal cost exceeds the marginal benefit, you don't pursue the activity any further. If the marginal benefit exceeds the marginal cost, you pursue the activity. The author sets up a criminal justice scenario for evaluating crime and punishment using marginal cost, marginal benefit analysis. If the marginal cost of the crime (punishment and the probability of being caught) is less than the marginal benefit, it is economically efficient to pursue the activity.   The legal system is not just based on economic decision making, thank goodness! The principles of fairness, justice, and morality are also employed in the decision making process!

Answers to Chapter 23

Key Term Matching Quiz

1. b	6. h	11. j
2. f	7. c	12. d
3. i	8. e	
4. k	9. g	
5. a	10. l	

True/False Questions

1. T.

2. T.

3. F.

4. F. Factual question, the leading importer to the U.S. is Canada.

5. T.

6. T. Example in text was wheat into TV sets.

7. F. Factual question, basis is comparative advantage.

8. T.

9. T.

10. T. Definitional question.

11. F. Theoretical question, gains *always* exceed losses from trade.

12. T.

13. F.

14. F. Definitional question, it measures the relative price ratio of the two items.

15. F. Theoretical question, Japan's trade partners have *not* had a loss.

16. F.

17. T. Theoretical question, trade is based on a difference of some sort.

18. T.

19. T.

20. T.

21. T.

22. T.

23. F. Definitional question, a country can save more than it invests by lending to other countries.

24. F. most economists see such a link.

25. F. Definitional question, a tariff is a tax.

True/False Questions (continued)

26. F. Theoretical question, welfare decreases.

27. T.

28. F. Factual question, the cost is about $22 billion per year.

29. T.

30. T.

31. F.

32. T.

Multiple Choice Questions

1. e	6. d	11. c
2. b	7. a	12. b
3. c	8. c	
4. a	9. c	
5. e	10. d	

Chapter Review (Fill in the Blanks)

1. surplus, deficit.
2. Canada.
3. less.
4. lower opportunity cost.
5. farm products, high-tech products.
6. increase, decrease.
7. consumers, producers.
8. producers, consumers.
9. technology, resources or inputs.
10. dynamic gains from trade, economies of scale, political gains from trade.
11. borrowing from.
12. tax on imports, quantity restriction on imports.
13. increase, decrease.
14. tariff.
15. $22 billion.
16. General Agreement on Tariffs and Trade (GATT), World Trade Organization (WTO).
17. European Union (EU), European Free Trade Association (EFTA).
18. dumping.

Short Answer Questions

1. Figure 23.2 shows that trade is a smaller percentage of GDP in the U.S. than in most other industrialize nations.

2. See section "Principle of Comparative Advantage."

3. The U.S. has a comparative advantage in farm products and high-tech products. This means that the U.S. can produce these goods while giving up less of other products than other nations can produce these goods.

4. Figure 23.10 illustrates that the static answer is "yes," because the exporter and importer both experience net gains.

5. Yes, it can be seen that way. (Doubtless those who seek to restrict trade will portray the matter differently.) Recall that rent-seeking is the use of time, money and other resources to try to get government benefits (spending, tax changes, or regulations targeted to some special interest group—see chapter 23).

6. See section "Reasons for Comparative Advantage."

7. Comparative advantage is based on opportunity cost of a good in terms of another. If a nation is very productive in all goods, it may still have a production possibilities curve with a slope that is different from that of other nations. See Table 23.5 for an illustration.

8. See the section "Balance of Trade and the Current Account."

9. The majority view is that budget deficits can cause trade deficits. The minority view emphasizes other possible causes, such as changes in tax policy, changes in tastes, and changes in technology. Figure 23.16 shows the current account deficit and the budget deficit for the U.S. since the late 1960's.

10. See section "Effects of Current Account Deficits."

11. See the section "Types of Trade Restrictions."

12. The gainers from restrictions (firms and their employees) have more political power than losers from restrictions (consumers).

13. See section on arguments to restrict trade. Note that restrictions may increase international tensions, and lead to war—not a wise way to obtain national security.

Basic Problems

1. Trade has increased as a fraction of GDP. Figure 23.1 is a model answer for this question.

2. When a nation trades, it produces one combination of goods, and trades to obtain (and consume) another combination. Figure 23.8 is a model answer for this question.

3. Figure 23.12 is a model answer to this question.

Basic Problems

4. Trade restrictions raise prices in protected industries, which reduces buying power of buyers of that good or service. Because buying power is less, demand for other goods and services will decrease, and destroy jobs in those other industries.

Advanced Problems

1. A nation (just like an individual) has the choice of producing something for itself or buying from another (by producing and selling a product). If buying the product has a lower opportunity cost (i.e., it takes fewer resources), then trade benefits a nation. Therefore, a nation which wishes to improve its standard of living will always compare the opportunity cost of buying an item to the cost of producing it.

2. See the section, "Winners and Losers: The Size of the Gain from Trade." Figure 23.10 is a model answer for this question.

3. Producers who fact import competition will seek trade restrictions, in order to protect their income and profits. Consumers (if they bother at all on this topic) will favor lower trade barriers. You will tend to raise barriers if industry and associated labor groups contribute money to your campaign, and you feel you need their votes at election time. You will tend to lower barriers if you want consumer votes, or if you find the economic theory of trade persuasive.

4. See section "Seven Arguments for Protectionism." Note that most are fallacious, or subject to stringent qualification before acceptance.

5. Students may suggest a variety of answers, but economists will welcome the unfair competition, and the free widgets and gadgets. Why pay for something if it is free?